TELECOMMUNICATION NETWORKS AND COMPUTER SYSTEMS

Series Editors

Mario Gerla
Aurel Lazar
Paul Kuehn

Raphael Rom   Moshe Sidi

Multiple Access Protocols
Performance and Analysis

With 41 Illustrations

Springer-Verlag
New York Berlin Heidelberg
London Paris Tokyo Hong Kong

Raphael Rom and Moshe Sidi
Electrical Engineering Department
Technion—Israel Institute of Technology
Haifa 32000, Israel

Series Editors

Mario Gerla
Department of Computer Science
University of California
Los Angeles, CA 90024, USA

Paul Kuehn
Institute of Communications
Switching and Data Technics
University of Stuttgart
D-7000 Stuttgart
Federal Republic of Germany

Aurel Lazar
Department of Electrical
Engineering
and Center for
Telecommunications Research
Columbia University
New York, NY 10027, USA

Library of Congress Cataloging-in-Publication Data
Rom, Raphael.
    Multiple access protocols : performance and analysis / Raphael
Rom, Moshe Sidi.
        p.   cm.—(Telecommunication networks and computer systems)
    Includes bibliographical references.
    ISBN 0-387-97253-6 (alk. paper)
    1. Computer network protocols.   2. Packet switching (Data
transmission)   3. Artifical satellites in telecommunication.
4. Local area networks (Computer networks)   I. Sidi, Moshe.
II. Title.   III. Series.
TK5105.5.R65   1990   90-31273
621.39'81—dc20

Printed on acid-free paper.

Camera-ready text supplied by the authors.
Printed and bound by R.R. Donnelley & Sons, Harrisonburg, Virginia.
Printed in the United States of America.

9 8 7 6 5 4 3 2 1

ISBN 0-387-97253-6 Springer-Verlag New York Berlin Heidelberg
ISBN 3-540-97253-6 Springer-Verlag Berlin Heidelberg New York

PREFACE

Computer communication networks have come of age. Today, there is hardly any professional, particularly in engineering, that has not been the user of such a network. This proliferation requires the thorough understanding of the behavior of networks by those who are responsible for their operation as well as by those whose task it is to design such networks. This is probably the reason for the large number of books, monographs, and articles treating relevant issues, problems, and solutions in this field.

Among all computer network architectures, those based on broadcast multiple access channels stand out in their uniqueness. These networks appear naturally in environments requiring user mobility where the use of any fixed wiring is impossible and a wireless channel is the only available option. Because of their desirable characteristics multiple access networks are now used even in environments where a wired point-to-point network could have been installed. The understanding of the operation of multiple access network through their performance analysis is the focus of this book.

In many aspects broadcast multiple access networks are similar, or even identical, to point-to-point networks. The major difference lies in the way in which the data channels are used by the network nodes. This book concentrates on mechanisms for channel access in multiple access communication systems including local area networks, satellite, and radio networks. The text has a mathematical orientation with emphasis on insight, that is, the analysis is mathematical in nature yet the purpose is understanding the operation of the systems through their analysis. We have assumed acquaintance with probabilistic modeling of systems, some knowledge in stochastic processes and just a bit of elementary queueing systems--all on the level of undergraduate studies. With this knowledge the reader should be able to follow all the mathematical derivations.

While some of the material covered in this book appeared in other books, the vast body of the text has appeared only in professional journals in their typical cryptic language and inconsistent notation. Some of the material appears here for the first time. Because of the inconsistent notation used in the diverse exposition of the material a great emphasis is placed on uniform notation-- identical concepts have been assigned the same notation throughout the book. This should make it ever so much easier to understand the concepts and compare derivations and results.

The subjects covered in the book were chosen judiciously. Each subsection presents a communication system whose nature differs from the others in the system characteristics, the purpose of the system, or the method of analysis. Via this approach we cover all types of multiple access systems known to date and most of the analytical methods used in their analysis.

The introduction chapter, presents our way of classifying the multiple access protocols. It is here that we present the concepts that dictate the order in which we address the protocols in the rest of the book. The introduction also includes a thorough definition of the model that is used throughout the book in the analysis of the protocols. The reader is encouraged to read this section before proceeding to the main text and to keep on referring to this chapter while studying the material. The main body of the book resides in Chapters 2 through 5. Chapter 2 addresses the traditional conflict-free protocols. In Chapter 3 we address the Aloha family of protocols that is so fundamental in the analysis of multiple access networks and is used mainly in satellite networks. Chapter 4 addresses carrier sensing protocols that are so popular in local area networks. In Chapter 5 we present the family of collision resolution protocols that are algorithmically somewhat more complex but that exhibit many other desirable features. Chapters 2, 3, and 5 are to some extent independent of one another, in the sense that one can be studied without the others and because different analytical techniques are used (Chapter 4 uses the same tools and approach as does Chapter 3). We do, however, feel that studying the subjects in the order presented contributes significantly to the understanding of the material. Finally, in Chapter 6 we scan briefly other major subjects that have been studied and published in the open literature but that are beyond the scope of this book.

This book is aimed both at the student and the professional engineer. From a curriculum standpoint the material here contains more than can be covered in a single semester of studies. However, with sufficient mathematical background an in-depth course can be constructed covering enough material so that the student could complete the rest of the material by himself. A small set of problems and exercises is included at the end of every chapter. These exercises are, in many cases, nontrivial and require a bit of time to solve; they are meant to enhance the reader's knowledge and train him in the analytical techniques covered in the text.

To enhance its use as a reference for professionals, the book points the reader to variations and other systems through an extensive bibliography. One might expect the professional to study the basic material as presented in the book and then follow the bibliography to an analysis of a system that might be closer to the one he seeks.

Finally, we would like to thank Prof. Aurel Lazar from Columbia University for helping and directing us along the path that lead to the publishing of this book. Thanks are also due to the many colleagues whose critical review enhanced the presentation of the material, and to our students who were the guinea-pigs of earlier versions of the manuscript.

Haifa, Israel   Raphael Rom

October 1989   Moshe Sidi

CONTENTS

CHAPTER 1

INTRODUCTION

Three major components characterize computer communication networks: switches, channels, and protocols. The switches (or nodes) are the hardware entities that house the data communication functions; the protocols are the sets of rules and agreements among the communicating parties that dictate the behavior of the switches, and the channel is the physical medium over which signals, representing data, travel from one switch to another.

Traditional networks make use of point-to-point channels, that is, channels that are dedicated to an (ordered) pair of users. These channels, beyond being very economical, are advantageous due to their noninterference feature namely, that transmission between a pair of nodes has no effect on the transmission between another pair of nodes even if these two pairs have a common node. Point-to-point channels, however, require the topology to be fixed, mostly determined at network design phase. Subsequent topological changes are quite hard (and costly) to implement.

When point-to-point channels are not economical, not available, or when dynamic topologies are required broadcast channels can be used. Informally stated, a broadcast channel is one in which more than a single receiver can potentially receive every transmitted message. Broadcast channels appear naturally in radio, satellite, and some local area networks. The broadcast property has its advantages and disadvantages. If, indeed, a message is destined to a large number of destinations then a broadcast channel is clearly superior. However, in a typical case a message is destined to a single or a very small number of destinations and wasteful processing results in all those switches for whom the message is not intended. Moreover, transmissions over a broadcast channel interfere, in the sense that one transmission coinciding in time with another may cause none of them to be received. In other words, the success of a transmission between a pair of nodes is no longer independent of other transmissions. Important advantages of a broadcast system are the easy deployment of a network and the ability to support mobile users.

To make a transmission successful interference must be avoided or at least controlled. The channel then becomes the shared resource whose allocation is critical for proper operation of the network. This book focuses on access schemes to such channels known in the literature as *Multiple Access Protocols*. These protocols are nothing but channel allocation schemes that posses desirable performance characteristics. In terms of known layering models, such as the

OSI reference model, these protocols reside mostly within a special layer called the *Medium Access Control (MAC)* layer. The *MAC* layer is between the *Data Link Control (DLC)* layer and the *Physical* layer.

The need for multiple access protocols arises not only in communication systems but also in many other systems such as a computer system, a storage facility, or a server of any kind, where a resource is shared (and thus accessed) by a number of independent users. In this book we mainly address a shared communication channel. To briefly summarize the environment in which we are interested we assume, in general, that (1) sending a message to multiple users in a single transmission is an inherent capability, (2) users typically hear one another, (3) we confine ourselves to the *Medium Access Control* layer freeing us from worrying about network wide functions such as routing and flow control, and (4) interference is inherent, i.e., communication between one pair of nodes may influence the communication between other pairs. More precise definitions appear later in the introduction and in the description of the various protocols.

1.1. PROTOCOL CLASSIFICATION

The multiple access protocols suggested and analyzed to date are too numerous to be all mentioned here. We therefore classify these protocols and take samples of the various classes to be analyzed in the text. In the description of the classification we consider the channel as the focal point and refer to the nodes transmitting through the channel as its users.

There are various ways to classify multiple access protocols. Examples of such classifications appear in [KSY84] and [Sac88]. Our classification is presented in Figure 1.1. First and foremost, we are interested in noncentralized multiple access protocols. These are protocols in which all nodes behave according to the same set of rules. In particular there is no single node coordinating the activities of the others (whose protocol, by necessity, differs from the rest). This also excludes, for example, all polling-type access protocols. The classification of Figure 1.1 attempts to exhibit the underlying balance and symmetry behind existing multiple access protocols.

At the highest level of the classification we distinguish between conflict-free and contention protocols. Conflict-free protocols are those ensuring that a transmission, whenever made, is a successful one, that is, will not be interfered by another transmission. Conflict-free transmission can be achieved by allocating the channel to the users either statically or dynamically. The channel resources can be viewed, for this purpose, from a time, frequency, or mixed time-frequency standpoint. Hence, the channel can be divided by providing the entire frequency range (bandwidth) to a single user for a fraction of the time as done in Time Division Multiple Access (TDMA), or providing a fraction of the frequency range to every user all of the time as done in Frequency Division Multiple Access (FDMA), or providing every user a portion of the bandwidth for a fraction of the time as done in spread-spectrum based systems such as Code Division Multiple Access (CDMA).

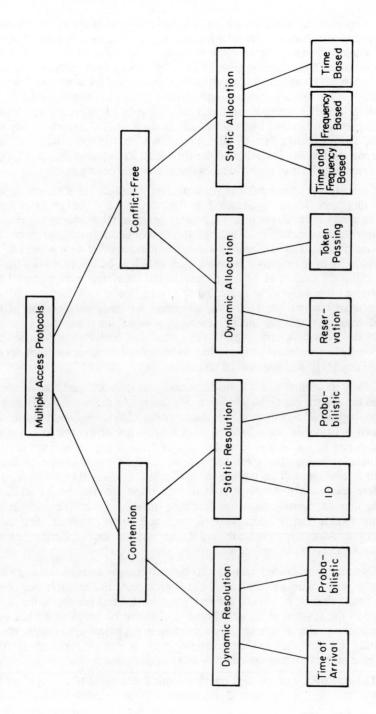

Figure 1.1: Classification of Multiple Access Protocols

To counter the static allocation, the dynamic one allocates the channel based on demand so that a user who happens to be idle uses only little, if at all, of the channel resources, leaving the majority of its share to the other, more active users. Such an allocation can be done by various reservation schemes in which the users first announce their intent to transmit and all those who have so announced will transmit before new users have a chance to announce their intent to transmit. Another common scheme is referred to as token passing in which a single (logical or physical) token is passed among the users permitting only the token holder to transmit, thereby guaranteeing noninterference. The Mini Slotted Alternating Priority (MSAP) and the Broadcast Recognition Access Method (BRAM) are examples of multiple access protocols that belong to this class.

Contention schemes differ in principle from conflict-free schemes since a transmitting user is not guaranteed to be successful. The protocol must prescribe a way to resolve conflicts once they occur so all messages are eventually transmitted successfully. The resolution process does consume resources and is one of the major differences among the various contention protocols. If the probability of interference is small, such as might be the case with bursty users, taking the chance of having to resolve the interference compensates for the resources that have to be expanded to ensure freedom of conflicts. Moreover, in most conflict-free protocols, idle users do consume a portion of the channel resources; this portion becomes major when the number of potential users in the system is very large to the extent that conflict-free schemes are impractical. In contention schemes idle users do not transmit and thus do not consume any portion of the channel resources.

When contention-based multiple access protocols are used, the necessity arises to resolve the conflicts, whenever they occur. As in the conflict-free case, here too, both static and dynamic resolutions exist. Static resolution means that the actual behavior is not influenced by the dynamics of the system. A static resolution can be based, for example, on user ID's or any other fixed priority assignment, meaning that whenever a conflict arises the first user to finally transmit a message will be the one with, say, the smallest ID (this is done in some tree-resolution protocols). A static resolution can also be probabilistic, meaning that the transmission schedule for the interfering users is chosen from a fixed distribution that is independent of the actual number of interfering users, as is done in Aloha-type protocols and the various versions of Carrier Sensing Multiple Access (CSMA) protocols.

Dynamic resolution, namely taking advantage and tracking system changes is also possible in contention-based protocols. For example, resolution can be based on time of arrival, giving highest (or lowest) priority to the oldest message in the system. Alternatively, resolution can be probabilistic but such that the statistics change dynamically according to the extent of the interference. Estimating the multiplicity of the interfering packets, and the exponential back-off scheme of the Ethernet standard fall into this category.

The main body of the text contains typical examples of multiple access protocols that are analyzed and discussed. These examples were chosen judiciously to cover the above classes of protocols. Each example presents a system or a protocol whose nature differs from the others either in the system characteristics, or in the purpose of the system, or in the method of analysis. Via this approach we cover all types of noncentralized multiple access protocols known to date and most of the analytical methods used in their analysis.

1.2. THE SYSTEM MODEL

In the analysis of the various multiple access protocols we are interested mainly in *throughput* and *delay* characteristics. We take the throughput of the channel to mean the aggregate average amount of data that is transported through the channel in a unit of time. In those cases where only a single transmission can be successful at any time (as is typical in many single-hop systems) the throughput, as thus defined, equals the fraction of time in which the channel is engaged in the successful transmission of user data. In delay calculations we generally consider the time from the moment a message is generated until it makes it successfully across the channel. Here one must distinguish between the user and the system measures as it is possible that the average delay measured for the entire system does not necessarily reflect the average delay experienced by any of the users. In "fair", or homogeneous systems we expect these to be almost identical. Two other criteria are also of great interest: system stability and message storage requirement (buffer occupancy). The notion of stability arises in this context because the protocol characteristics may be such that some message generation rates, even smaller than the maximal transmission rate in the channel, cannot be sustained by the system for a long time. Evaluation of those input rates for which the system remains stable is therefore essential. We postpone further definitions to the sections dealing directly with stability. Buffer occupancy is clearly an important performance measure since having to provide larger buffers generally translates into more costly and complex implementation. Higher buffer occupancy usually also means longer message delays and vice versa.

To analyze multiple access protocols one must make assumptions regarding the environment in which they operate. Hence, in each and every protocol we must address the following issues:

- *Connectivity.* In general, the ability of a node to hear the transmission of another node depends on the transmission power used, on the distance between the two nodes, and on the sensitivity of the receiver at the receiving node. In this text we assume a symmetric connectivity pattern, that is, every node can successfully transmit to every node it can hear. Basically, connectivity patterns can be classified into three categories known as single-hop, dual-hop and multihop topologies. In a single-hop topology all users hear one another, and hence no routing of messages is required. Dual-hop topologies are those in which messages from a source to a destination do not have to pass more than two hops, meaning that either the source and destination can communicate directly or there exists a node that communicates directly with both the source and the destination. This configuration is peculiar in a broadcast channel context since the intermediary node can be affected by the behavior of two other nodes that do not hear one another. The multihop topology is the most general one in which beyond (and in addition to) the problems encountered in the single and dual-hop topologies one must address routing issues that become complex if the topology is allowed to vary dynamically.

- *Channel type*. The channel is the medium through which data is transferred from its source to its destination. In this text we deal with an *errorless collision channel*. Collision is a situation in which, at the receiver, two or more transmissions overlap in time wholly or partially. A collision channel is one in which all the colliding transmissions are not received correctly and in most protocols have to be retransmitted. A channel is errorless, if a single transmission heard at a node is always received correctly. Other possible channels include the noisy channel in which errors may occur even if only a single transmission is heard at a node and, furthermore, the channel may be such that errors between successive transmissions are not independent. Another channel type is the capture channel in which one or more of the colliding transmissions "captures" the receiver and can be received correctly. Yet another case is a channel in which coding is used so that even if transmissions collide the receiver can still decode some or all of the transmitted information.

- *Synchronism*. Users are generally not assumed to be synchronized and are capable of accessing and transmitting their data on the channel at any time. Another important class of systems is that of *slotted* systems in which a global clock exists that marks equally long intervals of time called slots. In these systems transmissions of data start only at slot boundaries. Other operations, such as determining activities on the channel can be done at any time. Various degrees of synchronism are required in the slotted protocols we consider.

- *Feedback/Acknowledgment*. Feedback is the information available to the users regarding activities on the channel at prior times. This information can be obtained by listening to the channel, or by explicit acknowledgement messages sent by the receiving node. For every protocol we assume that there exist some instants of time (typically slot boundaries or end of transmissions) in which feedback information is available. Common feedback information indicates whether a message was successfully transmitted, or a collision took place, or the channel was idle. It is generally assumed that the feedback mechanism does not consume channel resources, for example, by utilizing a different channel or by being able to determine the feedback locally. Other feedback variations include indication of the exact or the estimated number of colliding transmissions, or providing uncertain feedback (e.g., in the case of a noisy channel). Recently no-feedback protocols have also been proposed.

- *Message size.* The basic unit of data generated by a user is a message. It is possible, though, that due to its length, a message cannot be transmitted in a single transmission and must therefore be broken into smaller units called *packets* each of which can be transmitted in a single channel access. A message consists of an integral number of packets although the number of packets in a message can vary randomly. Packet size is measured by the time required to transmit the packet once access to the channel has been granted. Typically, we assume all packets to be of equal size and variations include randomly varying packets.

- *Message generation.* All users are statistically identical and generate new messages according to a Poisson process. Variations include cases in which all users are not the same and in particular one heavy user and many identical small ones. Few analyses can be found in the literature accommodating non-Poisson generation processes.

- *User population.* The number of users in the system can be finite or infinite. Every user is a different, generally independent entity. One interesting observation is that most conflict-free protocols are useless if the user population increases beyond a certain amount. For such cases contention based protocols are the only possible solution.

- *Buffering capability.* Messages generated by the user are stored in a buffer. In a typical analysis it is assumed that every user has a buffer for a single message and that it does not generate new messages unless its buffer is empty. Other alternatives include more buffering, both infinite and finite, at each user.

A word about notation

Throughout the text we adopt a consistent notation as follows. A random variable is denoted by a letter with a tilde, e.g., $\tilde{x}$. For this random variable we denote by $F_{\tilde{x}}(x)$ its probability distribution function, by $f_{\tilde{x}}(x)$ its probability density function, by $F_{\tilde{x}}^*(s)$ the Laplace transform of $f_{\tilde{x}}(x)$, and by $\overline{x^k}$ its kth moment. If $\tilde{x}$ is a discrete random variable then $X(z)$ denotes its generating function. The expectation is denoted by $\overline{x}$ or just x. In general, a discrete stochastic process is denoted by $\{\tilde{x}_n, n \geq 0\}$.

CHAPTER 2

CONFLICT-FREE ACCESS PROTOCOLS

Conflict-free protocols are designed to ensure that a transmission, whenever made, is not interfered by any other transmission and is therefore successful. This is achieved by allocating the channel to the users without any overlap between the portions of the channel allocated to different users. An important advantage of conflict-free access protocols is the ability to ensure fairness among users and the ability to control the packet delay--a feature that may be essential in real-time applications.

The first three sections are devoted to static channel allocation strategies in which channel allocation is predetermined (typically at network design time) and does not change during the operation of the system. The two most well known protocols in this class are the Frequency Division Multiple Access (FDMA) in which a fraction of the frequency bandwidth is allocated to every user all the time, and the Time Division Multiple Access (TDMA) in which the entire bandwidth is used by each user for a fraction of the time.

For both the FDMA and the TDMA protocols no overhead, in the form of control messages, is incurred. However, due to the static and fixed assignment, parts of the channel might be idle even though some users have data to transmit. Dynamic channel allocation protocols attempt to overcome this drawback by changing the channel allocation based on the current demands of the users.

2.1. FREQUENCY DIVISION MULTIPLE ACCESS

With Frequency Division Multiple Access (FDMA) the entire available frequency band is divided into bands each of which serves a single user. Every user is therefore equipped with a transmitter for a given, predetermined, frequency band, and a receiver for each band (which can be implemented as a single receiver for the entire range with a bank of bandpass filters for the individual bands).

The main advantage of FDMA is its simplicity--it does not require any coordination or synchronization among the users since each can use its own frequency band without interference. This, however, is also the cause of waste especially when the load is momentarily uneven, since when one user is idle his share of the bandwidth cannot be used by other users. It should be noted that if the users have uneven long term demands, it is possible to divide the frequency range unevenly, i.e., proportional to the demands. FDMA is also not flexible; adding a new user to the network requires equipment modification (such as additional filters) in every other user. For more details the reader may consult any of the many texts treating FDMA that have been published, e.g., by Stallings [Sta85] or the one by Martin [Mar78].

To evaluate the performance of the FDMA protocol let us assume that the entire channel can sustain a rate of R bits/sec which is equally divided among M users--R/M bits/sec for each. Since the individual bands are disjoint, there is no interference among users' transmissions and the system can therefore be viewed as M independent queues (see Figure 2.1). Each of these queues has an individual input process governing the packet generation process for that user. If the packet length is a random variable P, then the service time afforded to every packet is the random variable $\tilde{T}=MP/R$. To evaluate the throughput of the individual user we note that every bit transmitted is a "good" bit and thus the individual throughput is the fraction of time the individual server is busy (i.e., nonempty system). The total throughput is M times the individual throughput while the average packet delay can be obtained by applying Little's result to the individual queue. In general, all parameters relating to FDMA can be obtained by applying known results of the corresponding queue discipline.

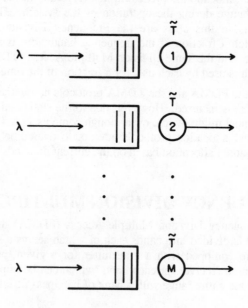

Figure 2.1: FDMA System Model

Consider a typical user that generates packets according to a Poisson process with rate λ packets/sec. and his buffering capabilities are not limited. The time required for the transmission of a packet is T. Each node can therefore be viewed as an M/G/1 queue. Thus, using the known system delay time formula for M/G/1 queueing systems we get that the expected delay of a packet is (see Appendix)

$$D = \bar{x} + \frac{\lambda \overline{x^2}}{2(1 - \lambda \bar{x})} = T + \frac{\lambda \overline{T^2}}{2(1 - \lambda T)}$$

where $T = E[\tilde{T}]$ and $\overline{T^2} = E[(\tilde{T})^2]$.

When all packets are of equal length consisting of P bits each then the transmission time of every packet is (deterministically) equal to $T = MP/R$ seconds. In this case the queueing model corresponds to an M/D/1 queue in which $\overline{T^2} = T^2$ and therefore

$$D = T + \frac{\lambda T^2}{2(1 - \lambda T)} = T\left[1 + \frac{\rho}{2(1 - \rho)}\right] = \frac{MP}{R}\left[1 + \frac{\rho}{2(1 - \rho)}\right] \quad (2.1)$$

where $\rho \triangleq \lambda T$.

For M/G/1 systems $\rho = \lambda \bar{x}$ is the fraction of time the server is busy. In our case, therefore, ρ equals the individual user's throughput. Normalizing the

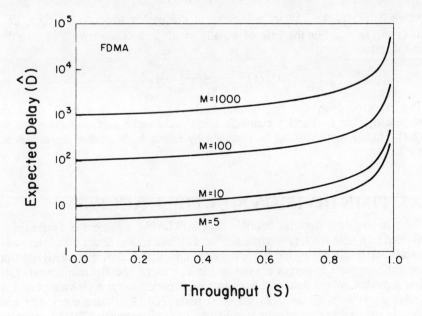

Figure 2.2: Throughput-Delay Characteristics for FDMA

expected delay given in (2.1) by P/R, the time required to transmit a packet in a channel with rate R, and substituting S for ρ we get the normalized expected delay, $\hat{D}$,

$$\hat{D} = \frac{D}{P/R} = \left[1 + \frac{S}{2(1-S)}\right] M = M\frac{2-S}{2(1-S)}$$

which is the desired throughput-delay characteristic for FDMA with constant packet size. Graphs depicting the throughput delay for various population sizes is depicted in Figure 2.2. Note that for a wide range the delay is rather insensitive to the throughput. For values of throughput beyond 0.8 the delay increases quickly to values which cannot be tolerated.

2.1.1. Delay Distribution

The delay distribution of FDMA is also taken directly from known M/G/1 results. Specifically, if $\tilde{D}$ is a random variable representing the packet delay, then the Laplace transform of the probability density function (pdf) of $\tilde{D}$, $D^*(s) = E[e^{-s\tilde{D}}]$, is given by (see Appendix)

$$D^*(s) = X^*(s)\frac{s(1-\rho)}{s - \lambda + \lambda X^*(s)}$$

where $X^*(s)$ is the Laplace transform of the packet transmission time, i.e., $X^*(s) = E[e^{-sT}]$. For the case of equally sized packets we have $X^*(s) = e^{-sT}$ and therefore

$$D^*(s) = \frac{s(1-\rho)}{\lambda + (s-\lambda)e^{sT}} \quad .$$

The expected delay can be obtained by taking the derivative of $D^*(s)$ with respect to s at $s=0$ and for equally sized packets the expression is given in (2.1). Higher moments can be obtained by taking higher order derivatives at $s=0$.

2.2. TIME DIVISION MULTIPLE ACCESS

In the time division multiple access (TDMA) scheme the time axis is divided into time slots, preassigned to the different users. Every user is allowed to transmit freely during the slot assigned to him, that is, during the assigned slot the entire system resources are devoted to that user. The slot assignments follow a predetermined pattern that repeats itself periodically; each such period is called a *cycle* or a *frame*. In the most basic TDMA scheme every user has exactly one slot in every frame (see Figure 2.3). More general TDMA schemes in which several slots are assigned to one user within a frame, referred to as generalized TDMA, are considered in the next section. Note that for proper operation of a TDMA scheme, the users must be synchronized so that each one knows exactly when and for how long he can transmit. Further details on

TDMA schemes can be found in texts such as [Kuo81,Sta85].

To analyze the performance of a TDMA scheme consider a system composed of M users each transmitting equally long packets of P bits each. If the total rate of transmission is R bits/sec then the packet transmission time is $T = P/R$ which is taken to be the slot size. The duration of the entire cycle is therefore $T_c = MT$. Assuming that the packet arrival processes of new packets to the different users are independent, it follows that the queueing behavior of the queue at one user is independent of the queueing behavior of all others. The reason is that a user transmits a packet, if he has any, every T_c seconds, independently of any event in any of the queues of other users. Consequently, in the following we concentrate on the characteristics of one user, and without loss of generality, assume that the user transmits a packet, if he has any, at the first slot of every frame.

Consider a typical packet generated by the user. The delay suffered by this packet has three components: (1) the time between its generation and the end of the current frame, (2) the queueing time to allow all the packets already queued to be transmitted and, (3) the packet transmission time itself. Of these components the first and the third are readily known. Since all frames are of equal length, the average time between the packet generation time and the end of the current frame is $\frac{1}{2}T_c$. Packet transmission time is T.

To compute the queueing time (once the end of the current frame is reached) we observe that the queue behaves exactly like one with deterministic service time of T_c. If we assume for each user a Poisson arrival process of λ packets/second and that the number of packets that can be stored in a queue is not bounded, then the queueing time is identical to the queueing time in an M/D/1 queueing system in which the deterministic service time $\bar{x}$ is T_c. We thus have that the expected queueing time of a packet, W_q, is given by (see Appendix)

$$W_q = \frac{\rho}{2(1-\rho)}\bar{x} = \frac{\rho}{2(1-\rho)}T_c = \frac{\rho}{2(1-\rho)}MT$$

where $\rho = \lambda T_c = \lambda MP/R$ (note that this is the same value for ρ as in the FDMA case). The total expected packet delay is therefore

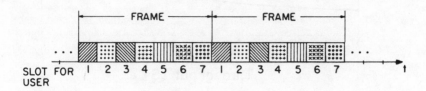

Figure 2.3: TDMA Slot Allocation

$$D = \frac{1}{2}T_c + W_q + T = \frac{1}{2}MT + \frac{\rho}{2(1-\rho)}MT + T = T\left[1 + \frac{M}{2(1-\rho)}\right].$$

As in the FDMA case, every bit transmitted should be counted in the throughput or, in other words, the throughput equals the fraction of time the server is busy, which for an M/D/1 queue equals ρ. Thus, as in the FDMA case, we have $S = \rho$ leading to

$$D = T\left[1 + \frac{M}{2(1-S)}\right],$$

and the normalized expected packet delay is obtained by dividing D by the time required to transmit a packet,

$$\hat{D} = \frac{D}{T} = 1 + \frac{M}{2(1-S)} \tag{2.2}$$

which is the desired throughput delay characteristic of a TDMA scheme. A family of graphs of the expected packet delay versus the throughput for various values of M is given in Figure 2.4. They are, not surprisingly, similar to those of the FDMA (Figure 2.2).

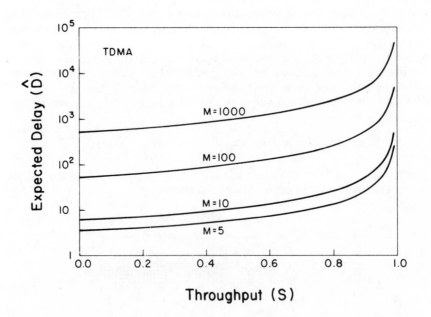

Figure 2.4: Throughput Delay for TDMA

2.2.1. FDMA - TDMA Comparison

Comparing the throughput delay characteristics of FDMA and TDMA we note that

$$D_{FDMA} = D_{TDMA} + \frac{P}{R}\left[\frac{M}{2} - 1\right] \geq D_{TDMA} \; .$$

We thus conclude that for $M \geq 2$ (i.e., every meaningful case) the TDMA expected delay is always less than that of FDMA and the difference grows linearly with the number of users and is independent of the load! The difference stems from the fact that the actual transmission of a packet in TDMA takes only a single slot while in FDMA it lasts the equivalent of an entire frame. This difference is somewhat offset by the fact that a packet arriving to an empty queue may have to wait until the proper slot when a TDMA scheme is employed, whereas in FDMA transmission starts right away.

It must be remembered, however, that at high throughput the dominant factor in the expected delay is inversely proportional to $(1-S)$ in both TDMA and FDMA and therefore the ratio of the expected delays between the two schemes approaches unity when the load increases.

As a practical matter, while FDMA performs slightly worse than TDMA, it is somewhat easier to implement since it does not require any synchronization among users, which is necessary to keep the TDMA users from transmitting in a slot which is not their own.

2.2.2. Message Delay Distribution

In the previous section we derived the expected packet delay in a TDMA system. In this section we generalize the arrival process and demonstrate how one can, with fairly straightforward queueing theory techniques, compute the *distribution* of the delay in such a system. The analysis presented is essentially due to Lam [Lam77].

As before, the queueing behavior of one user is independent of the queue-ing behavior of other users and therefore we consider a typical user in an M user system in which the slot size T equals the duration of *packet* transmission. The user transmits a packet, if he has any, in the first slot of every frame. At each arrival epoch a new *message* arrives. A message consists of a random bulk of $\tilde{L}$ packets. Let $L(z)$ be the generating function of $\tilde{L}$, L its mean and $\overline{L^2}$ its second moment, i.e.,

$$L(z) = \sum_{l=1}^{\infty} Prob[\tilde{L} = l]z^l \; ,$$

$$L = L'(z)|_{z=1} = \sum_{l=1}^{\infty} l \cdot Prob[\tilde{L} = l] \; ; \quad \overline{L^2} = L''(z)|_{z=1} + L = \sum_{l=1}^{\infty} l^2 \cdot Prob[\tilde{L} = l] \; .$$

We assume that messages arrive to the user according to a Poisson process at a rate of λ messages/sec. Notice that the arrival process considered here is somewhat more general than that considered in the previous section. If one takes $L(z)=z$, then each message consists of a single packet and the general arrival process we consider here degenerates to that of the previous section. The buffering capabilities of the user are not limited.

The *message delay* $\tilde{D}$ is defined as the time elapsing between the message arrival epoch until after the transmission of the last packet of that message is completed. In this section we derive the Laplace transform of the message delay distribution.

Consider an arbitrary "tagged" message arriving $T_c - \tilde{w}$ seconds after the beginning of the $(j+1)$st frame (i.e., $\tilde{w}$ seconds before its end). Assume that our tagged message is the $\tilde{k}+1$st message arriving in that frame, that is $\tilde{k} \geq 0$ messages arrived prior to it in the same frame ($\tilde{k}$ and $\tilde{w}$ are random variables and when $\tilde{w}$ is given, $\tilde{k}$ has a Poisson distribution with parameter $\lambda(T_c - \tilde{w})$). Figure 2.5 shows the relation among these quantities.

Denote by $\tilde{q}_j$ the number of packets awaiting transmission at the beginning of the $(j+1)$st frame. Then the delay of the tagged message is given by

$$\tilde{D} = \tilde{w} + \left[\max(\tilde{q}_j - 1, 0) + \sum_{i=1}^{\tilde{k}} \tilde{L}_i \right] T_c + \left[(\tilde{L}_{\tilde{k}+1} - 1)T_c + T \right] \qquad (2.3)$$

where the first term ($\tilde{w}$) represents the waiting time of the tagged message until

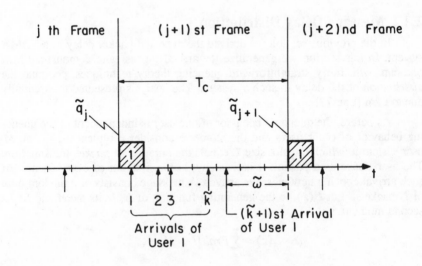

Figure 2.5: Packet Delay Components

the end of the $(j+1)$st frame. The second term in (2.3) represents the time required to transmit all the packets already queued in the user buffer upon the tagged message arrival. When messages are transmitted in a FIFO manner, this is the time the message will wait from the end of the $(j+1)$st frame until its first packet will be transmitted. This second term is composed of two components: the first $(T_c [\max(\bar{q}_j - 1, 0)])$ corresponds to waiting for transmission of packets present in the queue at the beginning of the $(j+1)$st frame. The other component $(T_c \sum_{i=1}^{k} \bar{L}_i)$ corresponds to waiting for transmission of packets that arrived since the beginning of the $(j+1)$st frame until the arrival of the tagged message. Finally, the third term in (2.3) represents the time required to transmit the tagged message itself: $(\bar{L}_{\bar{k}+1} - 1)T_c$ seconds to transmit all packets of the tagged message, except the last one that requires only T seconds.

The expression in (2.3) can be rewritten as

$$\bar{D} = \max(\bar{q}_j - 1, 0)T_c + \left[\bar{w} + T_c \sum_{i=1}^{\bar{k}} \bar{L}_i \right] + \left[\bar{L}_{\bar{k}+1} T_c + T - T_c \right] . \quad (2.4)$$

The three components in this expression are statistically independent of one another: the first contains quantities relating to previous frames, the second to the current frame up to the arrival of the tagged message, and the last one to the tagged message itself. Thus, $D^*(s)$, the Laplace transform of the probability density function of $\bar{D}$ is the product of the Laplace transforms of these three components.

Let $\bar{a}_j$ be the number of packets arriving during the jth frame. Because the number of messages arriving in a frame depends only on the arrival process and on the frame length, and because all frames are equally long we conclude that $\bar{a}_j$ is independent of j. The relation among the values of $\bar{q}$ in consecutive frames is therefore given by

$$\bar{q}_{j+1} = \bar{q}_j - \Delta(\bar{q}_j) + \bar{a} \quad (2.5)$$

where $\Delta(i)$ equals 0 for $i=0$ and equals 1 elsewhere. The explanation of (2.5) is simple. The packets awaiting transmission at the beginning of the $(j+1)$st frame are those packets that were queued up at the beginning of the jth frame, less the packet (if there were any) that has been transmitted in the first slot of the jth frame. In addition, the packets that arrived during the jth frame are also queued up at the beginning of the $(j+1)$st frame.

Let $Q_j(z)$ be the generating function of $\bar{q}_j$, i.e., $Q_j(z) = E[z^{\bar{q}_j}]$. From (2.5) we obtain,

$$Q_{j+1}(z) = E[z^{\bar{q}_{j+1}}] = E[z^{\bar{q}_j - \Delta(\bar{q}_j) + \bar{a}}] = E[z^{\bar{a}}]E[z^{\bar{q}_j - \Delta(\bar{q}_j)}] \quad (2.6)$$

where we used the fact that the arrival process is independent of the queue size, hence $\bar{a}$ is independent of $\bar{q}_j$.

Let $A(z)$ be the generating function of $\bar{a}$, i.e., $A(z) \stackrel{\Delta}{=} E[z^{\bar{a}}]$. The derivation of $A(z)$ is simple,

$$A(z) = E[z^{\tilde{a}}] = E\left\{ E[z^{\tilde{a}} \mid m \text{ messages arrive in a frame }]\right\}$$

$$= E\left\{ [L(z)]^m \right\} = \sum_{m=0}^{\infty} \frac{e^{-\lambda T_c}(\lambda T_c)^m}{m!} [L(z)]^m = e^{\lambda T_c [L(z)-1]} \tag{2.7}$$

where we used the fact that the generating function of the number of packets in a message is $L(z)$.

We now turn to compute the quantity $E[z^{\tilde{q}_j - \Delta(\tilde{q}_j)}]$ that appears in (2.6).

$$E[z^{\tilde{q}_j - \Delta(\tilde{q}_j)}] = \sum_{k=0}^{\infty} z^{k-\Delta(k)} P[\tilde{q}_j = k] = P[\tilde{q}_j = 0] + \frac{1}{z}\left[Q_j(z) - P[\tilde{q}_j = 0]\right]$$

$$= z^{-1} Q_j(z) + (1 - z^{-1}) P[\tilde{q}_j = 0] \; . \tag{2.8}$$

Combining (2.6) and (2.8) we obtain,

$$Q_{j+1}(z) = A(z)\left\{ z^{-1} Q_j(z) + (1-z^{-1}) P[\tilde{q}_j = 0]\right\} \; . \tag{2.9}$$

The chain $\{\tilde{q}_j, j=1,2,\cdots\}$ is clearly a Markov chain (see (2.5) and the Appendix). Assuming that this Markov chain is ergodic (as we discuss below), the existence of steady-state (invariant) probabilities for the queue size at the beginning of a frame is guaranteed. Let $Q(z)$ be the generating function of this invariant distribution, i.e., $Q(z) = \lim_{j\to\infty} Q_j(z)$ and let $P[\tilde{q}=0]$ be the probability that the queue will be empty at the beginning of a frame in steady-state. Then from (2.9) we obtain,

$$Q(z) = A(z)\left\{ z^{-1} Q(z) + (1 - z^{-1}) P[\tilde{q} = 0]\right\}$$

or

$$Q(z) = A(z) \frac{P[\tilde{q} = 0](z - 1)}{z - A(z)} \; .$$

The computation of $P[\tilde{q}=0]$ is now easy; we use the normalization condition that $Q(z)|_{z=1} = 1$ and obtain that $P[\tilde{q}=0] = 1 - A'(z)|_{z=1} = 1 - \lambda L T_c \triangleq 1 - \rho$ (we used L'Hopital's rule in this calculation). Therefore, using (2.7) we obtain

$$Q(z) = A(z)\frac{(1-\rho)(z-1)}{z - A(z)} = e^{\lambda T_c [L(z)-1]} \frac{(1-\rho)(z-1)}{z - e^{\lambda T_c [L(z)-1]}} \; . \tag{2.10}$$

The derivation of equation (2.10) holds if and only if $\rho < 1$, which renders the q's an ergodic Markov chain and an altogether stable system.

We now turn to compute the Laplace transform of the probability density function of the three components in equation (2.4). Starting with the first component we note that $\max(\tilde{q}_j - 1, 0) = \tilde{q}_j - \Delta(\tilde{q}_j)$. From (2.8) we have,

$$E\left[z^{\tilde{q}_j - \Delta(\tilde{q}_j)}\right] = z^{-1}Q_j(z) + (1-z^{-1})P\left[\tilde{q}_j = 0\right] \ . \tag{2.11}$$

We are interested in the steady-state behavior, hence we let $j \to \infty$ in (2.11) to obtain,

$$E\left[z^{\tilde{q} - \Delta(\tilde{q})}\right] = z^{-1}Q(z) + (1-z^{-1})P\left[\tilde{q} = 0\right] = \frac{(1-\rho)(z-1)}{z - A(z)} \tag{2.12}$$

where we used the expression for $Q(z)$ from (2.10). Consequently, we get (by substituting $z = e^{-sT_c}$)

$$E\left[\exp[-sT_c(\tilde{q} - \Delta(\tilde{q}))]\right] = E\left[[\exp(-sT_c)]^{\tilde{q} - \Delta(\tilde{q})}\right] = E\left[z^{\tilde{q} - \Delta(\tilde{q})}\right]_{z = \exp(-sT_c)} \ .$$

Substituting (2.12) and (2.7) into the last equation and denoting $L^*(s) \triangleq L(e^{-sT_c})$ we get

$$E\left[\exp[-sT_c(\tilde{q} - \Delta(\tilde{q}))]\right] = \frac{(1-\rho)[1 - \exp(-sT_c)]}{\exp\{\lambda T_c[L^*(s) - 1]\} - \exp\{-sT_c\}} \ . \tag{2.13}$$

To handle the second component of equation (2.4) we define $\tilde{y} \triangleq \tilde{w} + T_c \sum_{i=1}^{\tilde{k}} \tilde{L}_i$ and thus we need to compute $E[e^{-s\tilde{y}}]$. This is done by computing the conditional transform and then relaxing the conditions one by one as follows:

$$E[e^{-s\tilde{y}} \mid \tilde{k} = k, \tilde{w} = w] = E\left[\exp(-sw - sT_c \sum_{i=1}^{k} \tilde{L}_i)\right] = e^{-sw} E\left[\exp(-sT_c \sum_{i=1}^{k} \tilde{L}_i)\right]$$

$$= e^{-sw}\left[E[\exp(-sT_c\tilde{L})]\right]^k = e^{-sw}L^{*k}(s) \ .$$

Noting that for a given w, $\tilde{k}$ is distributed according to a Poisson distribution with mean $\lambda(T_c - w)$ we now remove the condition on $\tilde{k}$

$$E[e^{-s\tilde{y}} \mid \tilde{w} = w] = E[e^{-sw}L^{*\tilde{k}}(s) \mid \tilde{w} = w] = e^{-sw}E[L^{*\tilde{k}}(s) \mid \tilde{w} = w]$$

$$= e^{-sw}E[z^{\tilde{k}} \mid \tilde{w} = w]\,\Big|_{z = L^*(s)} = e^{-sw}e^{\lambda(T_c - w)(z-1)}\,\Big|_{z = L^*(s)}$$

$$= \exp\left[\lambda T_c[L^*(s) - 1]\right]\exp\left[-w[s - \lambda + \lambda L^*(s)]\right] \ .$$

Finally, relaxing the condition on $\tilde{w}$ and recalling that the latter is uniformly distributed on $[0, T_c]$ we get

$$E[e^{-s\tilde{y}}] = E\left[\exp\{\lambda T_c[L^*(s) - 1]\}\exp\{-\tilde{w}[s - \lambda + \lambda L^*(s)]\}\right]$$

$$= \exp\{\lambda T_c[L^*(s) - 1]\}E\left[\exp\{-\tilde{w}[s - \lambda + \lambda L^*(s)]\}\right] \tag{2.14}$$

$$= \frac{\exp\{\lambda T_c[L^*(s) - 1]\} - \exp\{-sT_c\}}{T_c[s - \lambda + \lambda L^*(s)]} \ .$$

This last result can be obviously computed directly by

$$E[e^{-s\tilde{y}}] = \int_{w=0}^{T_c} \frac{1}{T_c}\left[e^{-sw} \sum_{k=0}^{\infty} L^{*k}(s)\frac{[\lambda(T_c - w)]^k}{k!}e^{-\lambda(T_c - w)}\right] dw \quad.$$

Finally, treating the third component of equation (2.4) we get

$$E\left[\exp[-s(\tilde{L}_{k+1}T_c + T - T_c)]\right] = e^{-s(T_c - T)}E[e^{-s\tilde{L}T_c}] = e^{-s(T_c - T)}L^*(s) \quad. \qquad (2.15)$$

Putting together the results of equations (2.13), (2.14), and (2.15) we finally get

$$D^*(s) = \frac{1-\rho}{T_c}\cdot\frac{1-e^{-sT_c}}{s - \lambda + \lambda L^*(s)}e^{-s(T_c - T)}L^*(s) \qquad (2.16)$$

which is the desired result, i.e., the Laplace transform of the message delay.

To find the expected message delay we take derivative of $D^*(s)$ with respect to s computed at $s=0$ to obtain

$$D = T_c(L - \frac{1}{2}) + \frac{\lambda T_c^2\overline{L^2}}{2(1 - \lambda T_c L)} + T \quad,$$

and in a normalized form

$$\hat{D} = \frac{D}{T} = M(L - \frac{1}{2}) + \frac{M\overline{L^2}}{L}\frac{\rho}{2(1 - \rho)} + 1$$

which, for the case that each message consists of a single packet ($L=\overline{L^2}=1$), reduces to the previously obtained result given in equation (2.2).

2.3. GENERALIZED TDMA

The allocation of a single slot within a frame to each user is reasonable in a homogeneous system. However, when the communication requirements of the users in a system are unequal, the channel will be utilized more efficiently if users with greater requirements have more slots allocated within each frame than users with light traffic. This is done in the generalized TDMA scheme in which a user might be allocated more than one slot within a frame, with arbitrary distances between successive allocated slots. An example is depicted in Figure 2.6 where the frame consists of 7 slots and 4 users share the channel. Slots 1,2 and 4 are allocated to one user, slots 3 and 5 to another user, and slots 6 and 7 one to each of the other users. Consider a user to whom K slots are allocated in every frame and let $d(k)\geq 1$ $(1\leq k \leq K)$ be the distance between the $(k+1) \bmod K$ allocated slot and the $k \bmod K$ allocated slot. Notice that $\sum_{k=1}^{K} d(k)=T_c$. In each allocated slot, the user transmits one packet, if it has any. Without loss of generality we assume that the first slot in a frame belongs to our user. The analysis of the performance of a user in a generalized TDMA scheme is more complicated than the analysis presented in the previous section

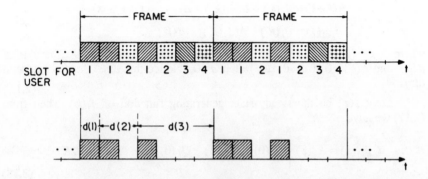

Figure 2.6: Generalized-TDMA Slot Allocation

for regular TDMA scheme. This chapter is interesting mainly due to the mathematical tools and techniques used.

2.3.1. Number of Packets at Allocated Slots - Distribution

Let $\bar{q}_j(k)$ be the number of packets awaiting transmission at the beginning of the kth allocated slot ($1 \le k \le K$) in the $(j+1)$st frame. We start by determining the generating function of the steady-state distribution of $\bar{q}_j(k)$ ($1 \le k \le K$). Steady-state distribution exists when

$$\rho \overset{\Delta}{=} \lambda L T_c / K < 1$$

since $\lambda L T_c$ is the expected number of packets arriving at the user during a frame and the user can transmit at most K packets during a frame. In steady-state the user's throughput is

$$S = K\rho = \lambda L T_c \ .$$

From the operation of generalized TDMA we have that the number of packets awaiting transmission at the beginning of the $(k+1)$st allocated slot ($1 \le k \le K-1$) in the $(j+1)$st frame equals the number of packets awaiting transmission at the beginning of the kth allocated slot, less the packet (if there were any) that has been transmitted in the kth allocated slot, plus the packets that arrived during $d(k)$. In addition, the number of packets awaiting transmission at the beginning of the first allocated slot in the $(j+1)$st frame equals the number of packets awaiting transmission at the beginning of the last (Kth) allocated slot in the jth frame, less the packet (if there were any) that has been transmitted in the Kth allocated slot, plus the packets that arrived during $d(K)$.

Therefore,

$$\bar{q}_j(k+1) = \bar{q}_j(k) - \Delta(\bar{q}_j(k)) + \bar{a}(k) \qquad 1 \le k \le K-1$$
$$\bar{q}_{j+1}(1) = \bar{q}_j(K) - \Delta(\bar{q}_j(K)) + \bar{a}(K) \tag{2.17}$$

where $\bar{a}(k)$ $(1 \le k \le K)$ is the number of packets arriving to the user during $d(k)$, and $\Delta(\bar{q})=0$ if $\bar{q}=0$, $\Delta(\bar{q})=1$ if $\bar{q}>0$. Notice that $\bar{a}(k)$ does not depend on j.

Let $Q_k(z)$ be the steady-state generating function of $\bar{q}_j(k)$. Then from (2.17) we have

$$Q_{k+1}(z) = A_k(z) \left\{ Q_k(0) + [Q_k(z) - Q_k(0)]z^{-1} \right\} \qquad 1 \le k \le K-1$$

$$Q_1(z) = A_K(z) \left\{ Q_K(0) + [Q_K(z) - Q_K(0)]z^{-1} \right\} \tag{2.18}$$

where $A_k(z) = E[z^{\bar{a}(k)}] = e^{\lambda d(k)[L(z)-1]}$ $(1 \le k \le K)$. In (2.18) we used the fact that $\bar{a}(k)$ is independent of $\bar{q}_j(k)$. The derivation of (2.18) is identical to that of equation (2.8) in the regular TDMA. From (2.18) we obtain

$$Q_k(z) = Q_1(z)z^{-(k-1)} \prod_{m=1}^{k-1} A_m(z) + (1-z^{-1}) \sum_{v=1}^{k-1} Q_v(0)z^{-(k-v-1)} \prod_{m=v}^{k-1} A_m(z) \qquad 2 \le k \le K$$

$$Q_1(z) = Q_1(z)z^{-K} \prod_{m=1}^{K} A_m(z) + (1-z^{-1}) \sum_{v=1}^{K} Q_v(0)z^{-(K-v)} \prod_{m=v}^{K} A_m(z) . \tag{2.20}$$

We therefore have

$$Q_1(z) = \frac{(z-1) \sum\limits_{u=1}^{K} Q_u(0)z^{u-1} \prod\limits_{m=u}^{K} A_m(z)}{z^K - \prod\limits_{m=1}^{K} A_m(z)} . \tag{2.21}$$

Had the boundary probabilities $Q_k(0) = Prob[q(k)=0]$ $(1 \le k \le K)$ been known, the generating functions $Q_k(z)$ $(1 \le k \le K)$ would be completely determined. To complete the calculation we must therefore compute these unknown probabilities which we do, using a standard method (see for instance the book by Hayes [Hay84]). The method exploits the fact that $Q_1(z)$, being a generating function, must be analytic within the unit disk and thus any zero of the denominator within the unit disk must also be a zero of the numerator.

The approach is to prove that there are exactly K zeroes of the denominator of equation (2.21) within the unit disk, all of them distinct. Let their values be denoted by z_n. These values must also be zeroes of the numerator of equation (2.21) which results in K linear equations in the K unknowns $Q_k(0)$.

Consider the zeroes of the denominator of (2.21) within the unit disk. Any such zero, $|z_n| \le 1$, satisfies the equation

$$z_n^K = \prod_{m=1}^{K} A_m(z) = e^{\lambda T_c [L(z_n)-1]} \ . \tag{2.22}$$

We first prove that each root $|z_n| \leq 1$ of (2.22) is a simple root. If there were a multiple root z_n, then the derivative of the denominator of (2.21) with respect to z computed at $z = z_n$ would also vanish, i.e.,

$$K z_n^{K-1} = \lambda T_c L'(z_n) e^{\lambda T_c [L(z_n)-1]}$$

which when substituted into (2.22) yields

$$K = \lambda T_c L'(z_n) z_n \ . \tag{2.23}$$

We also have

$$|L'(z_n)| = |\sum_{l=1}^{\infty} l \cdot z_n^{l-1} \cdot Prob[\bar{L}=l]| \leq \sum_{l=1}^{\infty} l \cdot Prob[\bar{L}=l] = L \ . \tag{2.24}$$

Equations (2.23) and (2.24) imply that $K \leq \lambda T_c L$ which contradicts the stability condition, and therefore each root $|z_n| \leq 1$ of (2.22) is a simple one.

Next we determine the number of roots of the denominator of (2.21) within the unit disk. To do so we apply Rouche's theorem.

Rouche's Theorem: Given two functions $f(z)$ and $g(z)$ analytic in a region R, consider a closed contour C in R; if on C we have $f(z) \neq 0$ and $|f(z)| > |g(z)|$, then $f(z)$ and $f(z)+g(z)$ have the same number of zeroes within C.

To apply this theorem we identify $f(z) = z^K$ and $g(z) = -e^{\lambda T_c [L(z)-1]}$. The region R is the disk of radius $1+\delta$ (i.e., $|z| < 1+\delta$) for some $\delta > 0$. If δ is small enough, z^K and $e^{\lambda T_c [L(z)-1]}$ are both analytic in R since they are analytic in $|z| \leq 1$. Also, because δ is strictly positive we can find some δ' such that $\delta > \delta' > 0$ so that $|z| = 1+\delta'$ is an appropriate contour for Rouche's theorem. If δ is small enough, we can use a Taylor series expansion to obtain

$$|z|^K = (1+\delta')^K \sim 1 + K\delta'$$
$$|e^{\lambda T_c [L(z)-1]}| \sim 1 + \lambda T_c L \delta' \ .$$

From the stability condition $\lambda L T_c < K$ we see that on the ring $|z| = 1+\delta'$ we have $|z|^K > |e^{\lambda T_c [L(z)-1]}|$, implying that z^K and $z^K - e^{\lambda T_c [L(z)-1]}$ have the same number of roots within $|z| = 1+\delta'$. But z^K has K roots in the unit circle (actually a root of multiplicity K at the origin), and hence the denominator of (2.21) has K roots within the unit circle, that are all distinct. One of these roots is $z_K = 1$. The other roots are denoted by $z_1, z_2, \cdots, z_{K-1}$.

We have already indicated that whenever the denominator of (2.21) vanishes within the unit disk, its numerator must vanish too. We can thus substitute the values of z_n ($1 \leq n \leq K-1$) into the numerator of (2.21) and obtain the following $K-1$ equations:

$$\sum_{v=1}^{K} Q_v(0) z_n^{v-1} \prod_{m=v}^{K} A_m(z_n) = 0 \qquad 1 \le n \le K-1 \; . \tag{2.25}$$

An additional equation comes from the normalization condition $Q_1(z)|_{z=1}=1$, namely (we use L'Hopital's rule in (2.21))

$$K - \lambda T_c L = \sum_{i=1}^{K} Q_i(0) \; . \tag{2.26}$$

It is not difficult to verify that the set of K equations (2.25)-(2.26) has a unique solution. For a complete description of the computation of the underlying determinant the interested reader is referred to the book by Hayes [Hay84]. The solution of equations (2.25)-(2.26) determines $Q_k(0)$ $(1 \le k \le K)$.

To summarize, the actual solution procedure is finding the roots of equation (2.22) within the unit disk and then solving the set of equations (2.25) and (2.26). The solutions are then substituted into equation (2.21). Solving (2.22) is, by all counts, the toughest part of the procedure. One quite efficient method to do it is due to Mueller [Mue56, CoB80]. This method is particularly useful since it is iterative, does not involve derivatives, obtains both real and complex roots even when these are not simple, and converges almost quadratically in the vicinity of a root. In addition, the roots are computed in an increasing absolute value order and therefore the roots within the unit disk are computed first. Another alternative for computing the boundary probabilities is to use Neuts' theory of matrix geometric computation [Neu81] as is described in [HoR87].

2.3.2. Expected Number of Packets at Allocated Slots

The expected number of packets at the beginning of an allocated slot in steady-state can be computed by evaluating the derivative of $Q_k(z)$ with respect to z at $z=1$ (see (2.20) and (2.21)). An alternative method (the one we employ here) is to use (2.17) directly. To that end, we square, take expectations of both sides of (2.17) and let $j \rightarrow \infty$. We obtain

$$E[\bar{q}^2(k+1)] = E[\bar{q}^2(k)] + E[\Delta(\bar{q}(k))^2] + E[\bar{a}^2(k)] + 2E[\bar{q}(k)\bar{a}(k)]$$

$$- 2E[\bar{q}(k)\Delta(\bar{q}(k))] - 2E[\Delta(\bar{q}(k))\bar{a}(k)] \qquad 1 \le k \le K-1$$

$$E[\bar{q}^2(1)] = E[\bar{q}^2(K)] + E[\Delta(\bar{q}(K))^2] + E[\bar{a}^2(K)] + 2E[\bar{q}(K)\bar{a}(K)]$$

$$- 2E[\bar{q}(K)\Delta(\bar{q}(K))] - 2E[\Delta(\bar{q}(K))\bar{a}(K)] \; .$$

Let $q(k) \triangleq E[\bar{q}(k)])$ and $a(k) \triangleq E[\bar{a}(k)]$ for $1 \le k \le K$. With these notations and using the independence between $\bar{q}$ and $\bar{a}$ and the identities $E[\Delta(\bar{q}(k))^2] = E[\Delta(\bar{q}(k))] = 1 - Q_k(0)$; $E[\bar{q}(k)\Delta(\bar{q}(k))] = E[\bar{q}(k)]$ (which stem from the structure of the $\Delta(\cdot)$ function) we obtain

$$q^2(k+1) = q^2(k) + E[\bar{a}^2(k)] + [1-Q_k(0)][1-2a(k)]$$
$$- 2q(k)[1-a(k)] \qquad 1 \le k \le K-1 \qquad (2.27)$$
$$q^2(1) = q^2(K) + E[\bar{a}^2(K)] + [1-Q_K(0)][1-2a(K)] - 2q(K)[1-a(K)] \ .$$

Summing (2.27) for all $k=1,2,\cdots,K$ we obtain

$$2\sum_{k=1}^{K}q(k)[1-a(k)] = \sum_{k=1}^{K}E[\bar{a}^2(k)] + \sum_{k=1}^{K}[1-Q_k(0)][1-2a(k)] \ . \qquad (2.28)$$

Using (2.17) we have

$$\sum_{k=1}^{K}q(k)[1-a(k)] = q(1)[1-a(1)] + \sum_{k=2}^{K}q(k)[1-a(k)]$$

$$= q(1)[1-a(1)] + \sum_{k=1}^{K-1}q(k)[1-a(k+1)]$$

$$+ \sum_{k=1}^{K-1}\left[a(k)-E[\Delta(\bar{q}(k))]\right][1-a(k+1)] \qquad (2.29)$$

$$= q(1)[2-a(1)-a(2)] + \sum_{k=1}^{K-1}\left[a(k)-E[\Delta(\bar{q}(k))]\right][1-a(k+1)]$$

$$+ \sum_{k=2}^{K-1}q(k)[1-a(k+1)] = \cdots =$$

$$= q(1)\left[K-\sum_{k=1}^{K}a(k)\right] + \sum_{k=1}^{K}[1-a(k)]\sum_{m=1}^{k-1}\left[a(m)-E[\Delta(\bar{q}(m))]\right]$$

where an empty sum vanishes. Substituting (2.29) into (2.28) we obtain

$$q(1) = \frac{\displaystyle\sum_{k=1}^{K}E[\bar{a}^2(k)] + \sum_{k=1}^{K}[1-Q_k(0)][1-2a(k)]}{2\left[K-\displaystyle\sum_{k=1}^{K}a(k)\right]}$$

$$- \frac{2\displaystyle\sum_{k=1}^{K}[1-a(k)]\sum_{m=1}^{k-1}\left[a(m)-E[\Delta(\bar{q}(m))]\right]}{2\left[K-\displaystyle\sum_{k=1}^{K}a(k)\right]} \qquad (2.30)$$

Because the arrival is Poisson we have $a(k)=E[\bar{a}(k)]=\lambda L d(k)$ and $E[\bar{a}^2(k)]=\lambda L^2 d(k)+\lambda^2 L^2 d^2(k)$. Also, from (2.26) $\sum_{k=1}^{K}[1-Q_k(0)]=\lambda L T_c$. Therefore, we obtain from (2.30)

$$q(1) = \frac{\lambda L T_c + \lambda \sum_{k=1}^{K} d(k) \left[\overline{L^2} + \lambda L^2 d(k) - 2L\left[1 - Q_k(0)\right]\right]}{2(K - \lambda L T_c)}$$

$$- \frac{2\sum_{k=1}^{K} \left[1 - \lambda L d(k)\right] \sum_{m=1}^{k-1} \left[\lambda L d(m) - 1 + Q_m(0)\right]}{2(K - \lambda L T_c)} ,$$

and finally from (2.17) we get

$$q(k) = q(1) + \sum_{m=1}^{k-1} \left[a(m) - E\left[\Delta(\bar{q}(m))\right]\right]$$

$$= q(1) + \sum_{m=1}^{k-1} \left[\lambda L d(m) - 1 + Q_m(0)\right] \quad 2 \le k \le K \ . \tag{2.31}$$

Note that once the expected number of packets at the beginning of allocated slots is determined, it is straight forward to compute the expected number of packets at the beginning of an arbitrary slot (see the Exercises section).

2.3.3. Message Delay Distribution

Consider a tagged message arriving within $d(k)$ $(1 \le k \le K)$, $\bar{w}(k)$ seconds before the beginning of the $(k+1)$st allocated slot and tag its last packet. The delay of the tagged message is the time elapsed from its arrival, until its last packet is transmitted, i.e., it is the delay of the tagged packet. Thus, if $\bar{l}(k)$ is a random variable representing the total number of packets that are to be transmitted before the tagged packet then the delay of the tagged packet is $\bar{w}(k)$ plus the time needed to transmit the $\bar{l}(k)$ packets plus the time to transmit the tagged packet itself (note that as in the regular TDMA $\bar{l}(k)$ depends on $\bar{w}(k)$).

Some insight into $\bar{l}(k)$ is appropriate. The quantity $\bar{l}(k)$ is actually the number of intervals that have to elapse before the interval in which the tagged packet is transmitted. This number can be (uniquely) decomposed into a number of complete frames and some leftover. In other words we can write

$$\bar{l}(k) = \bar{f}(k) \cdot K + \bar{J}(k) \quad 0 \le \bar{J}(k) \le K-1$$

where $\bar{f}$ designates the number of complete frames of delay and $\bar{J}$ designates the number of intervals left over. As a matter of fact $\bar{f}$ and $\bar{J}$ depend only on $\bar{l}(k)$ and not on k itself. We use the notation $\bar{f}(k)$ and $\bar{J}(k)$ (or $\bar{f}$ and $\bar{J}$) as a shorthand. Both $\bar{J}(k)$ and $\bar{f}(k)$ are non-negative integer-valued random variables and their distributions are derived in Appendix A at the end of this chapter.

The delay of the tagged message after waiting the initial $\bar{w}(k)$ seconds is $\bar{f}(k)T_c$ seconds (representing the number of complete frames) plus the time to transmit the $\bar{J}(k)$ left over packets which requires $\sum_{u=k+1}^{k+\bar{J}(k)} d(u)$ seconds if there are any packets left. In all cases, the transmission time of the tagged packet is

T. In summary, given $\tilde{w}(k)$ the total delay is

$$\tilde{D}(k \mid \tilde{w}(k),\tilde{l}(k)) = \begin{cases} \tilde{w}(k) + \tilde{f}(k)T_c + T & \tilde{J}(k) = 0 \\ \tilde{w}(k) + \tilde{f}(k)T_c + \sum_{u=k+1}^{k+\tilde{J}(k)} d(u) + T & 1 \le \tilde{J}(k) \le K-1 \end{cases}$$

where the summation wraps-around from K to 1 when necessary. The above can be rewritten (along with the relation $\tilde{f}K = \tilde{l} - \tilde{J}$) as follows:

$$\tilde{D}(k \mid \tilde{w}(k),\tilde{l}(k)) = \tilde{w}(k) + T + \tilde{l}(k)\frac{T_c}{K} - \tilde{J}(k)\frac{T_c}{K}$$

$$+ \sum_{u=k+1}^{k+1+\tilde{J}(k)} d(u) - d(k+1+\tilde{J}(k)) \ . \quad (2.32)$$

For notational convenience, let us define

$$V(J,k) \stackrel{\Delta}{=} \sum_{u=k+1}^{k+1+J(k)} d(u) - d(k+1+J(k))$$

which then turns equation (2.32) into

$$\tilde{D}(k \mid \tilde{w}(k),\tilde{l}(k)) = \tilde{w}(k) + T + \tilde{l}(k)\frac{T_c}{K} - \tilde{J}(k)\frac{T_c}{K} + V(\tilde{J},k) \ . \quad (2.33)$$

Note that $\tilde{l}$, and hence $\tilde{J}$ depend on $\tilde{w}(k)$. Moving to the Laplace transform domain, the above equation turns into

$$D_k^*(s \mid \tilde{w}(k),\tilde{l}(k)) = E\left[e^{-s\tilde{D}(k \mid \tilde{w}(k),\tilde{l}(k))} \right]$$

$$= e^{-sT} e^{-s\tilde{w}(k)} e^{-sT_c \tilde{l}(k)/K} e^{sT_c \tilde{J}(k)/K} e^{-sV(\tilde{J},k)} \ . \quad (2.34)$$

We proceed by eliminating the condition on $\tilde{l}$. Let $l_k(z,\tilde{w}(k))$ be the generating function of $\tilde{l}$ given $\tilde{w}$. Continuing from equation (2.34) we get

$$D_k^*(s \mid \tilde{w}(k)) = e^{-sT} e^{-s\tilde{w}(k)} E\left[e^{-sT_c \tilde{l}(k)/K} e^{sT_c \tilde{J}(k)/K} e^{-sV(\tilde{J},k)} \right]$$

$$= e^{-sT} e^{-s\tilde{w}(k)} \left[\sum_{l=0}^{\infty} e^{-sT_c l/K} e^{sT_c J/K} e^{-sV(\tilde{J},k)} Prob\,[\tilde{l}(k)=l] \right]$$

$$= e^{-sT} e^{-s\tilde{w}(k)} \sum_{f=0}^{\infty} \sum_{j=0}^{K-1} e^{-sT_c (fK+j)/K} e^{sT_c j/K} e^{-sV(j,k)} Prob\,[\tilde{l}(k)=fK+j]$$

$$= e^{-sT} e^{-s\tilde{w}(k)} \sum_{j=0}^{K-1} e^{-sV(j,k)} \left[\sum_{f=0}^{\infty} \left(e^{-sT_c/K} \right)^{fK} Prob\,[\tilde{l}(k)=fK+j] \right] \ .$$

We recognize the bracketted term as the basic relation derived in Appendix A at the end of this chapter, with z replaced by $z_s \stackrel{\Delta}{=} e^{-sT_c/K}$. Making the substitution we get

$$
\begin{aligned}
D_k^*(s \mid \bar{w}(k)) &= e^{-sT} e^{-s\bar{w}(k)} \sum_{j=0}^{K-1} e^{-sV(j,k)} \left[\sum_{m=0}^{K-1} \frac{1}{K} (z_s \beta_m)^{-j} l(z_s \beta_m, \bar{w}(k)) \right] \\
&= \frac{1}{K} e^{-sT} e^{-s\bar{w}(k)} \sum_{m=0}^{K-1} l(z_s \beta_m, \bar{w}(k)) \sum_{j=0}^{K-1} e^{-sV(j,k)} (z_s \beta_m)^{-j}
\end{aligned}
\tag{2.35}
$$

where $\beta_m = e^{i\frac{2\pi m}{K}}$ is the unit root of order K.

The next step is to remove the condition on $\bar{w}(k)$, but before doing so we must evaluate the generating function of $\tilde{l}$ since it depends on $\bar{w}(k)$. To do so we notice that given $\bar{w}(k)$, the total number of packets that are to be transmitted before the tagged packet, $\tilde{l}(k)$, is the sum of three independent random variables: (i) the packets already waiting at the beginning of the kth allocated slot less one packet (if there were any) that is transmitted in the kth allocated slot, i.e., $\tilde{q}(k) - \Delta(\tilde{q}(k))$ (generating function $[(1-z^{-1})Q_k(0) + z^{-1}Q_k(z)]$; see equation (2.8)), (ii) Packets arriving from the beginning of the kth allocated slot until the arrival of the tagged message (generating function $e^{\lambda[d(k)-\bar{w}(k)][L(z)-1]}$; see equation (2.7)), (iii) Packets of the tagged message, not including the tagged packet itself (generating function $L(z)z^{-1}$). Therefore,

$$
\begin{aligned}
l_k(z, \bar{w}(k)) &\triangleq E[z^{\tilde{l}(k)} \mid \bar{w}(k)] \\
&= [(1-z^{-1})Q_k(0) + z^{-1}Q_k(z)]e^{\lambda[d(k)-\bar{w}(k)][L(z)-1]}L(z)z^{-1} .
\end{aligned}
\tag{2.36}
$$

By defining

$$
h_k(z) \triangleq [(1-z^{-1})Q_k(0) + z^{-1}Q_k(z)]e^{\lambda d(k)[L(z)-1]}L(z)z^{-1} = Q_{k+1}(z)L(z)z^{-1}
$$

equation (2.36) can be written as

$$
l_k(z, \bar{w}(k)) = h_k(z)e^{\lambda \bar{w}(k)[1-L(z)]}
$$

and when substituted into (2.35) we get

$$
\begin{aligned}
D_k^*(s \mid \bar{w}(k)) &= \frac{1}{K} e^{-sT} e^{-s\bar{w}(k)} \sum_{m=0}^{K-1} h_k(z_s \beta_m) e^{\lambda \bar{w}(k)[1-L(z_s \beta_m)]} \sum_{j=0}^{K-1} e^{-sV(j,k)} (z_s \beta_m)^{-j} \\
&= \frac{1}{K} e^{-sT} \sum_{m=0}^{K-1} h_k(z_s \beta_m) \left[\sum_{j=0}^{K-1} e^{-sV(j,k)} (z_s \beta_m)^{-j} \right] e^{-\bar{w}(k)\{s-\lambda[1-L(z_s \beta_m)]\}} .
\end{aligned}
$$

Since $\bar{w}(k)$ is uniformly distributed between 0 and $d(k)$ we have from the above equation

$$
D_k^*(s) = E[e^{-s\tilde{D}(k)}] = E[D_k^*(s \mid \bar{w}(k))] = \frac{1}{d(k)} \int_0^{d(k)} D_k^*(s \mid w)dw
$$

$$
= \frac{1}{K} e^{-sT} \sum_{m=0}^{K-1} h_k(z_s \beta_m) \frac{1}{d(k)} \int_0^{d(k)} e^{-w\{s-\lambda[1-L(z_s \beta_m)]\}}dw \left[\sum_{j=0}^{K-1} e^{-sV(j,k)} (z_s \beta_m)^{-j} \right]
$$

$$= \frac{1}{K} e^{-sT} \sum_{m=0}^{K-1} h_k(z_s \beta_m) \frac{1 - e^{-d(k)\{s - \lambda[1 - L(z_s \beta_m)]\}}}{d(k)\{s - \lambda[1 - L(z_s \beta_m)]\}} \left[\sum_{j=0}^{K-1} e^{-sV(j,k)}(z_s \beta_m)^{-j} \right] .$$

Finally, the Laplace transform of the delay distribution is given by

$$D^*(s) = \sum_{k=1}^{K} \frac{d(k)}{T_c} D_k^*(s) \tag{2.37}$$

since $d(k)/T_c$ is the probability that the tagged message will arrive within $d(k)$.

2.3.4. Expected Message Delay

The expected delay of a message can be computed by evaluating the derivative of $D^*(s)$ with respect to s at $s=0$ (see (2.37)). An alternative method (the one we employ here) is to use (2.33) directly. To that end, we take expectation on (2.33) and obtain

$$D(k) = E[\tilde{w}(k)] + T + E[\tilde{l}(k)]\frac{T_c}{K} \tag{2.38}$$

$$- E[\tilde{J}(k)]\frac{T_c}{K} + E[V(\tilde{J},k)] \qquad 1 \le k \le K .$$

We now compute each of the terms in (2.38). Clearly,

$$E[\tilde{w}(k)] = \frac{1}{2} d(k) .$$

From (2.36) and (2.31),

$$E[\tilde{l}(k)] = q(k) - [1 - Q_k(0)] + \frac{1}{2}\lambda L d(k) + L - 1$$

$$= q(1) + L - 1 - \frac{1}{2}\lambda L d(k) + \sum_{m=1}^{k} [\lambda L d(m) - 1 + Q_m(0)] .$$

Using (2.36), the distribution of $\tilde{J}$ (from Appendix A at the end of this chapter) and the definition of $h_k(z)$ we have

$$E[\tilde{J}(k)] = E\left[E[\tilde{J}(k) | \tilde{w}(k)] \right] = E\left[\frac{K-1}{2} - \sum_{m=1}^{K-1} \frac{l_k(\beta_m, \tilde{w}(k))}{1 - \frac{1}{\beta_m}} \right]$$

$$= \frac{K-1}{2} - \sum_{m=1}^{K-1} \frac{E[l_k(\beta_m, \tilde{w}(k))]}{1 - \frac{1}{\beta_m}}$$

$$= \frac{K-1}{2} - \sum_{m=1}^{K-1} \frac{h_k(\beta_m)}{1 - \frac{1}{\beta_m}} E\left[e^{c_m \tilde{w}(k)}\right]$$

$$= \frac{K-1}{2} - \sum_{m=1}^{K-1} \frac{h_k(\beta_m)}{1 - \frac{1}{\beta_m}} \frac{1}{d(k)} \int_0^{d(k)} e^{c_m w} dw$$

$$= \frac{K-1}{2} - \sum_{m=1}^{K-1} \frac{h_k(\beta_m)}{1 - \frac{1}{\beta_m}} \frac{e^{c_m d(k)} - 1}{c_m d(k)}$$

where $c_m \triangleq \lambda[1 - L(\beta_m)]$. In a similar manner,

$$E[V(\tilde{J},k)] = E\left[E[V(\tilde{J},k)|\tilde{w}(k)]\right] = E\left[\sum_{J=0}^{K} V(J,k) Prob[\tilde{J}=J|\tilde{w}(k)]\right]$$

$$= E\left[\frac{1}{K} \sum_{J=0}^{K-1} V(J,k) \sum_{m=0}^{K-1} \beta_m^{-J} l_k(\beta_m, \tilde{w}(k))\right]$$

$$= \frac{1}{K} \sum_{J=0}^{K-1} \sum_{m=0}^{K-1} V(J,k) \beta_m^{-J} h_k(\beta_m) E\left[e^{c_m \tilde{w}(k)}\right] \quad .$$

Considering that $V(J,k) = 0$ for $J=0$, $\beta_0 = 1$, and $c_0 = 0$, the above yields

$$E[V(\tilde{J},k)] = \frac{1}{K} \sum_{J=1}^{K-1} V(J,k) + \frac{1}{K} \sum_{m=1}^{K-1} \sum_{J=1}^{K-1} V(J,k) \beta_m^{-J} h_k(\beta_m) \frac{e^{c_m d(k)} - 1}{c_m d(k)} \quad .$$

Combining all terms we obtain

$$D(k) = \frac{1}{2} d(k) + T$$

$$+ \frac{T_c}{K} \left[q(1) + L - 1 - \frac{1}{2} \lambda L d(k) + \sum_{m=1}^{k} [\lambda L d(m) - 1 + Q_m(0)] \right]$$

$$- \frac{T_c(K-1)}{2K} + \frac{1}{K} \sum_{J=1}^{K-1} V(J,k)$$

$$+ \frac{T_c}{Kd(k)} \sum_{m=1}^{K-1} h_k(\beta_m) \frac{e^{c_m d(k)} - 1}{c_m} \left[\frac{1}{1 - \frac{a}{\beta_m}} + \sum_{J=1}^{K-1} V(J,k) \beta_m^{-J} \right] \quad .$$

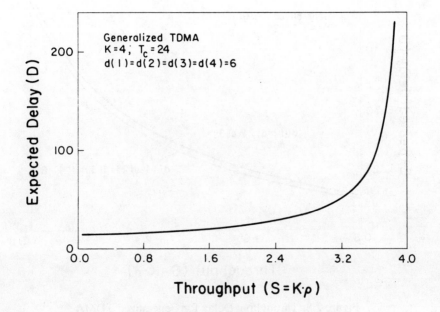

Figure 2.7: Throughput Delay for Generalized TDMA
$$L(z) = (z + z^2 + z^3 + z^4)/4$$

Finally, the expected delay of a message is

$$D = \sum_{k=1}^{K} \frac{d(k)}{T_c} D(k) .$$

Figures 2.7 and 2.8 contain some numerical results for a frame with 24 slots, four of which are allocated to the user under consideration. We assume that an arriving message can contain one, two, three or four packets with equal probabilities, i.e., $L(z) = (z + z^2 + z^3 + z^4)/4$. In Figure 2.7 the allocated slots are evenly spaced, so that $d(1) = d(2) = d(3) = d(4) = 6$. Figure 2.8 contains the evenly spaced case as well as the contiguous allocation in which the first four slots are allocated to the user, i.e., $d(1) = d(2) = d(3) = 1$, $d(4) = 21$. We observe that for the arrival pattern under consideration, the evenly spaced allocation is better, but the differences between the two allocations is rather small. It is interesting to mention that in this case the evenly spaced allocation gives the minimal expected delay and the contiguous allocation gives the maximal expected delay for all values of arrival rate. Thus any other allocation results in expected delay that is between the curves of Figure 2.8.

A natural question to ask is how to allocate the K slots available to a user in a frame in order to improve the performance. When the expected number of

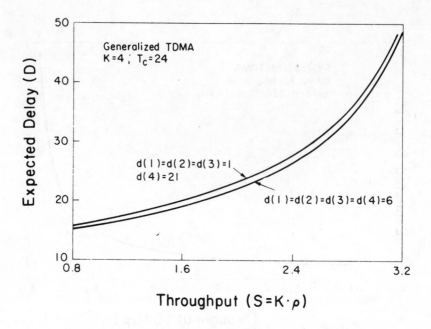

Figure 2.8: Throughput Delay for Generalized TDMA
$$L(z) = (z+z^2+z^3+z^4)/4$$

packets in the user's buffer is the performance measure, or equivalently, when expected *packet* delay is the measure, Hofri and Rosberg showed [HoR87] that the best allocation is the uniform one, namely, all the internal periods $d(k)$ $(1 \le k \le K)$ should be equal. Furthermore, this allocation remains optimal for all arrival rates.

When the expected *message* delay is used as the performance measure, numerical experimentation leads us to believe, that the optimal allocation depends both on the arrival rate λ and on the specific distribution of the message length. Whereas complete characterization of the optimal allocation pattern is still an open question, the following captures some of our observations.

When a message arrives at the user's buffer, its delay is affected by the number of packets ahead of it in the buffer. This number amounts to a number of whole frames plus some leftover; The allocation of slots within a frame can affect only this leftover. Thus, for heavy load ($\rho \to 1$), the expected message delay is not very sensitive to changes in the inter-allocation distances since the major portion of the delay is due to the large number of whole frames a message must wait before its transmission starts. For light load ($\rho \to 0$ or equivalently $\lambda \to 0$), the expected message delay might be sensitive to the allocation distances. Let γ_i $(1 \le i \le K)$ be the probability that a message transmission requires i slots beyond the number of whole frames, where γ_K means that the message requires a whole number of frames. In other words γ_i is the probability that a message length is $i \bmod K$ (clearly $\sum_{i=1}^{K}\gamma_i=1$). It can be shown (we leave the details as an exercise) that if $\gamma_i=\gamma_{K-i+1}$ for $i=1,2,\cdots,K$, then the expected delay is completely independent of the inter-allocation distances and if $\gamma_i=\gamma_{K-i+1}$ for $i=2,3,\cdots,K-1$, then for $\gamma_1 > \gamma_K$ the optimal allocation is the uniform (equidistant) one while for $\gamma_1 < \gamma_K$ the K slots should be contiguous in order to minimize $D_{\lambda\to 0}$.

2.4. DYNAMIC CONFLICT-FREE PROTOCOLS

Static conflict-free protocols such as the FDMA and TDMA protocols do not utilize the shared channel very efficiently, especially when the system is lightly loaded or when the loads of different users are asymmetric. The static and fixed assignment in these protocols, cause the channel (or part of it) to be idle even though some users have data to transmit. Dynamic channel allocation protocols are designed to overcome this drawback. With dynamic allocation strategies, the channel allocation changes with time and is based on current (and possibly changing) demands of the various users. The more responsive and better usage of the channel achieved with dynamic protocols does not come for free: it requires control overhead that is unnecessary with static protocols and consumes a portion of the channel.

As an example of a protocol that belongs to the family of dynamic conflict-free protocols we take the protocol known as Mini Slotted Alternating Priority (MSAP) protocol. It is designed for a slotted system, i.e., one in which the time axis is divided into slots of equal duration and where a user's transmission is limited to within the slot (the TDMA system is also such a system).

To ensure freedom of transmission conflicts it is necessary to reach an agreement among the users on who transmits in a given slot. This agreement entails collecting information as to who are the ready users, i.e., those who request channel allocation, and an arbitration algorithm by which one of these users is selected for transmission. This latter mechanism is nothing but imposing a priority structure on the set of users each of which constitutes a separate priority class. The MSAP protocol handles properly various such structures. The presentation here follows that of Kleinrock and Scholl [KlS80].

Let the users be numbered sequentially $0,1,\cdots,M-1$. The priority enforcement is based on the observation that if in the most recent slot the channel was allocated to user i then it must have been the one with the highest priority. Defining the priority structure is thus the determination of the transmission order after the transmission of some user. Given then, that user i transmitted last we define the following priority structures:

1. *Fixed Priorities.* Transmission order: $0,1,\cdots,M-1$.

2. *Round-Robin.* Transmission order: $i+1,i+2,\cdots,i+M$ (user arithmetic is modulo M).

3. *Alternating Priorities.* Transmission order: $i,i+1,\cdots,i+M-1$.

The fixed priority structure implies that user i has always higher priority than user $i+1$, thus it treats preferentially the smaller numbered users, and is somewhat "unfair" (although desired in some cases). The round-robin priority structure implies a channel that is allocated to the users in a cyclic order and ensures that between any two transmissions of any user *all* other users have a chance to transmit at least once. The alternating priorities structure allows a user to whom the channel is allocated to transmit *all* the messages in its buffer before the channel is allocated to another user; in other respects this structure is a round-robin one since the channel is allocated to the different users in a cyclic order.

Once the priority structure is decided upon the only issue left is to identify the one user with the highest priority among those wishing to transmit. MSAP does this by means of reservations as follows. Denote by τ the maximum system propagation delay, that is, the longest time it takes for a signal emitted at one end of the network to reach the other end. Let every slot consist of initial $M-1$ reservation "minislots" each of duration τ, followed by a data transmission period of duration T, followed by another minislot (see Figure 2.9). Only those users wishing to transmit in a slot take any action; a user that does not wish to transmit in a given slot remains quiet for the entire slot duration. Given that every user wishing to transmit knows his own priority they behave as follows:

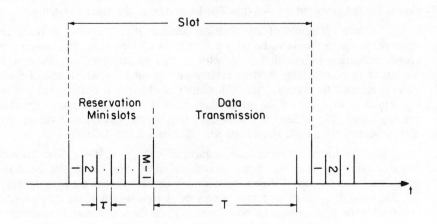

Figure 2.9: MSAP Slot Structure

- If the user of the highest priority wishes to transmit in this slot then he starts immediately. His transmission consists of an unmodulated carrier for a duration of $M-1$ minislots followed by a message of duration T.

- A user of the i th priority ($1 \le i \le M-1$) wishing to transmit in this slot will do so only if the first i minislots are idle. In this case he will transmit $M-1-i$ minislots of unmodulated carrier followed by a message of duration T.

The specific choice of the minislot duration ensures that when a given user transmits in a minislot all other users know it by the end of that minislot allowing them to react appropriately. The additional minislot at the end allows the data signals to reach every user of the network. This is needed to ensure that all start synchronized in the next slot, as required by the reservation scheme.

The evaluation of throughput is fairly simple. Since transmission is conflict-free every nonempty slot conveys useful data. However, the first $M-1$ minislots as well as the one after data transmission are pure overhead and should not be counted in the throughput. Thus if all slots are used, that is in the highest possible load circumstances, we get a channel capacity (maximum throughput) of

$$S_{\max} = \frac{T}{T + M\tau} = \frac{1}{1 + Ma}$$

where $a \overset{\Delta}{=} \tau/T$ is a characteristic parameter of the system. It is evident that the capacity increases both with the reduction of a and the number of users. For a typical value of $a = 0.01$ only a few tens of users can be tolerated before the capacity reduces below an acceptable level.

2.4.1. Expected Delay

Consider the problem in a somewhat more general setting. Let the arrival processes of packets at user i be Poisson with rate λ_i ($0 \le i \le M-1$). Let $\tilde{w}_i$ be the waiting time of a packet at user i (with mean w_i), and let $\tilde{x}_i$ be the transmission (service) time of a single packet (with mean x_i). Denote $\rho_i \overset{\Delta}{=} \lambda_i x_i$, and $\rho = \sum_{i=0}^{M-1} \rho_i$. In the following derivation we assume a fixed priority structure among the users; as we indicate later, some of the results apply also to other priority structures. In a fixed priority structure λ_i can be interpreted as the arrival rate of packets of the i th priority. We also assume that the buffering capabilities of each user are not limited.

Consider a random "tagged" packet that joins user k's buffer. Upon its arrival there are $\tilde{L}_i$ packets at the i th user already waiting. Let $\tilde{N}_i$ be the number of packets that arrive at user i during the waiting time of the tagged packet. The waiting time of the tagged packet is composed of waiting for the currently transmitting user to complete his transmission (or if there is no transmitting user the packet will wait until the channel is available for transmission), the transmission time of all packets with equal or higher priority (anywhere in the system) that are waiting upon his arrival, and the transmission time of all higher priority packets that will arrive (anywhere in the system) before he starts transmission. Denote by f the forced idle-time, that is an idle time imposed by the server (the channel) when it empties. With the above definitions we have

$$E[\bar{w}_k] = w_k = \left[\sum_{i=0}^{M-1} \rho_i \frac{E[\bar{x}_i^2]}{2E[\bar{x}_i]} + (1-\rho)\frac{E[f^2]}{2E[f]}\right]$$

$$+ \left[\sum_{i=0}^{k} E[\bar{x}_i]E[\bar{L}_i]\right] + \left[\sum_{i=0}^{k-1} E[\bar{x}_i]E[\bar{N}_i]\right] \ . \tag{2.39}$$

The first term in this equation is the average time before the next transmission starts. If the system is nonempty, then ρ_i is the probability that user i is transmitting, and the average residual transmission time is $E[\bar{x}_i^2]/(2E[\bar{x}_i])$. Similarly, a user encountering an empty system (probability $1-\rho$) must wait the residual forced idle-time. The second term denotes the total transmission time of all packets of equal or higher priority that are waiting for transmission. The third term is the total transmission time of all packets of higher priority that will arrive while the tagged packet is waiting. Note that within a priority class first come first serve (FCFS) order prevails.

Straightforward application of Little's formula yields $E[\bar{L}_i] = \lambda_i w_i$ and $E[\bar{N}_i] = \lambda_i w_k$ which, when substituted into equation (2.39) yields

$$w_k = \frac{\displaystyle\sum_{i=0}^{M-1} \rho_i \frac{E[\bar{x}_i^2]}{2E[\bar{x}_i]} + (1-\rho)\frac{E[f^2]}{2E[f]} + \sum_{i=0}^{k-1} \rho_i w_i}{1-\rho^{(k)}}$$

where $\rho^{(k)} \triangleq \sum_{i=0}^{k} \rho_i$. The above equation can be recursively evaluated to yield

$$w_k = \frac{\displaystyle\sum_{i=0}^{M-1} \rho_i \frac{E[\bar{x}_i^2]}{2E[\bar{x}_i]} + (1-\rho)\frac{E[f^2]}{2E[f]}}{(1-\rho^{(k)})(1-\rho^{(k-1)})} \ .$$

The mean packet delay, averaged over all priority levels is $\sum_{i=0}^{M-1} (\lambda_i/\lambda)w_i$ which in general cannot be evaluated in closed form. However, if the transmission times of all priority levels have the same distribution (that is $\bar{x}_i$ is independent of i) then

$$w = E[\bar{w}] = \sum_{i=0}^{M-1} \frac{\lambda_i}{\lambda}w_i = \frac{\rho \dfrac{E[\bar{x}^2]}{2E[\bar{x}]} + (1-\rho)\dfrac{E[f^2]}{2E[f]}}{1-\rho} \ . \tag{2.40}$$

If, in addition, f is distributed in the same way as $\bar{x}$ we get

$$E[\tilde{w}] = \frac{\dfrac{E[\tilde{x}^2]}{2E[\tilde{x}]}}{1-\rho} \ . \tag{2.41}$$

For the MSAP case, all the $\tilde{x}_i$ are indeed the same and equal the slot size namely $M\tau + T = T(1+Ma)$. The quantity f represents the forced idle-time incurred when the system becomes empty (a transmission can start only at slot boundaries) and is also deterministically equal to the slot size. Thus the conditions of equation (2.41) hold and when substituted yields

$$w_k = \frac{(1+Ma)T}{2(1-\rho^{(k)})(1-\rho^{(k-1)})}$$

with $\rho^{(k)} = (1+Ma)T\sum_{i=0}^{k}\lambda_i$. The mean packet delay is thus

$$D = \sum_{i=0}^{M-1}\frac{\lambda_i}{\lambda}D_i = \sum_{i=0}^{M-1}\frac{\lambda_i}{\lambda}[w_i + (1+Ma)T] = E[\tilde{w}] + (1+Ma)T$$

$$= (1+Ma)T\left[1 + \frac{1}{2(1-\rho)}\right]$$

which finally yields

$$\hat{D} = \frac{D}{T} = (1+Ma)\left[1 + \frac{1}{2(1-\rho)}\right] \ . \tag{2.42}$$

Note that since ρ is the fraction of periods in which transmission takes place and since $Ma/(1+Ma)$ of every slot is overhead, we conclude that $S = \rho/(1+Ma)$, or $\rho = (1+Ma)S$. When substituted into the last equation the throughput delay characteristic of MSAP results.

Although the preceding analysis was performed for fixed priorities the final results hold for other priority structures as well. The priority conservation law [Kle76] states that for any M/G/1 queue and any nonpreemptive work-conserving queueing discipline (which includes all those of concern here) $\sum \rho_i w_i = Const$. Thus, as surprising as it might appear, the average delay given by equations (2.40) and (2.42) holds for all priority structures mentioned in the beginning of this subsection. Higher moments are, as expected, different.

2.5. RELATED ANALYSIS

Conflict-free access protocols, especially the static ones, are the oldest and most popular protocols around. This is the reason for the large volume of analyses of such protocols. We suggest here several of those analyses along with some other conflict-free protocols.

FDMA and TDMA

A good treatment of TDMA and FDMA analysis can be found in [Hay84]. A sample path comparison between FDMA and TDMA schemes is carried out in [Rub79] where it is shown that the TDMA scheme is better than the FDMA scheme not only on the average. A TDMA scheme in which the packets of each user are serviced according to a priority rule is analyzed in [MoR84]. The question of optimal allocation of slots to the users in the generalized TDMA scheme is addressed in [ItR84] where the throughput of the system is maximized (assuming single buffers for each user) and in [HoR87] where the expected packet-delay in the system is minimized.

Code Division Multiple Access

Both FDMA and TDMA do not allow any time overlap of transmissions. A conflict-free scheme that does allow overlap of transmission both in the frequency and the time domains is the *code division multiple access (CDMA)* [Pur87]. The conflict-free property of CDMA is achieved by using orthogonal signals in conjunction with matched filters in the corresponding receivers. Interconnecting all users in the system requires that matched filters corresponding to all signals to be available at all receivers. The use of multiple orthogonal signals increases the bandwidth required for transmission. Yet, CDMA allows the coexistence of several systems in the same frequency bands, as long as different signals are used in different systems.

Reservation Protocols

The MSAP protocol presented in the text is a representative of an entire family of protocols that guarantee conflict-free transmissions by way of reservation. All these protocols have a sequence of preceding bits serving to reserve or announce upcoming transmissions (this is known as the reservation preamble). In MSAP there are $M-1$ such bits for every transmitted packet. We mention here those reservation protocols which basically do not involve contention for the reservation itself; such protocols are discussed in Section 3.5.

An improvement to the MSAP protocol is the bit-map protocol described in [Tan81]. The idea behind this protocol is to use a single reservation preamble to schedule more than a single transmission. This is done by utilizing the fact that all participating nodes are aware of the reservations made in the preamble. The bit-map protocol requires synchronization among the users that is somewhat more sophisticated than the MSAP protocol, but the overhead paid per transmitted packet is less than the overhead in the MSAP protocol.

Another variation of a reservation protocol has been described in [Rob75]. There, every user can make a reservation in every minislot of the reservation preamble, and if the reservation remains uncontested that reserving user will transmit. If there is a collision in the reservation minislot all users but the "owner" of that minislot will abstain from transmission. Altogether, this is a standard TDMA with idle slots made available to be grabbed by others. Several additional reservation and TDMA protocols are also analyzed in [Rub79].

One of the most efficient reservation protocols is the Broadcast Recognition Access Method (BRAM) [CFL79]. This is essentially a combination between the bit-map and the MSAP protocols. As in the MSAP protocol, a reservation preamble serves to reserve the channel for a single user but unlike the MSAP, the reservation preamble does not necessarily contain all $M-1$ minislots. The idea is that users start their transmission with a staggered delay not before they ensure that another transmission is not ongoing (the paper [KlS80] also refers to a similar scheme). Under heavy load BRAM reduces to regular TDMA.

EXERCISES

Problem 2.1

Assume that a portion y of every transmitted packet is overhead (e.g., address, sync bits, etc.).

(a)   What will be the throughput delay characteristic of an FDMA scheme?

(b)   What will be the throughput delay characteristic of a TDMA scheme?

Problem 2.2

Derive the Laplace transform of the message delay in FDMA in which every message contains a random number of packets. Compare the expected message delay with that of TDMA.

Problem 2.3

Compare the first two moments of the queueing time of FDMA with that of TDMA (Note: the queueing time does not include the actual transmission time).

Problem 2.4

Derive the steady-state distribution and the first two moments of the number of *messages* in a TDMA scheme where $L(z)$ is the generating function of the number of packets in a message.

Problem 2.5

Consider a TDMA scheme in which a user is assigned the first two slots of every frame but a message transmission will start only at the first slot in the frame. Assume a Poisson message arrival process with rate λ messages/second and the number of packets in a message distributed according to the generating function $L(z)$. We are interested in the message delay distribution at the user.

(a)   Define an appropriate set of random variables and write the equation for $\bar{D}$ --the delay of an arbitrary ("tagged") message.

(b)   Find the generating function of $\bar{f}$ the number of frames required to transmit a message containing $\bar{L}$ packets.

(c)   Compute the Laplace transform of the message delay and derive from it the average message delay.

Problem 2.6

For the generalized TDMA scheme derive the generating function of the number of packets at the beginning of an *arbitrary* slot. Compute also the expected number of packets at the beginning of an arbitrary slot.

Problem 2.7

Show that when the inter-allocation of slots in the generalized TDMA scheme is uniform, i.e., $d(k) = T_c / K$ for $1 \le k \le K$, then the Laplace transform of the delay distribution in (2.37) reduces to that in (2.16) (see Sections 2.2 and 2.3).

Problem 2.8

This problem addresses the optimal allocation of slots (i.e., choosing $d(k)$) in the generalized TDMA protocol when the load is very light, i.e., $\rho \to 0$ or equivalently $\lambda \to 0$. Let

$$F = 1 + \frac{1}{T_c} \sum_{i=1}^{K} \gamma_i \left[\frac{1}{2} \sum_{j=1}^{K} d^2(j) + \sum_{j=1}^{K} \sum_{l=j+1}^{j+i-1} d(j) d(l) \right]$$

where γ_i $(1 \le i \le K-1)$ is the probability that a message transmission requires i slots beyond the number of whole frames and γ_K is the probability that a message transmission requires a whole number of frames.

(a)   Show that it is sufficient to minimize F in order to minimize the expected delay under the light load circumstances.

(b)   Show that the expression for F reduces to

$$F = 1 + \frac{1}{2} T_c + \frac{1}{T_c} \sum_{l=1}^{K} \sum_{k=1}^{K-l} d(l) d(l+k) \sum_{i=k+1}^{K} (\gamma_i - \gamma_{K-i+1}) .$$

Note from the above expression that when $\gamma_i = \gamma_{K-i+1}$ for $i = 1, 2, \cdots, K$, then the light-load expected delay is independent of the inter-allocation distances.

(c)   Let $\gamma_i = \gamma_{K-i+1}$ for $i = 2, 3, \cdots, K-1$. What is the optimal allocation when $\gamma_1 > \gamma_K$ and when $\gamma_1 < \gamma_K$?

Problem 2.9

Referring to the delay analysis of the MSAP protocol. Prove that

$$w_k = \frac{\displaystyle\sum_{i=0}^{M-1} \rho_i \frac{E[\tilde{x}_i^2]}{2E[\tilde{x}_i]} + (1-\rho)\frac{E[t^2]}{2E[t]}}{(1-\rho^{(k)})(1-\rho^{(k-1)})}$$

(with $\rho^{(k)} = \sum_{i=0}^{k}\rho_i$) is a solution of the general equation, and that if all $\tilde{x}_i$ have the same distribution then

$$E[\tilde{w}] = \sum_{i=0}^{M-1} \frac{\lambda_i}{\lambda} w_i = \frac{\rho\dfrac{E[\tilde{x}^2]}{2E[\tilde{x}]} + (1-\rho)\dfrac{E[t^2]}{2E[t]}}{1-\rho} \ .$$

APPENDIX A

Distribution of the Mod Function

Let $\tilde{l}$ be a non-negative integer valued random variable with a known distribution and a generating function $l(z)$, and let K be a known positive integer constant. The quantity $\tilde{l}$ can be uniquely decomposed into

$$\tilde{l} = \tilde{f} \cdot K + \tilde{J} \qquad 0 \le \tilde{J} \le K-1 \ .$$

In another form this can be written as $\tilde{J} = \tilde{l} \bmod K$ and $\tilde{f} = \left\lfloor \tilde{l}/K \right\rfloor = (\tilde{l} - \tilde{J})/K$. We would like to compute the distributions of $\tilde{J}$ and $\tilde{f}$ from that of $\tilde{l}$.

Let β_m be the unit roots of order K namely, $\beta_m = e^{i \frac{2\pi m}{K}}$. These roots obey

$$\frac{1}{K} \sum_{m=0}^{K-1} \beta_m^n = 1 - \Delta(n \bmod K) = \begin{cases} 1 & K \text{ divides } n \\ 0 & \text{otherwise} \end{cases}$$

Our most basic relation is derived as follows:

$$\frac{1}{K} \sum_{m=0}^{K-1} (z \beta_m)^{-n} l(z \beta_m) = \frac{1}{K} \sum_{m=0}^{K-1} (z \beta_m)^{-n} \sum_{l=0}^{\infty} Prob\,[\tilde{l}=l](z \beta_m)^l$$

$$= \frac{1}{K} \sum_{l=0}^{\infty} Prob\,[\tilde{l}=l] z^{l-n} \sum_{m=0}^{K-1} (\beta_m)^{l-n}$$

$$\hspace{6cm} (2A.1)$$

$$= \sum_{l=0}^{\infty} Prob\,[\tilde{l}=l] z^{l-n} [1 - \Delta((l-n) \bmod K)]$$

$$= \sum_{f=0}^{\infty} Prob\,[\tilde{l}=f\,K+n] z^{f\,K} \ .$$

By setting $z=1$ in equation (2A.1) we get

$$Prob\,[\tilde{J}=n] = \sum_{f=0}^{\infty} Prob\,[\tilde{l}=f\,K+n] = \frac{1}{K} \sum_{m=0}^{K-1} \beta_m^{-n} l(\beta_m) \qquad 0 \le n \le K-1$$

which gives us the distribution of $\tilde{J}$. From this $J(z)$, the generating function of $\tilde{J}$, can be computed as follows:

$$\sum_{n=0}^{K-1} Prob\,[\tilde{J}=n] z^n = \sum_{n=0}^{K-1} \left[\frac{1}{K} \sum_{m=0}^{K-1} \beta_m^{-n} l(\beta_m) \right] z^n$$

$$= \frac{1}{K} \sum_{m=0}^{K-1} \left[\sum_{n=0}^{K-1} \left(\frac{z}{\beta_m} \right)^n \right] l(\beta_m) = \frac{1}{K} \sum_{m=0}^{K-1} \frac{1 - \left(\frac{z}{\beta_m} \right)^K}{1 - \frac{z}{\beta_m}} l(\beta_m)$$

$$= \frac{1}{K} \sum_{m=0}^{K-1} \frac{1 - z^K}{1 - \frac{z}{\beta_m}} l(\beta_m) = \frac{1 - z^K}{K} \sum_{m=0}^{K-1} \frac{l(\beta_m)}{1 - \frac{z}{\beta_m}}$$

where in the step before last we used the fact that $\beta_m^K = 1$. Overall, we thus have

$$J(z) = \frac{1 - z^K}{K} \sum_{m=0}^{K-1} \frac{l(\beta_m)}{1 - \frac{z}{\beta_m}} = \frac{1 - z^K}{K(1 - z)} + \frac{1 - z^K}{K} \sum_{m=1}^{K-1} \frac{l(\beta_m)}{1 - \frac{z}{\beta_m}} .$$

Taking the derivative at $z = 1$ yields the expectation

$$E[\tilde{J}] = \frac{K-1}{2} - \sum_{m=1}^{K-1} \frac{l(\beta_m)}{1 - \frac{1}{\beta_m}} .$$

We turn now to calculate the generating function of $\tilde{f}$. Clearly

$$Prob[\tilde{f} = f] = \sum_{n=0}^{K-1} Prob[\tilde{l} = f K + n] \qquad f \geq 0$$

and thus

$$F(z) = \sum_{f=0}^{\infty} Prob[\tilde{f} = f] z^f = \sum_{f=0}^{\infty} \left[\sum_{n=0}^{K-1} Prob[\tilde{l} = f K + n] \right] z^f$$

$$= \sum_{n=0}^{K-1} \left[\sum_{f=0}^{\infty} Prob[\tilde{l} = f K + n] z^f \right] .$$

We note that the bracketted term in the summation appears in equation (2A.1) when $z^{1/K}$ is substituted for z. Hence

$$F(z) = \sum_{n=0}^{K-1} \left[\frac{1}{K} \sum_{m=0}^{K-1} (z^{1/K} \beta_m)^{-n} l(z^{1/K} \beta_m) \right]$$

$$= \frac{1}{K} \sum_{m=0}^{K-1} \left[\sum_{n=0}^{K-1} (z^{1/K} \beta_m)^{-n} \right] l(z^{1/K} \beta_m)$$

$$= \frac{1}{K} \sum_{m=0}^{K-1} \frac{1 - (z^{1/K} \beta_m)^{-K}}{1 - (z^{1/K} \beta_m)^{-1}} l(z^{1/K} \beta_m)$$

$$= \frac{1}{K} \sum_{m=0}^{K-1} \frac{1 - z^{-1}}{1 - (z^{1/K} \beta_m)^{-1}} l(z^{1/K} \beta_m) = \frac{1 - z^{-1}}{K} \sum_{m=0}^{K-1} \frac{l(z^{1/K} \beta_m)}{1 - (z^{1/K} \beta_m)^{-1}} \ .$$

Calculating the expected value of $\tilde{f}$ can be done by taking the derivative of the above equation at $z=1$ or using the direct approach, i.e.,

$$E[\tilde{f}] = \frac{E[\tilde{l}] - E[\tilde{J}]}{K} = \frac{1}{K} E[\tilde{l}] - \frac{K-1}{2K} + \frac{1}{K} \sum_{m=1}^{K-1} \frac{l(\beta_m)}{1 - \frac{1}{\beta_m}} \ .$$

$$\frac{\partial ...}{K ...} = \sum ... \frac{...}{...} ...$$

Calculating the canonical value ..., can be done b... Using the derivative of the ... with respect to ... for the direct demand ...

$$\frac{\partial ...}{\partial ...} = ...$$

CHAPTER 3

ALOHA PROTOCOLS

The Aloha family of protocols is probably the richest family of multiple access protocols. Its popularity is due first of all to seniority, as it is the first random access technique introduced. Second, many of these protocols are so simple that their implementation is straightforward. Many local area networks of today implement some sophisticated variants of this family's protocols.

With the conflict-free protocols that were discussed in Chapter 2, every scheduled transmission is guaranteed to succeed. The Aloha family of protocols belongs to the contention-type or random retransmission protocols in which the success of a transmission is not guaranteed in advance. The reason is that whenever two or more users are transmitting on the shared channel simultaneously, a collision occurs and the data cannot be received correctly. This being the case, packets may have to be transmitted and retransmitted until eventually they are correctly received. Transmission scheduling is therefore the focal concern of contention-type protocols.

Because of the great popularity of Aloha protocols, analyses have been carried out for a very large number of variations. The variations present different protocols for transmission and retransmission schedules as well as adaptation to different circumstances and channel features. This chapter covers a few of these variations.

3.1. PURE ALOHA

The *pure Aloha* protocol is *the* basic protocol in the family of the Aloha protocols. It considers a single-hop system with an infinite population generating packets of equal length T according to a Poisson process with rate λ packets/sec. The channel is error-free without capture: whenever a transmission of a packet does not interfere with any other packet transmission, the transmitted packet is received correctly while if two or more packet transmissions overlap in time, a collision is caused and none of the colliding packets are received correctly and they have to be retransmitted. The users whose packets collide with one another are called the *colliding users*. At the end of every transmission each user knows whether his transmission was successful or a collision took place.

The pure Aloha protocol is very simple [Abr70]. It states that a newly generated packet is transmitted immediately hoping for no interference by others. Should the transmission be unsuccessful, every colliding user, independently of the others, schedules his retransmission to a random time in the future. This randomness is required to ensure that the same set of packets does not continue to collide indefinitely. A simple example of the operation of the protocol is depicted in Figure 3.1 where the arrows indicate arrival instants, successful transmissions are indicated by blank rectangles and collided packets are hatched.

Since the population is infinite each packet can be considered as if it belongs to a different user. Hence, each newly arrived packet can be assigned to an idle user i.e., one that does not have a packet to retransmit. This allows us to interchange the roles of users and packets and consider only the points in time when packet transmission attempts are made.

Observing the channel over time we define a point process consisting of scheduling points, i.e., the points in which packets are scheduled for transmission. The scheduling points include both the generation times of new packets and the retransmission times of previously collided packets. Let the rate of the scheduling points be g packets/sec. The parameter g is referred to as the *offered load* to the channel. Clearly, since not all packets are successful on their first attempted transmission, $g > \lambda$.

The exact characterization of the scheduling points process is extremely complicated. To overcome this complexity it is assumed that this process is a Poisson process (with rate g, of course). This assumption can, however, be a good approximation at best (as has indeed been shown by simulation). The reason is that a Poisson process implies independence between events in nonoverlapping intervals, which cannot be the case here because of the dependence between the interval containing the original transmission and the interval containing a retransmission of the same packet. It can be shown, however, that if the retransmission schedule is chosen uniformly from an arbitrarily large interval then the number of scheduling points in any interval approaches a Poisson distribution. The Poisson assumption is used because it makes the analysis of Aloha-type systems tractable and predicts successfully their maximal throughput.

Pure Aloha is a single-hop system. Hence, the throughput is the fraction of time the channel carries useful information, namely noncolliding packets. The channel capacity is the highest value of arrival rate λ for which the rate of departure (throughput) equals the total arrival rate (but see the discussion of stability in Section 3.4).

Consider a packet (new or old) scheduled for transmission at some time t (see Figure 3.1). This packet will be successful if no other packet is scheduled for transmission in the interval $(t-T, t+T)$ (this period of duration $2T$ is called the *vulnerable* period). The probability of this happening, that is, the probability of success P_{suc}, is the probability that no packet is scheduled in an interval of length $2T$. Since the scheduling points correspond to a Poisson process, we have

$$P_{suc} = e^{-2gT} .$$

Now, packets are scheduled at a rate of g per second of which only a fraction P_{suc} are successful. Thus, the rate of successfully transmitted packets is gP_{suc}. When a packet is successful the channel carries useful information for a period of T seconds; in any other case it carries no useful information at all. Using the definition that the throughput is the fraction of time that useful information is carried on the channel we get

$$S = gTe^{-2gT}$$

which gives the channel throughput as a function of the offered load. Defining $G \overset{\Delta}{=} gT$ to be the *normalized offered load* to the channel, i.e., the rate (per packet transmission time) packets are transmitted on the channel, we have

$$S = Ge^{-2G} .$$

The relation between S and G is depicted in Figure 3.2, which is typical to many Aloha type protocols. At $G=\frac{1}{2}$, S takes on its maximal value of $1/2e \approx 0.18$. This value is referred to as the capacity of the pure Aloha channel.

We recall that for a system to be stable the long term rate of input must equal the long term rate of output meaning that stability requires $S = \lambda T$. Larger values of λ clearly cannot result in stable operation. Note however, that even for smaller values of λ there are two values of G to which it corresponds--one larger and one smaller than $\frac{1}{2}$. The smaller one is (conditionally) stable while the other one is conditionally unstable, meaning that if the offered load increases beyond that point the system will continue to drift to higher load and lower throughput. Thus, without additional measures of control, the stable throughput of pure Aloha is 0. We return to the stability issue in Section 3.4. (It is appropriate to add that this theoretical instability is rarely a severe problem in real systems, where the long term load including, of course, the "off hours" load, is fairly small although temporary problems may occur).

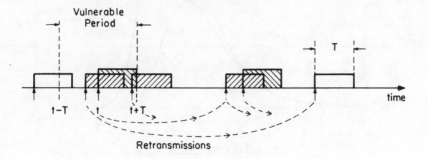

Figure 3.1: Pure Aloha Packet Timing

3.2. SLOTTED ALOHA

The *slotted Aloha* variation of the Aloha protocol is simply that of pure Aloha with a slotted channel. The slot size equals T--the duration of packet transmission. Users are restricted to start transmission of packets only at slot boundaries. Thus, the vulnerable period is reduced to a single slot. In other words, a slot will be successful if and only if exactly one packet was scheduled for transmission sometime during the previous slot. The throughput is therefore the fraction of slots (or probability) in which a single packet is scheduled for transmission. Because the process composed of newly generated and retransmitted packets is Poisson we conclude that

$$S = gTe^{-gT}$$

or using the definition of the normalized offered load $G = gT$

$$S = Ge^{-G} \ .$$

This relation is very similar to that of pure Aloha, except of increased throughput (see Figure 3.2). Channel capacity is $1/e \approx 0.36$ and is achieved at $G = 1$. The above results were first derived by Roberts [Rob72].

We would like to introduce an additional method of calculating throughput which will be useful later and which can be easily demonstrated in

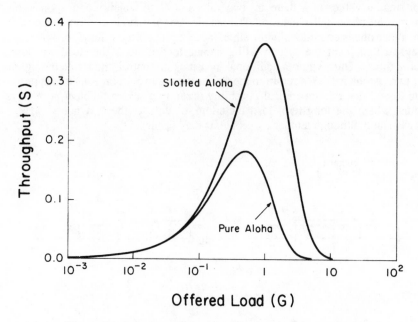

Figure 3.2: Throughput-Load of Pure and Slotted Aloha

the slotted Aloha case.

When observing the channel over time we notice a cyclic behavior of busy and idle periods (see Figure 3.3 in which up-arrows point at arrival instants, blank rectangles refer to successful slots, and hatched rectangles denote colliding packets, i.e., unsuccessful slots). A busy period is a succession of slots in which transmission takes place (successful or not). The idle period is defined as the interval between two busy periods. The starting times of every cycle (just before the start of the busy period) define renewal points. In fact, these are points of a regenerative process, since the system is memoryless in the sense that its behavior in a given cycle does not depend on the behavior in any previous cycle. As such, the expected fraction of time the system is in a given state equals the expected fraction of time *during a single cycle* that the system is in that state (see Appendix).

Let $\bar{I}$ be a random variable describing the number of slots in the idle period. The random variable $\bar{I}$ must be strictly positive since there must be at least one empty slot in an idle period. The probability that the idle period consists of a single slot is the probability that there were some packets scheduled during that slot that will be transmitted in the next slot. Thus,

$$P[\bar{I}=1] = P[Some\ packets\ scheduled\ in\ first\ slot]$$

$$= 1 - P[No\ packets\ scheduled\ in\ first\ slot] = 1 - e^{-gT} .$$

The probability that the idle period lasts exactly two slots is the probability of the event that no packets were scheduled in the first slot and some were scheduled in the second (to be transmitted in the third slot). Thus,

$$P[\bar{I}=2] = e^{-gT} \cdot (1 - e^{-gT}) .$$

In general, the length of the idle period is seen to be geometrically distributed, namely

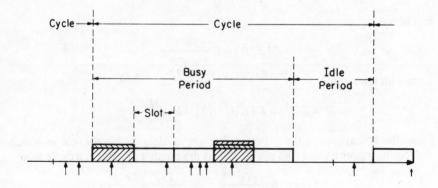

Figure 3.3: Slotted-Aloha Packet Timing

$$P[\tilde{I}=k] = \left[e^{-gT}\right]^{k-1}\left[1-e^{-gT}\right] \quad k = 1,2,\cdots$$

yielding an average length (measured in slots) of

$$I = \frac{1}{1-e^{-gT}} \ .$$

Similarly, let us define $\tilde{B}$ as the number of slots in the busy period. Clearly $\tilde{B}>0$. An argument similar to that used in calculating the distribution of the idle period leads to the derivation of the distribution of $\tilde{B}$. For the busy period to be $k>0$ slots long, packets must be scheduled for transmission in each and every one of the first $k-1$ slots and none scheduled in the kth. This leads to

$$P[\tilde{B}=k] = \left[1-e^{-gT}\right]^{k-1}e^{-gT} \quad k = 1,2,\cdots$$

yielding an expected value of

$$B = \frac{1}{e^{-gT}} \ .$$

Since not all the slots in the busy period are successful, let $\tilde{U}$ denote the number of useful, or successful slots in a cycle and let U be its expected value. The probability that a given slot in the busy period is successful is

$$\frac{gTe^{-gT}}{1-e^{-gT}}$$

which is the probability of a single arrival in a slot given that we are in the busy period (i.e., some arrivals do occur). Thus, given that the duration of the busy period is $\tilde{B}$ slots we have

$$P[\tilde{U}=k\,|\tilde{B}] = \binom{\tilde{B}}{k}\left[\frac{gTe^{-gT}}{1-e^{-gT}}\right]^k\left[1-\frac{gTe^{-gT}}{1-e^{-gT}}\right]^{(\tilde{B}-k)} \quad 0 \le k \le n$$

and hence

$$E[\tilde{U}\,|\tilde{B}] = \tilde{B}\frac{gTe^{-gT}}{1-e^{-gT}}$$

from which we get

$$U = E[\tilde{U}] = E[E[\tilde{U}\,|\tilde{B}]] = B\cdot\frac{gTe^{-gT}}{1-e^{-gT}} \ .$$

Now, the throughput is the expected fraction of slots within a cycle in which successful transmissions take place. If $\tilde{C}$ is the number of slots in a cycle then

$$S = \frac{E[\tilde{U}]}{E[\tilde{C}]} = \frac{U}{B+I} = \frac{B\cdot\dfrac{gTe^{-gT}}{1-e^{-gT}}}{B+I} = \frac{\dfrac{1}{e^{-gT}}\cdot\dfrac{gTe^{-gT}}{1-e^{-gT}}}{\dfrac{1}{e^{-gT}}+\dfrac{1}{1-e^{-gT}}} = gTe^{-gT}$$

which is the result obtained previously. The technique of using regenerative processes as done above is an important tool in deriving the throughput of more complicated protocols.

3.3. SLOTTED ALOHA - FINITE NUMBER OF USERS

To make the previous model more realistic we analyze here the case of an Aloha system with a finite number of users. The analysis of this model enables us to derive packet delays which we were unable to do in the previous model. The following analysis is based on that of Kleinrock and Lam [KlL75]. We consider a case in which slotted Aloha is used by a group of M users each with a single packet buffer (this less general case makes the comparison with the infinite population cases more meaningful since there too every user had only a single buffer). All packets are of the same size, requiring T seconds for transmission, which is also the slot-duration.

To gain insight into the relation between transmission of new packets and retransmission of old ones we build the following packet-scheduling model (referred to as the linear feedback model). Let every user be in one of two states--*thinking* and *backlogged*. In the thinking state the user does not have a packet in his buffer and does not participate in any scheduling activities. When in this state, the user generates a packet in every slot with probability σ and does not generate a packet in a slot with probability $1-\sigma$; packet generation is independent of any other activity. The preceding means that packet generation is an independent process distributed geometrically with mean $1/\sigma$. Once a packet is generated its transmission is attempted immediately, that is, in the next slot. If the transmission was successful the user remains in the thinking state and the packet generating process starts anew. If packet transmission was unsuccessful the user moves to the backlogged state and schedules the retransmission of the packet according to an independent geometric distribution with parameter ν. In other words, in every slot the user will retransmit the packet with probability ν and will refrain from doing so with probability $1-\nu$. While in the backlogged state the user does not generate any new packets. When the packet is finally successfully transmitted the user moves back to the thinking state.

Let the slots of the system be numbered sequentially $k=0,1,\cdots$ and let $\tilde{N}(k)$ denote the number of backlogged users at the beginning of the kth slot. The random variable $\tilde{N}(k)$ is referred to as the *state* of the system. The number of backlogged users at the beginning of the $(k+1)$st slot depends on the number of backlogged users at the beginning of the kth slot and the number of users that moved from state to state within the slot. Since state-transition of the users is independent of the activities in any previous slot the process $\{\tilde{N}(k), k=0,1,\cdots\}$ is a Markov chain. Because the number of backlogged users cannot exceed M this chain is finite; thus, if all states communicate (as we subsequently indicate) this Markov chain is also ergodic, meaning that a steady-state distribution exists.

The transition diagram for the system is shown in Figure 3.4. "Upward" transitions are possible between every state and all the higher-numbered states, since a collision among any number of packets is possible. "Downward" transitions are possible only to the adjacent state since only one packet can be successfully transmitted in a slot, at which time the backlog is reduced by unity. Note also the missing transition from state 0 to state 1 which is clear since if all users were thinking and a single user generated and transmitted a packet he could not cause a collision and become backlogged. The fact that all states communicate is evident from the diagram.

Steady-State Probabilities

For analysis purposes we introduce the following notation (see Appendix). Let π_i be the steady-state probability of the system being in state i, that is $\pi_i = \lim_{k \to \infty} Prob\,[\tilde{N}(k) = i]$. Further, let p_{ij} be the steady-state transition probability, i.e., $p_{ij} = \lim_{k \to \infty} Prob\,[\tilde{N}(k) = j \mid \tilde{N}(k-1) = i]$. Finally, denote by P the matrix whose elements are p_{ij} and by π the row vector whose elements are π_i. From the above argumentation it follows that the steady-state probability vector is the solution to the finite set of linear equations

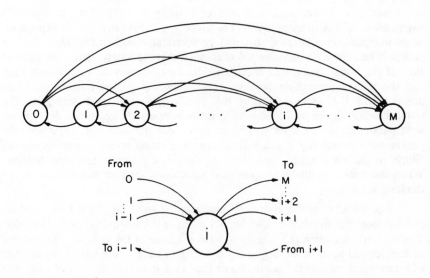

Figure 3.4: State Transitions of Finite Population Aloha

$$\pi = \pi P \qquad \sum_i \pi_i = 1$$

to which the existence of a unique solution is guaranteed. We must therefore construct the matrix P and derive the desired solution.

Since the retransmission process of every user is an independent geometric process, the probability that i out of the j backlogged users will schedule a retransmission in a given slot is binomially distributed, namely

Prob [i backlogged users transmit in a slot | j in backlog]

$$= \begin{bmatrix} j \\ i \end{bmatrix} v^i (1-v)^{j-i} . \tag{3.1}$$

In a similar manner, we obtain for the thinking users

Prob [i thinking users transmit in a slot | j in backlog]

$$= \begin{bmatrix} M-j \\ i \end{bmatrix} \sigma^i (1-\sigma)^{M-j-i} \tag{3.2}$$

since when j users are backlogged, $M-j$ users are thinking.

The matrix P can be constructed by applying equations (3.1) and (3.2) as follows.

Clearly, a transition from state i to state $j < i-1$ is impossible implying that $p_{ij} = 0$ for those cases. Consider the transition from state i to state $i-1$. This indicates a reduction in the backlog which is possible only if a single backlogged packet was transmitted (and no new packet was generated, of course).

The transition from state i to the very same state can come about from two distinct reasons. The first results from the circumstance in which no new packet was generated (and transmitted) while several backlogged users attempted transmission. The transmitting users clearly collide and remain in the backlog; because no transmission of new packets was attempted the backlog did not change. A special case of this latter one is when the slot remains idle-- neither a transmission of a new packet is attempted nor is a retransmission attempted. The second reason for this transition results from a situation in which none of the backlogged users attempt retransmission and a single thinking user transmits. In this case the thinking user succeeds and therefore remains in the thinking state leaving the system in the same state. The above can be summarized by the union of the two independent events: "No backlogged user succeeds and no thinking user attempts" and "No backlogged user attempts and a single thinking user attempts".

The next transition to consider is from state i to state $i+1$. Since the backlog increased, a collision must have taken place. Furthermore, since the backlog increased by unity, exactly one thinking user has attempted together with at least one attempt from the backlog.

The last case is the transition from state i to a state $j > i+1$. Here the backlog increased by two or more meaning that $j-i$ thinking users generated packets and, of course, collided. The activity of the backlogged users is immaterial in this case since the collision is generated by the thinking users alone.

The above can be summarized in the following formulae (where the bracketed terms correspond to the events described in the preceding explanation):

$$
p_{ij} = \begin{cases}
0 & j < i-1 \\[2mm]
\left[i v(1-v)^{i-1} \right] (1-\sigma)^{M-i} & j = i-1 \\[2mm]
\left[1-i v(1-v)^{i-1} \right](1-\sigma)^{M-i} + \left[(M-i)\sigma(1-\sigma)^{M-i-1} \right](1-v)^i & j = i \\[2mm]
\left[(M-i)\sigma(1-\sigma)^{M-i-1} \right]\left[1-(1-v)^i \right] & j = i+1 \\[2mm]
\binom{M-i}{j-i} \sigma^{j-i}(1-\sigma)^{M-j} & j > i+1
\end{cases} \tag{3.3}
$$

It can be easily verified that $\sum_j p_{ij} = 1$ as required. Also, note that p_{01} turns out to be identically zero; this result is correct and expected since it takes at least two colliding packets to increase the backlog and because no users were backlogged before, it is impossible to have a single backlogged user at the end of the slot.

Solving the set of equations $\pi = \pi P$ for the above matrix cannot be done in closed form. However, the special structure of the P matrix--having nonzero elements in the upper right triangle and in the first sub-diagonal--allows fairly easy computation.

Consider the homogeneous set of equations $x(I-P)=0$ where I is the identity matrix. This is the same set of equations rewritten with x replacing π. It can be shown that the rank of $I-P$ is M which means, among others, that nontrivial solutions exist and are all collinear. To find one of these solutions assume $x_0 = 1$. The first equation, namely $x_0(1-p_{00}) - x_1 p_{10} = 0$ yields $x_1 = (1-p_{00})/p_{10}$. From the second equation we have $-x_0 p_{01} - x_1(1-p_{11}) - x_2 p_{21} = 0$, from which x_2 can be calculated. Proceeding similarly, every step involves a simple computation and results in determining the value of an additional x_i. Having done this M times and calculated the values of all x_i we then compute

$$
\pi_i = \frac{x_i}{\sum_j x_j} .
$$

The value of π thus computed is collinear with x and therefore solves the original set of equations. The π_i clearly sum up to 1. This is therefore the desired solution.

Throughput Analysis

To evaluate the throughput of the system consider the epochs at the beginning of every slot. Since the activity within a given slot is independent of the activity in any previous slot these epochs are renewal points. Hence, the long term fraction of time the channel carries useful information--the throughput-- equals the expected fraction of slots containing useful transmission. If we denote by P_{suc} the probability of a successful slot then

$$S = P_{suc} .$$

For a slot to be successful only a single transmission must take place within it. This means that either all backlogged users remain silent and a single new user transmits, or a single backlogged user transmits while no new packet is generated. Given that there are i backlogged users this can be stated as

$$P_{suc}(i) \triangleq Prob\,[Successful\ slot\ /\ i\ users\ in\ backlog]$$
$$= (1-v)^i (M-i)\sigma(1-\sigma)^{M-i-1} + iv(1-v)^{i-1}(1-\sigma)^{M-i} . \qquad (3.4)$$

The total throughput is therefore

$$S = P_{suc} = E\,[P_{suc}(i)] = \sum_{i=0}^{M} P_{suc}(i)\pi_i . \qquad (3.5)$$

Note that since all users are statistically identical, the individual throughput is given by the value of S from the last equation divided by M.

As a special case, consider a situation in which we do not distinguish between backlogged packets and new packets, i.e., we set $v = \sigma$. Substituting this into equation (3.4) yields

$$P_{suc}(i) = M\sigma(1-\sigma)^{M-1}$$

indicating that $P_{suc}(i)$ is independent of i. This result is, of course, not surprising since if we cease to distinguish between backlogged and thinking users we cannot expect the probability of success to depend on the number of backlogged users. Moreover, because $P_{suc}(i)$ is independent of i we obtain from equation (3.5) a closed form expression for the throughput, namely

$$S = E\,[P_{suc}(i)] = M\sigma(1-\sigma)^{M-1} . \qquad (3.6)$$

Let us continue a bit with this line of thought, i.e., not distinguishing the backlogged from the thinking users. In previous sections we denoted by G the total, system wide, average number of transmissions per slot; in our case this equals $M\sigma$. Substituting this value into the throughput equation above yields

$$S = G\left[1 - \frac{G}{M}\right]^{M-1} .$$

Under these circumstances, letting M increase to infinity we find that in the limit $S = Ge^{-G}$, a result identical to the one derived in Section 3.2 for the infinite population slotted Aloha scheme. We might conclude, therefore, that the infinite population model is indeed in some sense the limit of the finite population model if backlogged users are not distinguished from the thinking ones and if the number of users is increased under the constraint that the total average arrival rate remains finite.

Expected Delay

The previous derivation considered the throughput from the departure standpoint since P_{suc} is the average rate of packet departure from the system. If the system is to be stable then this rate must equal the average rate of new packet generation. Now, when the system is in state i there are $M-i$ thinking users each generating packets in every slot with probability σ. Thus, the average rate of new packet generation when in state i is $(M-i)\sigma$. Taking expectation yields

$$S = E[(M-i)\sigma] = \sum (M-i)\sigma \pi_i = (M-\overline{N})\sigma \qquad (3.7)$$

where $\overline{N}$ is the average number of backlogged users.

Denote by b the average rate at which packets (actually, users with packets) join the backlog; then according to Little's formula, the average amount of time spent in the backlog is the ratio of the average number of backlogged users to the average rate of joining or $\overline{N}/b$. Not all packets going through the system are backlogged--the lucky ones make it the first time. Since b is the rate of packets joining the backlog and S (the throughput) is the rate of packets leaving the system then a fraction $(S-b)/S$ of the packets are never backlogged. These packets suffer a delay of 1 slot only. All the others (whose fraction is b/S) suffer the backlog delay mentioned above plus the one slot in which their transmission is successful. Measured in slots (i.e., normalized to the packet transmission time) the average delay is

$$\hat{D} = \frac{S-b}{S} \cdot 1 + \frac{b}{S}(\frac{\overline{N}}{b} + 1) = 1 + \frac{\overline{N}}{S} \ .$$

Using the value of $\overline{N}$ from equation (3.7) finally yields

$$\hat{D} = 1 - \frac{1}{\sigma} + \frac{M}{S} \qquad (3.8)$$

with the value of S taken from equation (3.5). This last equation is the desired throughput delay relation. It should be noted that this representation is parametric since σ influences the value of S. Throughput delay characteristics for several parameter choices are depicted in Figure 3.5. Each of the curves in the figure represents one value of ν with σ varying from 0 to 1 along the curve. Thus, the throughput first increases with σ until capacity is achieved (for that value of ν); thereafter the throughput decreases with increasing load. The delay, as intuitively expected, increases monotonically with σ.

Consider again the special case in which $\sigma = \nu$, for which the throughput is given in equation (3.6). Substituting this into equation (3.8) yields

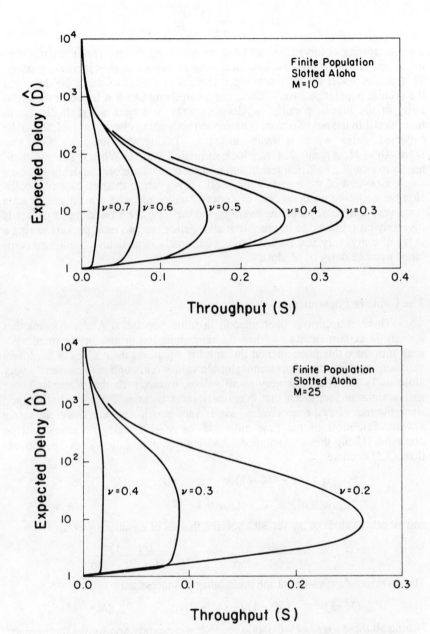

Figure 3.5: Throughput-Delay of Finite Population Slotted Aloha
(a) 10 Users
(b) 25 Users

$$\hat{D} = 1 + \frac{1 - (1-\sigma)^{M-1}}{\sigma(1-\sigma)^{M-1}} \; .$$

Two interesting observations can be made regarding this last result. First, keeping the product $M\sigma$ constant and increasing M shows an ever increasing delay. That is, the model we have developed cannot be used to evaluate the delay for the infinite population case. This is not a surprising fact and is due to the instability of the infinite-population Aloha systems, a subject we shall discuss in more detail in the next Section. The second interesting observation relates to the expected delay when σ tends to zero. Taking the limit we find that $\hat{D}(\sigma \to 0) \to M$, a result that may look surprising at first. When σ is very small, hardly ever will a collision result, and in most cases therefore the delay will be a single slot--that of the transmission itself. However, in the rare case of a collision the colliding users become of course backlogged, and remain in this state for a very long time since the average waiting time for a backlogged packet is inversely proportional to σ. Putting it all together we find most packets having a delay of unity, very few packets having extremely large delays, yielding a combined average delay of M slots.

The Capture Phenomenon

There is a curious phenomenon in finite population Aloha systems that appears in certain situations when the retransmission probability is small. We shall introduce this phenomenon through the equations themselves. Consider a situation in which σ accepts nonnegligible values (although not necessarily very close to 1) and ν accepts very small values, in fact such that $M\nu \ll 1$. These assumptions in fact mean that eventually most users will become backlogged since the rate of exit from the backlog is very small. One can therefore safely assume that most of the time either M or $M-1$ backlogged users will be observed. Using these assumptions, and approximating $(1-\nu)^i$ as $1 - i\nu$ equations (3.3) become

$$p_{M-1,M-1} = 1 - (M-1)\nu\sigma \quad ; \quad p_{M-1,M} = (M-1)\nu\sigma$$

$$p_{M,M-1} = M\nu \quad ; \quad p_{M,M} = 1 - M\nu$$

and all other values of p_{ij} vanish. Solving this set of equations yields

$$\pi_{M-1} = \frac{M}{M + (M-1)\sigma} \quad ; \quad \pi_M = \frac{(M-1)\sigma}{M + (M-1)\sigma} \; .$$

The corresponding values of the probability of success are

$$P_{suc}(M-1) = \sigma + (M-1)\nu + (M-2)\nu\sigma \quad ; \quad P_{suc}(M) = M\nu \; .$$

Putting all these together we obtain the following expression for the throughput

$$S = M\frac{\sigma + (M-1)\nu + (M-3)\nu\sigma}{M + (M-1)\sigma} \approx \frac{M\sigma}{M + (M-1)\sigma} \; .$$

   This expression is interesting because it indicates that the throughput increases with the load σ. Furthermore, substituting these values into equation (3.8) yields

$$\hat{D} = 1 + (M - 1)\frac{1 + \sigma}{\sigma} = M + \frac{M - 1}{\sigma}$$

indicating that the average delay is actually decreasing with increasing load! Furthermore, both the throughput and the average delay do not depend on ν hence these systems exhibit identical performance for various values of ν. The phenomenon is demonstrated in Figure 3.6 where the throughput-delay curve for a system with $M = 10$ is shown (this figure depicts the result of equation (3.8)). One can clearly observe that as long as σ is small delay increases with throughput as one might generally expect. At higher values of σ we note a decrease of the delay while the throughput increases, which is rather strange and is indicative of a curious phenomenon. Also note that the graphs for the various values of ν coincide for larger values of σ, demonstrating the previous observation that system performance under these conditions is almost independent of ν.

   To understand the nature of this phenomenon, recall that the retransmission rate is very small and that backlogged users remain in that state for a fairly long time. Since the rate of new packet generation σ is nonnegligible, eventually all users will become backlogged. With this situation in place consider a

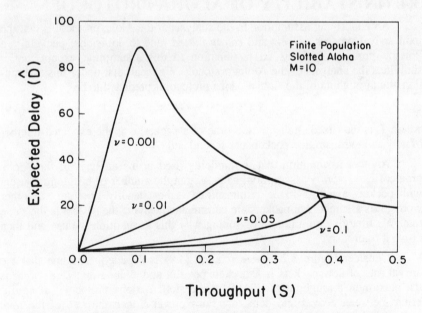

Figure 3.6: Throughput-Delay of finite population Aloha under Capture

user that retransmits his packet and (usually) succeeds. This user will generate another packet after a relatively short time and, having generated a new packet, is very likely to succeed again since the probability that his transmission will be interfered with that of a backlogged user is slight. This chain of events continues for quite a while until the "unfortunate" event that a retransmission of a backlogged user is scheduled at which time either a collision occurs immediately, or there are two thinking users that are likely to collide. When this happens all users are backlogged again, remaining so for quite a while, since retransmission rate is small. Eventually, however, another user retransmits and usually succeeds and the previous scenario repeats itself. What actually happens is that a random user *captures* the channel for a while, i.e., transmits successfully a succession of packets. Performance clearly improves with increasing σ because the more packets generated in between two retransmissions the better the throughput. When σ becomes sufficiently high, the throughput approaches 0.5 because the capturing user transmits in one slot and generates a new packet in the next and so forth.

This capture effect appears in all finite-population Aloha-like protocols such as all the variants of the carrier-sensing protocols, with and without collision detection (see, for example, [ShH82]).

3.4. (IN)STABILITY OF ALOHA PROTOCOLS

An underlying assumption in the analysis of the Aloha protocol is that the joint arrival process of *new* and *retransmitted* (due to collisions) packets is a Poisson process. There is no justification to this assumption except that it simplifies the analysis of the Aloha protocol. We recall that under this assumption, the throughput of the slotted Aloha protocol is predicted to be

$$S = gTe^{-gT} = Ge^{-G} \tag{3.9}$$

where T is the (fixed) transmission time of a packet, g is the expected number of new and retransmitted packets per second and $G = gT$.

Another assumption that is implicitly used in the analysis of the Aloha protocol is a *stability* assumption, namely, that the number of backlogged users with packets awaiting to be retransmitted is not steadily growing. In other words, it is assumed that packets are entering and leaving the system at the same rate. We first give an intuitive reasoning why this assumption is false and then prove it rigorously.

Consider Figure 3.2 where relation (3.9) is depicted. Assume that the arrival rate of new packets is λ packets per slot and assume that $\lambda < e^{-1}$ (e^{-1} is the maximum throughput predicted for the slotted Aloha protocol). If equilibrium between arrival and departure rates prevails, then the rate of the total traffic on the channel (new and retransmitted packets) $G = gT$ will be $G_1 = g_1 T$, as is shown in Figure 3.7. This is of course an "average" rate, and, over any fixed interval of time, the actual rate will fluctuate around this mean. If the actual traffic rate moves a little above G_1, the actual throughput increases a little above λ. Thus, packets leave the system faster than they arrive, which causes the actual traffic rate to decrease back to G_1. If the actual traffic rate moves a little below G_1, the actual throughput decreases a little below λ. Thus, packets leave the system slower than they arrive, which causes the actual traffic rate to increase back to G_1. Consequently, the point $(S,G) = (\lambda, G_1)$ is a conditionally stable point, namely, it is stable under small variations in G_1. However, if a large variation (and this will happen with probability one) causes the actual traffic to exceed G_2 in Figure 3.7 then the actual throughput decreases below λ. Thus, packets leave the system at a slower rate than they enter, which causes further increase in the actual traffic rate, a further decrease in actual throughput, etc. The system never returns to the point (λ, G_1), but rather drifts relentlessly toward the catastrophic, unconditionally stable, point $(S,G) = (0,\infty)$. We conclude that the maximum stable throughput of the Aloha protocol is *zero*.

In the following, this result is established in a more precise and formal manner. The following is based on the analysis by Fayolle et. al. [FLB74]. We first describe the concrete model that is used in the analysis.

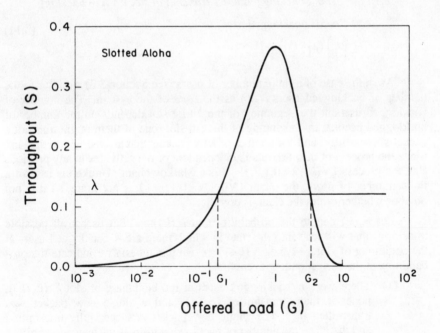

Figure 3.7: Demonstrating the Instability of Slotted Aloha

3.4.1. Analysis

Consider the slotted Aloha system with an infinite population of users, so that each new packet that arrives to the system is associated with a new user. Let $\bar{A}(k)$ be the number of new packets that are generated (arrive) during the kth slot. These packets are transmitted in slot $k+1$. It is assumed that $\{\bar{A}(k), k=0,1,2, \cdots\}$ is a sequence of independent and identically distributed (i.i.d.) random variables with a common distribution

$$Prob\,[\bar{A}(k) = i] = Prob\,[\,i\ new\ packets\ arrive\ in\ slot\ k\,] = a_i \qquad i \geq 0 \qquad (3.10)$$

and mean λ packets/slot ($\lambda = \sum_{i=1}^{\infty} i a_i$). Notice that if the arrival process of new packets is Poisson, $a_i = \lambda^i e^{-\lambda}/i!$.

Let $\bar{N}(k)$ be the number of backlogged users at the beginning of slot k ($k=0,1,2, \cdots$). Backlogged users have packets that collided, and that have to be retransmitted. We assume that $\bar{N}(0)=0$. The retransmission delay of a packet is assumed to be geometric, namely, a user that is backlogged at the beginning of slot k, retransmits its packet during slot k with probability ν, independently of any other event in the system. From these definitions we have:

$$b_i(n) \overset{\Delta}{=} Prob\,[i\ backlogged\ users\ transmit\ in\ slot\ k \mid n\ in\ backlog]$$

$$= Prob\,[i\ backlogged\ users\ transmit\ in\ slot\ k \mid \bar{N}(k) = n] \qquad (3.11)$$

$$= \begin{bmatrix} n \\ i \end{bmatrix} \nu^i (1-\nu)^{n-i} \ .$$

As in the case of a finite number of users (see Section 3.3) we refer to the number of backlogged users $\bar{N}(k)$ as the *state* of the system. The number of backlogged users at the beginning of the $k+1$st slot depends on the number of backlogged users at the beginning of the kth slot (one of them might transmit a packet successfully) and the number of new packets that arrived within the slot. Since the process of new arrivals is independent of the activities in any previous slot, the process $\{\bar{N}(k), k=0,1,2, \cdots\}$ is a Markov chain. Unlike the case of a finite number of users, the chain $\{\bar{N}(k), k=0,1, \cdots\}$ is not finite, so it is not obvious whether or not the chain is ergodic.

Let $\pi_n(k)$ denote the probability that $\bar{N}(k)=n$. Let us list all possible transitions that will lead into the state in which there are n backlogged users at the beginning of slot $k+1$, i.e., $\bar{N}(k+1)=n$ (in parenthesis we indicate the probabilities of the corresponding events):

(1) There were n backlogged users at the beginning of slot k ($\pi_n(k)$), none of them transmitted ($b_0(n)$) and a single new packet was transmitted (a_1). The single new packet is successfully transmitted and therefore the number of backlogged users is unchanged.

(2) There were n backlogged users at the beginning of slot k ($\pi_n(k)$), at least two of them transmitted ($1-b_0(n)-b_1(n)$) and hence collided, and no new packet was transmitted (a_0). The number of backlogged users is unchanged.

(3) There were n backlogged users at the beginning of slot k ($\pi_n(k)$), none of them transmitted ($b_0(n)$) and no new packet was transmitted (a_0). This corresponds to an idle slot and the number of backlogged users is unchanged.

(4) There were $n+1$ backlogged users at the beginning of slot k ($\pi_{n+1}(k)$), exactly one of them transmitted ($b_1(n+1)$) and no new packet was transmitted (a_0). In this case, the transmission of the backlogged user was successful, and therefore the number of backlogged users decreases by one.

(5) There were $n-1$ backlogged users at the beginning of slot k ($\pi_{n-1}(k)$), at least one of them transmitted ($1-b_0(n-1)$) and a single new packet was transmitted (a_1). In this case a collision occurs and the user with the new packet joins the backlogged users.

(6) There were $n-j$, $2 \le j \le n$ backlogged users at the beginning of slot k ($\pi_{n-j}(k)$) and at least two new packets were transmitted (a_j, $2 \le j \le n$). In this case a collision occurs and all users with the new packets join the backlogged users.

Summarizing the above, the following balance equation can be written:

$$\pi_n(k+1) = \pi_n(k)b_0(n)a_1 + \pi_n(k)[1 - b_0(n) - b_1(n)]a_0 + \pi_n(k)b_0(n)a_0$$

$$+ \pi_{n+1}(k)b_1(n+1)a_0 \tag{3.12}$$

$$+ \pi_{n-1}(k)[1 - b_0(n-1)]a_1 + \sum_{j=2}^{n} \pi_{n-j}(k)a_j \ .$$

Notice that (3.12) is valid for all $n \ge 0$ if one adopts the convention that $\pi_i(k)=0$ for $i<0$.

The Markov chain $\{\bar{N}(k), \ k=0,1,2,\cdots\}$ is aperiodic and irreducible. It is ergodic if an invariant probability distribution $\{\pi_n, \ n=0,1,2,\cdots\}$ exists satisfying (3.12) such that $\pi_n>0$ for all n, $\sum_{n=0}^{\infty}\pi_n=1$ and $\pi_n=\lim_{k\to\infty}\pi_n(k)$. Assuming the latter limit exists, we obtain from (3.12) :

$$\pi_n = \pi_n[b_0(n)a_1 - b_1(n)a_0] + \pi_{n+1}b_1(n+1)a_0$$

$$- \pi_{n-1}b_0(n-1)a_1 + \sum_{j=0}^{n}\pi_{n-j}a_j \ . \tag{3.13}$$

Define

$$P_N = \sum_{n=0}^{N} \pi_n \tag{3.14}$$

and sum (3.13) for $n=0,1,\cdots,N$:

$$P_N = \sum_{n=0}^{N} \pi_n = \sum_{n=0}^{N} \pi_n [b_0(n)a_1 - b_1(n)a_0] + \sum_{n=0}^{N} \pi_{n+1} b_1(n+1)a_0$$

$$- \sum_{n=0}^{N} \pi_{n-1} b_0(n-1))a_1 + \sum_{n=0}^{N} \sum_{j=0}^{n} \pi_{n-j} a_j$$

$$= \sum_{n=0}^{N} \pi_n [b_0(n)a_1 - b_1(n)a_0] + \sum_{n=0}^{N} \pi_{n+1} b_1(n+1)a_0 \qquad (3.15)$$

$$- \sum_{n=0}^{N} \pi_{n-1} b_0(n-1))a_1 + \sum_{j=0}^{N} a_j \sum_{n=j}^{N} \pi_{n-j}$$

$$= \pi_N b_0(N)a_1 - \pi_0 b_1(0)a_0 + \pi_{N+1} b_1(N+1)a_0 + \sum_{j=0}^{N} a_j P_{N-j} \; .$$

Using the fact that $b_1(0)=0$ we have:

$$P_N = \pi_N b_0(N)a_1 + \pi_{N+1} b_1(N+1)a_0 + \sum_{j=0}^{N} a_j P_{N-j} \qquad (3.16)$$

or

$$P_N(1 - a_0) = \pi_N b_0(N)a_1 + \pi_{N+1} b_1(N+1)a_0 + \sum_{j=1}^{N} a_j P_{N-j}$$

$$\leq \pi_N b_0(N)a_1 + \pi_{N+1} b_1(N+1)a_0 + P_{N-1} \sum_{j=1}^{N} a_j \qquad (3.17)$$

$$\leq \pi_N b_0(N)a_1 + \pi_{N+1} b_1(N+1)a_0 + P_{N-1}(1 - a_0)$$

where the first inequality above is due to the fact that P_N does not decrease as N increases, and the second inequality is due to the fact that $\sum_{j=1}^{N} a_j \leq \sum_{j=1}^{\infty} a_j = 1 - a_0$.

From (3.17) we have:

$$\pi_N(1 - a_0) = (P_N - P_{N-1})(1-a_0) \leq \pi_N b_0(N)a_1 + \pi_{N+1} b_1(N+1)a_0 \quad (3.18)$$

or (we use (3.11))

$$\frac{\pi_{N+1}}{\pi_N} \geq \frac{1 - a_0 - b_0(N)a_1}{b_1(N+1)a_0} = \frac{1 - a_0 - (1-v)^N a_1}{(N + 1)v(1 - v)^N a_0} \qquad (3.19)$$

for any $N \geq 0$. The inequality in (3.19) implies that the ratio (π_{N+1}/π_N) increases without limit as $N \to \infty$. Therefore, the sum $P_\infty \overset{\Delta}{=} \lim_{N \to \infty} P_N$ exists only if $\pi_N = 0$ for all finite values of N; otherwise, P_∞ is divergent, which cannot be the case when the π_n, $n \geq 0$ define a probability distribution. Thus, the Markov chain $\{\tilde{N}(k), \ k=0,1,2, \cdots \}$ representing the number of backlogged users is not ergodic, and the Aloha protocol is not stable. Furthermore, we will see that the throughput of the system is *zero*.

Let $S_n(k)$ be the conditional probability that one packet is successfully transmitted during the kth slot, given that $\tilde{N}(k) = n$. The throughput of the system is then

$$S = \lim_{k \to \infty} \sum_{n=0}^{\infty} S_n(k)\pi_n(k) . \tag{3.20}$$

A packet will be successfully transmitted only if exactly one backlogged user is transmitting and no new packet is transmitted or no backlogged user is transmitting and exactly one new packet is transmitted. Hence,

$$S_n(k) = b_1(n)a_0 + b_0(n)a_1 \tag{3.21}$$

($S_n(k)$ does not depend on k). Therefore,

$$\begin{aligned}
S &= \lim_{k \to \infty} \sum_{n=0}^{\infty} [b_1(n)a_0 + b_0(n)a_1]\pi_n(k) = \sum_{n=0}^{\infty} [b_1(n)a_0 + b_0(n)a_1]\pi_n \\
&= \lim_{N \to \infty} \sum_{n=0}^{N} [b_1(n)a_0 + b_0(n)a_1]\pi_n = 0
\end{aligned} \tag{3.22}$$

where we used the conclusion from (3.19) that $\pi_n = 0$ for any finite n.

The facts that the Markov chain $\{\tilde{N}(k), \ k = 0,1,2, \cdots \}$ is not ergodic and that the throughput of the system is zero, indicate that the number of backlogged users will eventually grow to infinity, no packets will be successfully transmitted, and the expected delay of a packet will be infinite.

3.4.2. Stabilizing the Aloha System

From the intuitive arguments given at the beginning of this chapter and from the analysis presented in the previous section, it is clear that the Aloha system (with infinitely many users) cannot be stable for a *policy* of retransmission of collided packets that does not take into account (somehow) the system state. The schemes presented thus far use fixed retransmission probabilities, meaning that the retransmission policy is independent of system state, rendering these schemes unstable. In order to stabilize the system, the retransmission probabilities must somehow adapt in accordance with the state of the system.

Assuming that some coordination among the backlogged users is possible prior to each slot, it is not difficult to develop retransmission policies that stabilize the Aloha system. For instance, consider the following *threshold policy*: At most θ (the threshold) of the backlogged users at the beginning of slot k, retransmit their packets during slot k, each of them with probability v independently of the other users. In other words, when the number of backlogged users does not exceed θ, each of them retransmits its packet with probability v. If the number exceeds θ, a subset of size θ is chosen from the backlogged users and each user in this subset retransmits its packet with probability v. All other backlogged users remain silent during that slot.

The implementation of the threshold policy is not specified but is clearly not simple; it is not clear how the number of backlogged users would be known, and even if it is known, it is not clear how the backlogged users coordinate to choose the subset of size θ. Nevertheless, it is instructive to see why this policy stabilizes the Aloha system for a certain range of arrival rate.

To prove the stabilizing properties of the threshold policy, we use a lemma due to Pakes [Pak69] that is often useful in proving ergodicity of homogeneous Markov chains.

Pakes' Lemma: Let $\{\tilde{Z}_k, \ k=0,1,2,\cdots\}$ be an irreducible, aperiodic homogeneous Markov chain whose state space is the set of nonnegative integers. The following two conditions are sufficient for the Markov chain to be ergodic:

(a) $|E[\tilde{Z}_{k+1} - \tilde{Z}_k \,|\, \tilde{Z}_k = i]| < \infty \quad \forall i$;

(b) $\underset{i \to \infty}{limsup} \ E[\tilde{Z}_{k+1} - \tilde{Z}_k \,|\, \tilde{Z}_k = i] < 0$.

It is clear that the Markov chain $\{\tilde{N}(k), \ k=0,1,2,\cdots\}$ is irreducible, aperiodic and homogeneous for the threshold policy. Assume that $\tilde{N}(k)=i$ and $i < \theta$. In this case we have only to show that condition (a) of Pakes' Lemma ($\tilde{N}$ plays the role of $\tilde{Z}$) holds, since $\tilde{N}(k)$ cannot increase to infinity in this case. Given that $\tilde{N}(k)=i$ we have

$$\tilde{N}(k+1) = \begin{cases} i-1 & \text{with probability } b_1(i)a_0 \\ i & \text{with probability } [1-b_1(i)]a_0 + b_0(i)a_1 \\ i+1 & \text{with probability } [1-b_0(i)]a_1 \\ i+j, j \geq 2 & \text{with probability } a_j \end{cases} \tag{3.23}$$

The explanation of (3.23) is similar to that of (3.12). From (3.23) we obtain

$$E[\tilde{N}(k+1) - \tilde{N}(k)\,|\,\tilde{N}(k)=i] = E[\tilde{N}(k+1)\,|\,\tilde{N}(k)=i] - E[\tilde{N}(k)\,|\,\tilde{N}(k)=i]$$

$$= (i-1)b_1(i)a_0 + i\{[1-b_1(i)]a_0 + b_0(i)a_1\}$$

$$+ (i+1)[1-b_0(i)]a_1 + \sum_{j=2}^{\infty}(i+j)a_j - i \tag{3.24}$$

$$= \sum_{j=0}^{\infty}(i+j)a_j - i - b_1(i)a_0 - b_0(i)a_1 = \lambda - b_1(i)a_0 - b_0(i)a_1 \ .$$

Hence, condition (a) holds if $\lambda < \infty$.

Consider now the case that $\tilde{N}(k)=i$ and $i \geq \theta$. As in (3.23) we have:

$$\tilde{N}(k+1) = \begin{cases} i-1 & \text{with probability } b_1(\theta)a_0 \\ i & \text{with probability } [1-b_1(\theta)]a_0 + b_0(\theta)a_1 \\ i+1 & \text{with probability } [1-b_0(\theta)]a_1 \\ i+j, j \geq 2 & \text{with probability } a_j \end{cases} \quad (3.25)$$

The above stems from the fact that at most θ users are transmitting when the threshold policy is employed. From (3.25) we have

$$E[\tilde{N}(k+1) - \tilde{N}(k) | \tilde{N}(k) = i] = (i-1)b_1(\theta)a_0 + i\{[1-b_1(\theta)]a_0 + b_0(\theta)a_1\}$$

$$+ (i+1)[1-b_0(\theta)]a_1 + \sum_{j=2}^{\infty}(i+j)a_j - i \quad (3.26)$$

$$= \lambda - b_1(\theta)a_0 - b_0(\theta)a_1 .$$

Hence, both conditions (a) and (b) hold if

$$\lambda < b_1(\theta)a_0 + b_0(\theta)a_1 . \quad (3.27)$$

Therefore, if λ satisfies (3.27), the system is stable.

In summary, we saw that by limiting the number of backlogged users that contend for the channel, it is possible to stabilize the Aloha system. Moreover, we derived a condition on the arrival rate, (3.27), that guarantees stability.

Let us now consider another stable policy for the Aloha system that requires only the knowledge of the number of backlogged users at the beginning of each slot. This policy is based on adaptively controlling the retransmission probabilities. Specifically, assuming that the number of backlogged users is known, we allow the retransmission probability v to be a function of that number. Denoting this function by $v(n)$ where n is the number of backlogged users we have (see (3.11)):

$$b_i(n) = \binom{n}{i} [v(n)]^i [1 - v(n)]^{n-i} . \quad (3.28)$$

For this retransmission policy, equation (3.23) holds for all i and therefore (see (3.24)):

$$E[\tilde{N}(k+1) - \tilde{N}(k) | \tilde{N}(k) = i] = \lambda - b_1(i)a_0 - b_0(i)a_1 \quad \forall i .$$

Consequently, conditions (a) and (b) of Pakes' Lemma will hold if

$$\lambda < \limsup_{n \to \infty} \{b_1(n)a_0 + b_0(n)a_1\} . \quad (3.29)$$

Let us now quantify this value of λ. Define

$$S_n(v) \triangleq b_1(n)a_0 + b_0(n)a_1 = [1 - v(n)]^n a_1 + n v(n)[1 - v(n)]^{n-1}a_0 . \quad (3.30)$$

By differentiating $S_n(v)$ with respect to v and setting the result equal to zero, one observes that $S_n(v)$ is maximized for

$$v^*(n) = \frac{a_0 - a_1}{na_0 - a_1} \ .$$

The maximum value of $S_n(v)$ is

$$S_n^*(v^*) = a_0 \left[\frac{n-1}{n - a_1/a_0} \right]^{n-1} \ .$$

Taking the limit as $n \to \infty$ (see equation (3.29)) we see that the system will be stable for

$$\lambda < e^{\log a_0 + \frac{a_1}{a_0} - 1} \ .$$

It is interesting to note that if the arrival process is Poisson, $a_1/a_0 = -\log a_0 = \lambda$ and therefore the system would be stable if $\lambda < e^{-1}$, exactly as was predicted for constant retransmission probabilities. However, one should not forget that the Aloha system with constant retransmission probabilities is unstable for any arrival rate. The stabilizing policy presented above, namely retransmitting with probabilities that are (approximately) inversely proportional to the number of backlogged users, requires the knowledge of this number and it is not clear how the users would know this number.

There exist retransmission policies that do not require the knowledge of the exact number of backlogged users. These policies are based on updating the retransmission probabilities recursively in each slot, according to what happened during that slot. The general structure of these policies is:

$$v_{k+1} = f(v_k, feedback\ of\ slot\ k) \ , \tag{3.31}$$

namely, the retransmission probability (of a backlogged user) in slot $k+1$ is some function f of the retransmission probability in the previous slot and of the event that occurred in slot k. In essence, all such policies (namely, all the functions f that are used) increase the retransmission probability when an idle slot occurs and decrease it when a collision occurs. Examples of such policies and their analysis can be found in the work by Hajek and Van Loon [HaL82]. The policies of the form (3.31) were proved to yield maximal stable throughput of at most e^{-1}.

To summarize, the virtue of the Aloha protocol is its simplicity. However, the simple protocol yields an unstable system. The protocols that stabilize the Aloha system are no longer as simple as the original protocol, and yet, they only guarantee throughput of at most e^{-1}. The reason for this low throughput is that in all the stabilizing policies discussed in this chapter (excluding the threshold policy that is not practical), all backlogged users are using the same retransmission probability. In Chapter 5 we shall see that if the decisions of users whether to transmit or not are based both upon their own history of retransmissions and the feedback history, higher stable throughput can be obtained.

3.5. RELATED ANALYSIS

Numerous variations of the environment under which the Aloha protocol operates have been addressed in the literature. We considered a very small part of these variations; slotted and non-slotted system; finite and infinite population; fixed length packets and Poisson arrivals. Several books such as [Kle76, Tan81, Hay84, Tas86, HaO86, BeG87] cover part of these and other variations. In the following we list a few of the variations that we did not describe. In addition, we refer to some papers in which performance measures, other than the throughput, have been computed for the Aloha protocol.

Variable-length packets

Abramson [Abr77] studied the performance of the infinite population pure Aloha system with two different possible packet lengths. Ferguson [Fer77b] and Bellini and Borgonovo [BeB80] considered a system with an arbitrary packet length distribution. It is interesting to note that it was shown in [BeB80] that constant length packets yield the maximum throughput over all packet length distributions (see Exercises).

Arbitrary interarrival distribution

Sant [San80] studied the performance of the pure Aloha system where packet interarrival times are statistically independent and identically distributed (i.i.d.), but not necessarily exponential.

Capture

The assumption that whenever two or more packets overlap at the receiver, all packets are lost, is overly pessimistic. In radio systems the receiver might correctly receive a packet despite the fact that it is time-overlapping with other transmitted packets. This phenomenon is known as *capture* and it can happen as a result of various characteristics of radio systems. Most studies [Abr77, Met76, Sha84, Lee87] considered power capture, namely the phenomenon whereby the strongest of several transmitted signals is correctly received at the receiver. Thus, if a single high powered packet is transmitted then it is correctly received regardless of other transmissions and hence the utilization of the channel increases. Some other works (for instance, Davis and Gronemeyer [DaG80]) studied the effect of delay capture (the receiver captures a packet since it arrived a short time before any other packet that is transmitted during the same slot) in slotted Aloha protocol (see Exercises).

Buffered users

In some practical systems the users can provide buffer space for queueing of exogenous packets that arrive at the user. The case of a single buffer per user has been considered in Section 3.3. When a finite number of buffers are available at each user, the analysis proceeds along the same lines, although the number of states increases dramatically. When the buffering capability at each user is not limited, one faces a very complicated queueing problem due to the strong interaction among the various queues of the system. Specifically, the success probability of a transmission of a certain user depends on the activity of the other users that have packets to transmit. Exact analysis of a two-user system has been carried by Sidi and Segall [SiS83]. Approximate analysis of an M-user system has been carried out by Saadawi and Ephremides [SaE81] and by Sidi and Segall [SiS83] for a symmetric system, and by Ephremides and Zhu [EpZ87] for a non-symmetric system. Bounds for the expected queue lengths have been derived by Szpankowski [Szp86]. Sufficient conditions for ergodicity of the system have been provided by Tsybakov and Mikhailov [TsM79] and Tsybakov and Bakirov [TsB88].

Reservation and adaptive protocols

Reservation schemes are designed to have the advantages of both the Aloha and the TDMA approaches. The operation of such schemes is discussed in Section 2.5, where only conflict-free reservation schemes are discussed. An immediate extension is, of course, to use a reservation scheme with contention, i.e., that users contend during a reservation period and those who succeed in making reservations transmit without interference. These schemes derive their efficiency from the fact that reservation periods are shorter than transmission periods by several orders of magnitude.

In the category of reservation schemes fall the works by Binder [Bin75] that requires knowledge of the number of users (or an upper bound thereof), and the works by Crowther et. al. [CRW73] and Roberts [Rob75] that do not require this knowledge. Approximate analysis of a reservation Aloha protocol can be found in [Lam80]. Additional variations of reservation protocols and their analysis can be found in [ToK76, Tal84, TsC86]. A TDMA scheme in which a group of users are contending for an allocated slot is analyzed in [Rub78]. Another approach in which previously contended users do not mix with new ones is known as the Split Reservation Upon Collision (SRUC) protocol and is described in [BoF78].

Another kind of protocols that are designed to operate as the Aloha protocol in light load and according to a TDMA scheme in heavy load are known as adaptive protocols. The urn scheme [KlY78] is an example of such a protocol.

Delay and interdeparture times

Ferguson presented an approximate analysis of the delay in the Aloha protocol [Fer75, Fer77b] and compared it to TDMA [Fer77a]. Exact packet delay and interdeparture time distribution for a finite population slotted Aloha system with a single buffer per each user has been derived in [Tob82b]. The interdeparture process of the Aloha protocols has been studied in [TaK85b].

Stability

Instability issues of the Aloha protocol were first identified in [CaH75] and [LaK75]. Later, similar issues were identified for the CSMA family of protocols in [ToK77] (see next chapter). Other papers that discussed these issues are [Jen80, MeL83, OnN85].

Stable protocols for the Aloha system of the form (3.31) have been suggested in several studies. For instance, Kelly [Kel85] proposed an additive rule for determining v_{k+1} (as opposed to the multiplicative rule suggested in [HaL82]). Another additive rule known as the pseudo-bayesian rule has been suggested in [Riv87] and analyzed in [Tsi87].

The operation of the stable algorithms depends very strongly on the feedback information that is obtained in each slot (see (3.31)). Therefore, if the feedback information is not reliable, the tuning of the algorithms should be adjusted as is discussed in [MeK85].

EXERCISES

Problem 3.1 (Busy period of pure Aloha [TaK85b])

Consider a pure Aloha system with Poisson offered load g packets/second and packets of equal size 1 ($T=1$). Denote by $\bar{F}$ the length of an unsuccessful transmission period.

(a)   Let $\bar{A}_i$ ($i=1,2,\cdots$) be the ith interarrival time between packets arriving within a single unsuccessful transmission period. Find $F_A(t)$, the distribution of $\bar{A}$, its pdf $f_A(t)$, and its Laplace transform $F_A^*(s)$.

(b)   Let $\bar{L}$ be the number of transmissions in an unsuccessful transmission period. Find $L(z)=E[z^L]$.

(c)   By conditioning on $\bar{L}$ find $F_F^*(s)$ the Laplace transform of the probability density function of $\bar{F}$. Compute the expectation and variance of $\bar{F}$.

(d)   Using the result of part (c) find the average length of a transmission period (successful or not) and the throughput of the system.

Problem 3.2 (Slotted Aloha with acknowledgements)

Consider a system that employs the slotted Aloha protocol. After each successful transmission the receiving station sends an acknowledgement packet indicating the transmission was successful. Acknowledgement packets are transmitted on the same channel used for data packets and their length is the same as that of a data packet. A collision between a data packet and an acknowledgement packet destroys both of them. Consequently, the collided data packets and the data packet that has been acknowledged by the collided acknowledgement packet have to be retransmitted. In the following use the standard Poisson assumptions.

(a)   Find the relation between the throughput S and the offered load G in this system. What is the maximal throughput of this system?

(b)   Draw S as a function of G for this system and for slotted Aloha without acknowledgements on the same figure.

Problem 3.3 (Slotted Aloha with time capture)

Consider a slotted Aloha system with a large number of terminals transmitting to a central station. Typically, when two or more packets are transmitted concurrently all are lost. However, if the first packet arrives at the station θ seconds before any other packet in that slot, the receiver of the station "locks on" the packet and can receive it correctly. This phenomenon is called *time capture*.

The terminals are evenly distributed around the station so that in terms of propagation time the most remote terminal is τ seconds away from the station. The slot size is T seconds and packets arrive for transmission on the channel according to a Poisson process with average g packets per second.

In the following we would like to compute the probability of capture and the channel throughput. Let t_1 be the time of the first arrival at the station in the given slot and let t_2 be the time of the second arrival at the station in the given slot. (In questions (a) and (b) below we compute the quantities conditioned on the event that k packets are ready to transmit at the beginning of the slot).

(a)   Define $t = t_2 - t_1$. Find the pdf $f_t(w)$ (conditioned on k).

(b)   What is the probability of capture in a slot (conditioned on k)?

(c)   What is the (unconditional) probability of capture in a slot?

(d)   What is the throughput S of the system?

(e)   Show that regardless of θ, maximum throughput is achieved for $gT > 1$. Explain this result.

Problem 3.4 (Slotted Aloha with power capture [Met76])

This problem deals with a different model for the capture phenomenon. As explained in Problem 3.3, a capture means receiving correctly a packet even when other packets are transmitted during the same time. The model used here is typical to *power capture*, namely, that some users transmit with higher power than others.

Assume that the population of users in the system is divided into K classes all using the slotted Aloha protocol. If a single user of class i ($2 \le i \le K$) is transmitting simultaneously with any number of users of classes $1, 2, \cdots, i-1$, then the transmitted packet of user i is captured and thus successfully received. All other users that transmitted during the slot have to retransmit their packets at some later time.

Let S_i denote the rate of generation of new packets (per slot) by users of class i ($1 \le i \le K$) and let G_i denote the total rate of transmitted packets (per slot) by users of class i. Use the standard Poisson assumptions.

(a)   Let $S = \sum_{i=1}^{K} S_i$ be the total throughput of the systems. Determine the maximal throughput for $K = 2$.

(b)   Determine the maximal throughput for any K. How should the G_i's ($1 \le i \le K$) be chosen in order to obtain the maximal throughput? What happens when $K \to \infty$?

(c)   For $K = 2$, determine the possible values of the couple (S_1, S_2). Draw your result.

Problem 3.5 (Pure Aloha with variable length packets [BeB80])

Consider a network whose users transmit (arbitrarily distributed) variable length packets according to the pure Aloha protocol.

Observe that long packets are more likely to collide than short packets. Therefore, the length distribution of packets that are successfully transmitted is different from the length distribution of an arbitrary packet transmitted in the channel.

Let $\tilde{x}_0$ be a random variable representing the length of packets (the time required to transmit a packet) generated by the users (this random variable represents also the length of packets that are successfully transmitted). Let $X_0(x)$ be its distribution function, $x_0(x)$ its density function, $X_0^*(s)$ its Laplace transform, and x_0 its mean. In a similar manner we define $\tilde{x}_c$, $X_c(x)$, $x_c(x)$, $X_c^*(s)$ and x_c for the packets transmitted on the channel (new packets and those that are retransmitted because of collisions).

Assume that new packets are generated according to a Poisson process with mean λ_0 and the total traffic on the channel is also Poisson with mean λ_c. Let $S = \lambda_0 x_0$ and $G = \lambda_c x_c$.

(a)   Prove that the probability $P_{suc}(x)$ for successful transmission of a packet whose length is $\tilde{x}_c = x$ (the packet is from the total traffic on the channel) is given by:

$$P_{suc}(x) = exp\{-\lambda_c(x_c + x)\}$$

Note that $P_{suc}(x)$ depends only on x_c and not on the distribution of $\tilde{x}_c$.

(b)   Prove the following relationships:

$$X_c^*(s) = \frac{X_0^*(s - \lambda_c)}{X_0^*(-\lambda_c)}$$

$$X_0^*(s) = \frac{X_c^*(s + \lambda_c)}{X_c^*(\lambda_c)}$$

(c)   Prove that the throughput is given by:

$$S = -\frac{Ge^{-G}}{x_c} X_c^{*(1)}\left(\frac{G}{x_c}\right) = -\frac{x_0 Ge^{-G}}{X_0^{*(1)}\left(\frac{-G}{x_c}\right)}$$

where $X_0^{*(1)} = \dfrac{dX_0^*(s)}{ds}$; $X_c^{*(1)} = \dfrac{dX_c^*(s)}{ds}$.

(d)   Let $\lambda_0(x) = \lambda_0 x_0(x)$ and $\Lambda_0^*(s) = \int_{0^-}^{\infty} e^{-sx} \lambda_0(x) dx$. Prove that

$$\Lambda_0^*(s) = \lambda_c X_c^*(s + \lambda_c) exp\{-\lambda_c x_c\}$$

$$S = -\left. \frac{d\Lambda_0^*(s)}{ds} \right|_{s=0}$$

(e)   Find the relation between S and G in the following three special cases:

(1)   Constant packet length: ($\tilde{x}_0 = x_0$ with probability 1).

(2)   Dual packet size: $x_0(x) = \alpha\delta(x - x_1) + (1 - \alpha)\delta(x - x_2)$; There are packets of two types - those with constant length x_1 and those with constant length x_2 ($x_1 < x_2$). The probability that a packet is of the first type is α.

(3)   Exponential packet length: $x_0(x) = \mu e^{-\mu x}$.

(f)   Prove that the throughput of a pure Aloha system is maximized when the packet length distribution is deterministic i.e., all packets have the same constant length.

Problem 3.6   (Aloha with K channels)

Consider a system consisting of K separate slotted channels (with slot boundaries synchronized). The system operates according to the slotted Aloha protocol with the specific channel chosen according to some rule.

(a)   Find the throughput of such a system for the infinite population case if the channels are selected uniformly at random.

(b)   For the finite population case find (and compare) the throughput delay characteristics if

(i)   The users are divided in advance into K equally sized groups each assigned one channel.

(ii)   Each user selects randomly and uniformly one of the K channels and performs all its activity on that channel.

(iii)   Every user and for every packet transmission (or retransmission) selects randomly, uniformly, and independent of the past the channel over which this specific packet is to be transmitted.

(iv)   Every user upon generating a new packet selects randomly and uniformly one channel to be used for transmission and all retransmissions of that packet.

CHAPTER 4

CARRIER SENSING PROTOCOLS

The Aloha schemes, described in the previous chapter, exhibited fairly poor performance which can be attributed to the "impolite" behavior of the users namely, whenever one has a packet to transmit he does so without consideration of others. It does not take much to realize that even little consideration can benefit all. Consider a behavior that we generically characterize as "listen before talk", that is, every user before attempting any transmission listens whether somebody else is already using the channel. If this is the case the user will refrain from transmission to the benefit of all; his packet will clearly not be successful if transmitted and, further, disturbing another user will cause the currently transmitted packet to be retransmitted, possibly disturbing yet another packet.

The process of listening to the channel is not that demanding. Every user is equipped with a receiver anyway. Moreover, to detect another user's transmission does not require receiving the information; it suffices to sense the carrier that is present when signals are transmitted. The carrier sensing family of protocols is characterized by sensing the carrier and deciding according to it whether another transmission is ongoing.

Carrier sensing does not, however, relieve us from collisions. Suppose the channel has been idle for a while and two users concurrently generate a packet. Each will sense the channel, discover it is idle, and transmit the packet to result in collision. "Concurrently" here does not really mean at the very same time; if one user starts transmitting it takes some time for the signal to propagate and arrive at the other user. Hence "concurrently" actually means within a time window of duration equal to signal propagation time. This latter quantity becomes therefore a crucial parameter in the performance of these protocols.

All the carrier sense multiple access (CSMA) protocols share the same philosophy: when a user generates a new packet the channel is sensed and if found idle the packet is transmitted without further ado. When a collision takes place every transmitting user reschedules a retransmission of the collided packet to some other time in the future (chosen with some randomization) at which time the same operation is repeated. The variations on the CSMA scheme are due to the behavior of users that wish to transmit and find (by sensing) the channel busy. Most of these variations were introduced and first analyzed in a series of papers by Tobagi and Kleinrock [KlT75, ToK75, ToK77].

For more detail the reader is referred to any of the many books and surveys that deal with various aspects of CSMA protocols such as Tannenbaum's [Tan81], Stallings' [Sta85], or Clark Pogran and Reed's [CPR78].

4.1. NONPERSISTENT CARRIER SENSE MULTIPLE ACCESS

In the nonpersistent versions of CSMA (NP-CSMA) a user that generated a packet and found the channel to be busy refrains from transmitting the packet and behaves exactly as if its packet collided, i.e, it schedules (randomly) the retransmission of the packet to some time in the future. The following analysis is based on Kleinrock and Tobagi [KIT75].

Throughput Analysis

To evaluate the performance of NP-CSMA let us adopt a model similar to that used in the evaluation of the performance of the Aloha protocol (Section 3.1). We assume an infinite population of users aggregately generating packets according to a Poisson process with parameter λ. All packets are of the same length and require T seconds of transmission. When observing the channel, packets (new and retransmitted) arrive according to a Poisson process with parameter g packets/sec.

In addition to the assumptions of the model used to analyze the Aloha protocol, the model used for CSMA deals also with system configuration which is manifested by a propagation delay among users. Denote by τ the maximum propagation delay in the system (measured in seconds) and define $a \overset{\Delta}{=} \tau/T$ to be the normalized propagation time. We assume that all users are "τ seconds apart" that is, τ is the propagation delay between every pair of users. With this assumption the following analysis provides a lower bound to the actual performance.

Consider an idle channel and a user scheduling a transmission at some time t (see Figure 4.1). This user senses the channel, starts transmitting at time t and does so for T seconds; once he is done it will take τ additional seconds before the packet arrives at the destination. This transmission therefore causes the channel to be busy for a period of $T+\tau$ seconds. If, at time $t' > t+\tau$ another user scheduled a packet for transmission, that user would sense the channel busy and refrain from transmission. If, however, some other user scheduled a packet for transmission during the period $[t, t+\tau]$, that user would sense the channel idle, transmit its packet, and cause a collision. The initial period of the first τ seconds of transmission is called the *vulnerable period* since only within this period is a packet vulnerable to interference. Figure 4.1(b) depicts a situation in which a packet transmission starting at time t is interfered by two other transmissions that start in the interval $[t, t+\tau]$. In the case of a collision the channel will therefore be busy for some (random) duration between $T+\tau$ and

$T+2\tau$. This period in which a transmission takes place is referred to as the *transmission period* (TP). In the case of NP-CSMA the transmission period coincides with the busy period. Having completed a transmission period the channel will be idle for some time until the next packet transmission is scheduled.

   We therefore observe along the time axis a succession of cycles each consisting of a transmission period followed by an idle period (see Figure 4.1(a)). Because packet scheduling is memoryless, the times in which these cycles start are renewal points. As we did before, we denote by $\tilde{B}$ the duration of the busy (transmission) period, and by B its mean. Let $\tilde{U}$ be the time duration within the transmission period in which a successful packet is being transmitted (with

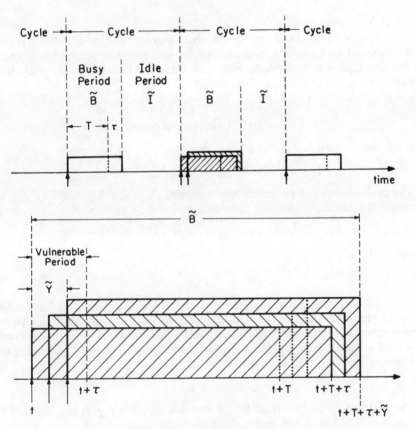

Figure 4.1: Nonpersistent CSMA Timing
(a) Cycle Structure
(b) Unsuccessful Transmission Period

mean U), and let $\tilde{I}$ the duration of the idle period (with mean I). The cycle length is clearly $\tilde{B}+\tilde{I}$ and the throughput is given by $S = U/(B+I)$. We now derive these quantities.

Consider first the idle period. Its duration is the same as the duration between the end of packet transmission and the arrival of the next packet. Because packet scheduling is memoryless we get

$$F_I(x) = Prob\,[\tilde{I} \le x] = 1 - Prob\,[\tilde{I} > x]$$

$$= 1 - P\,[No\ packet\ scheduled\ during\ x] = 1 - e^{-gx}$$

which means that $\tilde{I}$ is exponentially distributed with mean

$$I = \frac{1}{g} .$$

The expected useful time U can also be easily computed. When a packet is successful the channel carries useful information for a duration of T seconds--the time it takes to transmit the packet; in the unsuccessful case no useful information is carried at all or, in other words

$$\tilde{U} = \begin{cases} T & Successful\ period \\ 0 & Unsuccessful\ period \ . \end{cases}$$

If P_{suc} denotes the probability that a transmitted packet is successful then

$$U = E[\tilde{U}] = T \cdot P_{suc} + 0 \cdot (1 - P_{suc}) = T \cdot P_{suc} .$$

The probability of a successful transmission, P_{suc}, is the probability that no packet is scheduled during the vulnerable period $[t, t+\tau]$. Hence,

$$P_{suc} = Prob\,[No\ arrival\ in\ the\ period\ [t, t+\tau]\,] = e^{-g\tau}$$

and thus

$$U = Te^{-g\tau} .$$

To compute B, the average transmission period duration, let $\tilde{Y}$ be a random variable such that $t+\tilde{Y}$ denotes the time at which the *last* interfering packet was scheduled within a transmission period that started at time t (see Figure 4.1(b)). Clearly, $\tilde{Y} < \tau$ and for a successful transmission period $\tilde{Y}=0$. Using this notation the duration of the transmission period is

$$\tilde{B} = T + \tau + \tilde{Y} .$$

The period $\tilde{Y}$ is characterized by the fact that no other packet is scheduled for transmission during the period $[t+\tilde{Y}, t+\tau]$ for otherwise the packet that is transmitted at $t+\tilde{Y}$ would not have been the last packet to be transmitted in $[t+\tilde{Y}, t+\tau]$. Thus, the probability distribution function of $\tilde{Y}$ is

$$F_Y(y) = Prob\,[\tilde{Y} \le y] = Prob\,[No\ packet\ arrival\ during\ \tau-y] = e^{-g(\tau-y)} .$$

The above relation holds for $0 \le y \le \tau$. For negative values of y the probability distribution function vanishes and for values greater than τ it equals unity. It is important to notice that $F_Y(y)$ has a discontinuity at $y=0$ which means that care must be taken when the probability density function is derived. Denoting by $\delta(t)$ the Dirac impulse function we get

$$f_Y(y) = e^{-g\tau}\delta(y) + ge^{-g(\tau-y)} \tag{4.1}$$

from which

$$E[\breve{Y}] = \tau - \frac{1-e^{-g\tau}}{g} \tag{4.2}$$

and finally

$$B = E[T + \tau + \breve{Y}] = T + 2\tau - \frac{1-e^{-g\tau}}{g} \ .$$

Putting all these results together we get

$$S = \frac{U}{B+I} = \frac{Te^{-g\tau}}{T + 2\tau - \dfrac{1-e^{-g\tau}}{g} + \dfrac{1}{g}} = \frac{gTe^{-g\tau}}{g(T+2\tau) + e^{-g\tau}}$$

which is the desired relation we were seeking.

As before we normalize the quantities with respect to the packet transmission time. To that end, let G denote the average scheduling rate of packets measured in packets per packet transmission time; in other words $G=gT$. With our previous definition of the normalized propagation time a we get

$$S = \frac{Ge^{-aG}}{G(1+2a) + e^{-aG}} \ .$$

A sketch of the throughput versus the normalized offered load G for various values of the normalized propagation time a is shown in Figure 4.2. These graphs have the same shape as those for the Aloha system except for the evidently improved throughput. As is expected, the lower a the better the performance. In fact, the extreme case of $a \to 0$ yields a throughput of $G/(1+G)$ which does not decrease to zero with increasing load. We remark also that having the same characteristic shape as the Aloha protocol means that NP-CSMA (as the other protocols in this family) suffers from the same instability problems from which Aloha suffers.

4.2. 1-PERSISTENT CARRIER SENSE MULTIPLE ACCESS

With nonpersistent CSMA there are situations in which the channel is idle although one or more users have packets to transmit. The 1-persistent CSMA (1P-CSMA) is an alternative to nonpersistent CSMA that avoids such situations. This is achieved by applying the following rule: A user that senses the channel and finds it busy, persists to wait and transmits as soon as the channel becomes

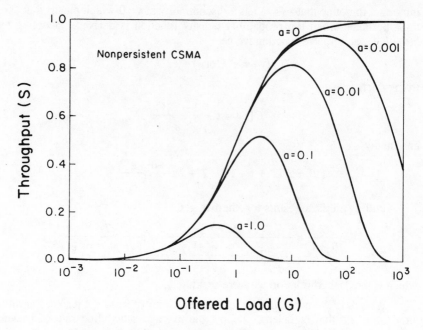

Figure 4.2: Throughput-Load of Nonpersistent CSMA

idle. Consequently, the channel is always used if there is a user with a packet.

The performance of the 1-persistent CSMA scheme was first analyzed by Kleinrock and Tobagi [KlT75]. The analysis presented in the following is considerably simpler and is based on Sohraby et. al. [SMV87].

Throughput Analysis

We adopt the same model as the one used in the analysis of nonpersistent CSMA. When observing the channel over time, one sees a sequence of cycles, each consisting of an idle period (no packet is scheduled for transmission during this period), followed by a busy period that consists of several successive *transmission periods* (see Figure 4.3). All users that sense the channel busy in some transmission period, transmit their scheduled packets at the beginning of the successive transmission period. If no packet is scheduled for transmission during some transmission period, then an idle period begins as soon as this transmission period ends.

Notice that a transmission period starts either with the transmission of a single packet (call it type 1 transmission period), or with the transmission of at least two packets (call it type 2 transmission period). A transmission period that follows an idle period is always a type 1 transmission period. The type of a transmission period that follows another transmission period depends on the

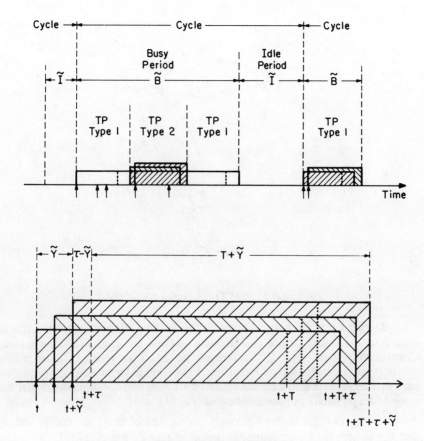

Figure 4.3: 1-Persistent CSMA Timing
(a) Cycle Structure
(b) Unsuccessful Transmission Period

number of those persistent users waiting for the current transmission to end. For consistency, an idle period is also viewed as a transmission period that starts with no transmitted packets (call it type 0 transmission period). This is depicted in Figure 4.3.

Define the state of the system at the beginning of a transmission period to be the type of that transmission period. These states (0,1 and 2) correspond to a three-state Markov chain embedded at the beginning of the transmission periods. The knowledge of the system state at the beginning of some transmission period (together with the scheduling points of packets during this transmission period) is sufficient to determine the system state at the beginning of the successive transmission period. The possible transitions among the three states of the embedded Markov chain are depicted in Figure 4.4.

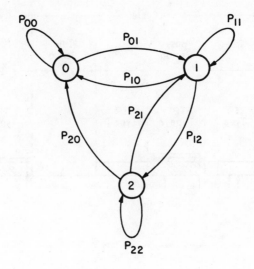

Figure 4.4: State Transitions of 1P-CSMA

During a type 0 transmission period no packets are transmitted and during type 2 transmission periods two or more packets are transmitted and collide. Consequently, only type 1 transmission periods may result in a successful transmission. Yet, for a type 1 transmission period to be successful, it is necessary that no packets arrive during its first τ seconds that constitute its vulnerable period (the probability of the latter event is $e^{-g\tau}$).

Let π_i $i=0,1,2$ be the stationary probability of being in state i, namely that the system is in a transmission period of type i. Let $\tilde{T}_i$ $i=0,1,2$ be a random variable representing the length of type i transmission period and let $E[\tilde{T}_i]=T_i$. Since the length of a packet is T seconds, and from the same renewal arguments we used before the throughput is given by

$$S = T \frac{\pi_1 e^{-g\tau}}{\sum_{i=0}^{2} \pi_i T_i} .$$

$$(4.3)$$

To compute the throughput we still have to compute π_i and T_i, $i=0,1,2$, which we do next.

Transmission Period Lengths

The nature of the idle period in 1-persistent CSMA is identical to that of nonpersistent CSMA, i.e., exponentially distributed with mean $1/g$, hence $T_0=1/g$. Regarding the random variables $\tilde{T}_1$ and $\tilde{T}_2$ the important observation is that they have the same distribution. The reason is that the length of a transmission period with either a single packet or with two or more packets, is determined only by the time of arrival of the *last* packet (if any) within the vulnerable period (the first τ seconds of the transmission period), and does not depend at all on the type of the transmission period.

The computation of $\tilde{T}_1$ and $\tilde{T}_2$ is identical to that of $\tilde{B}$ in the nonpersistent CSMA (Figure 4.1(b)). Let a transmission period start at time t and let $\tilde{Y}$ be a random variable representing the time (after t) of the *last* packet that arrived during the vulnerable period $[t, t+\tau]$ of a transmission period that started at time t ($\tilde{Y}=0$ if no packets arrive during $[t, t+\tau]$). Then

$$\tilde{T}_1 = \tilde{T}_2 = T + \tau + \tilde{Y} \ . \tag{4.4}$$

We already derived the probability distribution function and probability density function of $\tilde{Y}$ and found (see equations (4.1) and (4.2))

$$f_{\tilde{Y}}(y) = e^{-g\tau}\delta(y) + ge^{-g(\tau-y)} \qquad 0 \le y \le \tau \tag{4.5}$$

$$E[\tilde{Y}] = \tau - \frac{1-e^{-g\tau}}{g} \ . \tag{4.6}$$

Combining (4.4) and (4.6) we obtain

$$T_1 = T_2 = T + \tau + E[\tilde{Y}] = T + 2\tau - \frac{1-e^{-g\tau}}{g} \ . \tag{4.7}$$

State Probabilities

From the state diagram in Figure 4.4 we have,

$$\pi_0 = \pi_1 P_{10} + \pi_2 P_{20}$$
$$\pi_1 P_{12} = \pi_2 (P_{21} + P_{20}) \tag{4.8}$$
$$\pi_0 + \pi_1 + \pi_2 = 1 \ .$$

When a type 1 or a type 2 transmission period starts, the type of the next transmission period is determined (only) by those packets scheduled for transmission *after* the transmission period begins. Specifically, if no packets arrive within the transmission period, the next transmission period will be of type 0. If a single packet arrives within the transmission period, at least τ seconds after it begins, the next transmission period will be of type 1. Finally, if at lease two packets arrive within the transmission period, at least τ seconds after it begins, the next transmission period will be of type 2. Therefore,

$$P_{1j} = P_{2j} \qquad j = 0,1,2 \ . \tag{4.9}$$

Using (4.8) and (4.9) we have,

$$\pi_0 = \frac{P_{10}}{1 + P_{10}} \quad ; \quad \pi_1 = \frac{P_{10} + P_{11}}{1 + P_{10}} \quad ; \quad \pi_2 = \frac{1 - P_{10} - P_{11}}{1 + P_{10}} \quad . \tag{4.10}$$

Assume that a type 1 transmission period starts at time t. Conditioning on $\bar{Y} = y$, the next transmission period will be of type 0 (namely, an idle period) only if no packet is scheduled for transmission after time $t + \tau$ and before the end of the type 1 transmission period (namely, time $t + y + T + \tau$). The probability of this event is $e^{-g(T+y)}$. Unconditioning, we obtain

$$P_{10} = \int_0^\tau e^{-g(T+y)} f_{\bar{Y}}(y) dy = \int_0^\tau e^{-g(T+y)} \left[e^{-g\tau} \delta(y) + g e^{-g(\tau-y)} \right] dy \tag{4.11}$$

$$= (1 + g\tau) e^{-g(T+\tau)} \quad .$$

In a similar manner we obtain

$$P_{11} = \int_0^\tau g(T+y) e^{-g(T+y)} f_{\bar{Y}}(y) dy$$

$$= \int_0^\tau g(T+y) e^{-g(T+y)} \left[e^{-g\tau} \delta(y) + g e^{-g(\tau-y)} \right] dy \tag{4.12}$$

$$= g e^{-g(T+\tau)} \left[T + g\tau(T + \frac{\tau}{2}) \right] \quad .$$

Combining (4.3), (4.7), (4.10), (4.11), and (4.12) we obtain the throughput

$$S = \frac{gT e^{-g(T+2\tau)} [1 + gT + g\tau(1 + gT + g\tau/2)]}{g(T + 2\tau) - (1 - e^{-g\tau}) + (1 + g\tau) e^{-g(T+\tau)}}$$

or in a normalized form:

$$S = \frac{G e^{-G(1+2a)} [1 + G + aG(1 + G + aG/2)]}{G(1 + 2a) - (1 - e^{-aG}) + (1 + aG) e^{-G(1+a)}} \quad .$$

This relation is depicted in Figure 4.5. While, generally, these graphs have the same form as those of the nonpersistent CSMA, performance is less than expected. Recall that the 1-persistent CSMA was devised in an attempt to improve the performance of the nonpersistent CSMA by reducing the extent of the idle periods. This attempt is, evidently, not quite successful since for high load the nonpersistent CSMA outperforms the 1-persistent CSMA. In particular note that,

$$S_{a \to 0} = \frac{G(1 + G)}{1 + G e^G}$$

and thus, in the best possible case, $S \to 0$ when $G \to \infty$; the maximum for S in this case is obtained for $G \sim 1.03$. For low load, however, 1-persistent CSMA shows a slightly better throughput and improved performance.

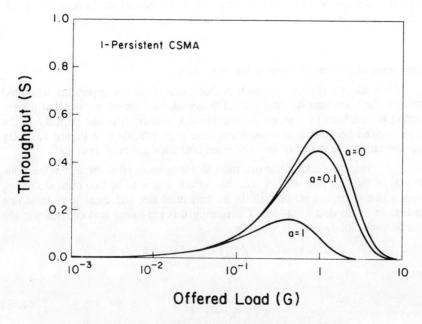

Figure 4.5: Throughput-Load of 1-Persistent CSMA

4.3. SLOTTED CARRIER SENSE MULTIPLE ACCESS

Consider an environment similar to that described for the CSMA protocols except for a slotted time axis. Let the slot size equal the maximum propagation delay τ which means that any transmission starting at the beginning of a slot reaches (and could be sensed by) each and every user by the end of that slot. These slots are sometimes referred to as *mini-slots* since they are shorter than the time required to transmit a packet. As in every slotted system users are restricted to start transmissions only at mini-slot boundaries. We assume that carrier sensing can be done in zero time (we may assume that τ includes the propagation delay as well as the carrier sensing time). All packets are of the same length and require T seconds for transmission. We also assume that the packet size T is an integer multiple of the propagation delay τ and denote by a the ratio between τ and T ($1/a$ is therefore an integer).

Users behave as follows. When a packet is scheduled for transmission at a given time the user waits to the beginning of the next mini-slot at which time it senses the channel and if idle transmits its packet for T seconds, i.e., $1/a$ mini-slots (the packet occupies the channel one more mini-slot before all other users have received it). If the channel is sensed busy, then the corresponding CSMA protocol is applied, namely, for nonpersistent CSMA the packet is rescheduled to some randomly chosen time in the future, and for 1P-CSMA the user waits until the channel becomes idle and then starts transmission. In both cases collided packets are retransmitted at some random time in the future.

Throughput of Slotted Nonpersistent CSMA

We adopt a similar approach to that taken in the corresponding unslotted systems (see Sections 4.1 and 4.2). Observing the channel we see that a busy period $\bar{B}$ consists of consecutive transmission periods. The idle period $\bar{I}$ is the time elapsed between every two successive busy periods (see Figure 4.6). By our definition, the length of an idle period is at least one mini-slot.

For the idle period to be one mini-slot long means that there is at least one arrival in the first mini-slot of the idle period. For it to be two mini-slots long means that there are no arrivals in its first mini-slot and there is at least one arrival in its second mini-slot. Continuing this reasoning and considering the Poisson scheduling process we have,

$$P(\bar{I}=k\tau) = (e^{-g\tau})^{k-1}(1 - e^{-g\tau}) \qquad k = 1,2,\cdots$$

so,

$$I = \frac{\tau}{1 - e^{-g\tau}} \, . \tag{4.13}$$

An outcome of the definition of the model is the fact that both successful and unsuccessful transmission periods last $T+\tau$ seconds (see Figure 4.6). A collision occurs if two or more packets arrive within the same mini-slot and are scheduled for transmission in the next mini-slot. A busy period will contain k transmission periods if there is at least one arrival in the last mini-slot of each of

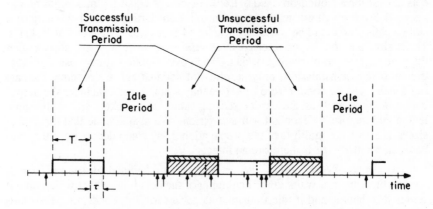

Figure 4.6: Slotted Nonpersistent CSMA Packet Timing

the first $k-1$ transmission periods, and no arrival in the last mini-slot of the kth transmission period. Thus,

$$Prob\,[\tilde{B}=k\,(T+\tau)] = (1 - e^{-g\tau})^{k-1}e^{-g\tau} \qquad k = 1,2,\cdots$$

so,

$$B = \frac{T+\tau}{e^{-g\tau}}.$$

Following a similar approach to that used in the slotted Aloha case we define a cycle as the period consisting of a busy period followed by an idle period and denote by $\tilde{U}$ the amount of time within a cycle during which the channel carries useful information. When a transmission period is successful the channel carries useful information for T seconds, while it carries no useful information in unsuccessful transmission periods. Since the number of transmission periods during $\tilde{B}$ is $\tilde{B}/(T+\tau)$, we have

$$U = E\,[\tilde{U}] = T\frac{B}{T+\tau}P_{suc}$$

where P_{suc} is the probability of a successful transmission period. We have

$$P_{suc} = Prob\,[successful\ transmission\ period]$$

$$= Prob\left[\begin{array}{c} single\ arrival\ in\ last\ mini\text{-}slot\ before \\ the\ transmission\ period \end{array}\,\middle|\ some\ arrivals\right]$$

$$= \frac{Prob\,[single\ arrival\ in\ a\ mini\text{-}slot]}{Prob\,[Some\ arrivals\ in\ a\ mini\text{-}slot]} = \frac{g\tau e^{-g\tau}}{1 - e^{-g\tau}}.$$

The division by the probability of "some arrivals" is noteworthy. It is necessary because we are computing the probability of a single arrival in the last mini-slot of the preceding transmission period knowing that there was at least one arrival, since a transmission period has been initiated.

Putting all these together we get

$$S = \frac{U}{B+I} = \frac{T\dfrac{B}{T+\tau}P_{suc}}{B+I} = \frac{\dfrac{T}{e^{-g\tau}}\dfrac{g\tau e^{-g\tau}}{1 - e^{-g\tau}}}{\dfrac{T+\tau}{e^{-g\tau}} + \dfrac{\tau}{1 - e^{-g\tau}}} = \frac{Tg\tau e^{-g\tau}}{T+\tau-Te^{-g\tau}}.$$

Using $a=\tau/T$ and $G=gT$ we have

$$S = \frac{aGe^{-aG}}{1+a - e^{-aG}}.$$

When a is very small we obtain:

$$S_{a\to 0} = \frac{G}{1+G}$$

which is identical to the nonslotted case when $a \to 0$.

Throughput of Slotted 1P-CSMA

The analysis of the slotted 1P-CSMA is similar to that of slotted nonpersistent CSMA. The mean of the idle period is given by (4.13) . The distribution of the busy period is

$$Prob\,[\tilde{B}=k\,(T+\tau)] = (1 - e^{-g\,(T+\tau)})^{k-1}e^{-g\,(T+\tau)} \qquad k = 1,2,\cdots$$

since a busy period will contain k transmission periods if at least one packet arrives in each of the first $k-1$ transmission periods (as opposed to mini-slots in the nonpersistent case), and no packet arrives in the kth transmission period. So,

$$B = \frac{T+\tau}{e^{-g\,(T+\tau)}} \; .$$

The probability of success in the first transmission period in a busy period, P_{suc_1}, is different from the success probability in any other transmission period within the busy period, P_{suc_2}. For the first transmission period in a busy period to be successful we need the last mini-slot of the idle period to contain exactly one arrival (notice that we know there is at least one arrival there, since it is the *last* mini-slot of the idle period). Hence,

$$P_{suc_1} = Prob\left[\begin{array}{c} successful\ transmission\ in\ the\ first \\ transmission\ period\ of\ a\ busy\ period \end{array}\right]$$

$$= Prob\,[\ single\ arrival\ in\ a\ mini\text{-}slot\ |\ at\ least\ one\ arrival\ ] = \frac{g\,\tau e^{-g\tau}}{1 - e^{-g\tau}} \; .$$

For any transmission period in a busy period, other than the first, to be successful we must have exactly one arrival during the previous transmission period, i.e.,

$$P_{suc_2} = Prob\,[\ successful\ transmission\ in\ non\text{-}first\ period\ in\ a\ busy\ period\ ]$$

$$= Prob\,[\ single\ arrival\ in\ a\ transmission\ period\ /\ at\ least\ one\ arrival\ ]$$

$$= \frac{g\,(T+\tau)e^{-g\,(T+\tau)}}{1 - e^{-g\,(T+\tau)}} \; .$$

The channel carries useful information only during successful transmission periods. The probability of success of the first transmission period in a busy period is P_{suc_1} and therefore $T{\cdot}P_{suc_1}$ is the expected amount of time the channel carries useful information during these periods. The expected number of transmission periods (other than the first) in a busy period is $B\,/(T+\tau)-1$, since each transmission period lasts $T+\tau$ seconds. The probability of success in each of these transmission periods is P_{suc_2} and therefore $[B\,/(T+\tau)-1]{\cdot}T{\cdot}P_{suc_2}$ is the expected amount of time the channel carries useful information during these periods. In summary, the expected amount of time within a cycle that the channel carries useful information is

$$U = T \left[P_{suc_1} + \frac{B - (T + \tau)}{T + \tau} P_{suc_2} \right] .$$

The throughput is therefore given by

$$S = \frac{U}{B + I} = \frac{gTe^{-g(T+\tau)}[T + \tau - Te^{-g\tau}]}{(T + \tau)[1 - e^{-g\tau}] + \tau e^{-g(T+\tau)}}$$

or in a normalized form

$$S = \frac{Ge^{-(1+a)G}[1 + a - e^{-aG}]}{(1 + a)[1 - e^{-aG}] + ae^{-(1+a)G}} .$$

This relation is depicted in Figure 4.7. For the case of a very small mini-slot size we have

$$S_{a \to 0} = \frac{Ge^{-G}[1 + G]}{G + e^{-G}} .$$

Comparing these graphs with those of the corresponding unslotted systems we note, as expected, a slightly better performance of the slotted systems.

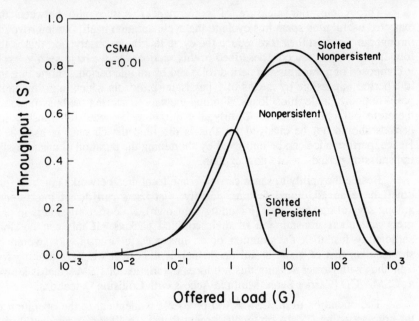

Figure 4.7: Throughput-Load of Slotted 1-Persistent and Nonpersistent CSMA

Practically speaking, the very small gain achieved is probably not worth the cost of keeping the users synchronized. From a theoretical standpoint the close performance means that the slotted system can serve as an approximation of the unslotted one. This is advantageous since analysis of slotted systems is often much simpler than the unslotted ones.

4.4. CARRIER SENSE MULTIPLE ACCESS WITH COLLISION DETECTION

The Aloha family of protocols suffers from the inherent interference of concurrently transmitted packets, that is, whenever the transmission of two or more packets overlap in time, even a bit, all are lost and must be retransmitted. The pure Aloha protocol suffers most, as no precautions to reduce collisions are taken. CSMA reduces the level of interference caused by overlapping packets by allowing users to sense the carrier due to other users' transmissions, and inhibit transmission when the channel is in use and a collision is inevitable. CSMA protocols appear to be the best possible solution since their performance depends only on the end-to-end propagation delay--a quantity that is not alterable (except by a different topological design). To further improve performance, a new avenue must therefore be sought.

Throughput, our measure of performance, is the ratio between the expected useful time spent in a cycle to the cycle duration itself. To improve the throughput we must therefore reduce the cycle length, an observation that is the foundation of the protocols described in this section. As we have seen, a cycle is composed of a transmission period followed by an idle period. Shortening the idle period is possible by means of 1-persistent protocols which, unfortunately, perform poorly under most loads. Finding the way to shorten the busy period is therefore our only recourse. Clearly, the duration of successful transmission periods should not be changed for this is the time the channel is used best. Hence, performance can be improved by shortening the duration of unsuccessful transmission periods, as we now explain.

Beside the ability to sense carrier, some local area networks (such as Ethernet) have an additional feature, namely, that users can detect interference among several transmissions (including their own) while transmission is in progress and abort transmission of their collided packets. If this can be done sufficiently fast then the duration of an unsuccessful transmission would be shorter than that of a successful one which is the effect we were looking for. Together with carrier sensing this produces a variation of CSMA that is known as CSMA/CD (Carrier Sense Multiple Access with Collision Detection).

The operation of all CSMA/CD protocols is identical to the operation of the corresponding CSMA protocols, except that if a collision is detected during transmission, the transmission is aborted and the packet is scheduled for transmission at some later time.

In all CSMA protocols, a transmission that is initiated when the channel is idle reaches all users after at most one end-to-end propagation delay, τ. Beyond this time, the channel will be sensed busy. The space-time diagram of Figure 4.8 captures this situation. In this figure we consider two users A and B, the propagation between whom is τ. Suppose that user A starts transmission at time t_0 when the channel is idle, then its transmission reaches user B at $t_0+\tau$. Suppose, further, that B initiates a transmission at time $t_1<t_0+\tau$ (when B still senses an idle channel). It takes τ_{cd} for a user to detect the collision, so that at time $t_0+\tau+\tau_{cd}$ user B positively determines the collision. In many local area networks such as Ethernet, every user upon detection of a collision initiates a *consensus reenforcement* procedure, which is manifested by jamming the channel with a collision signal for a duration of τ_{cr} to ensure that all network users indeed determine that a collision took place. Thus, at $t_0+\tau+\tau_{cd}+\tau_{cr}$ user B completed the consensus reenforcement procedure which reaches user A at $t_0+2\tau+\tau_{cd}+\tau_{cr}$. From user A's standpoint this transmission period lasted

$$\gamma = 2\tau + \tau_{cd} + \tau_{cr} \ .$$

By similar calculation, user B completes this transmission period at time $t_1+\gamma$. The channel is therefore busy for a period of $\gamma+t_1-t_0$. In the worst case user B starts transmission just prior to the arrival of A's packet, i.e., at time $t_1=t_0+\tau$; hence in the worst case, in an unsuccessful transmission period the channel remains busy for a duration of $\gamma+\tau$. Denoting by $\bar{x}$ the length of the transmission period we have

$$\bar{x} = \begin{cases} T+\tau & \textit{Successful transmission period} \\ \gamma+\tau & \textit{Unsuccessful transmission period} \end{cases}$$

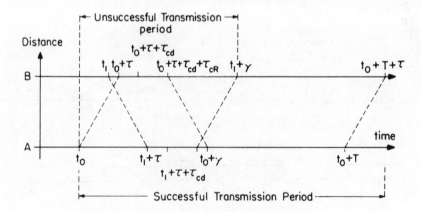

Figure 4.8: Collision Detection Timing

In the following we analyze the slotted versions of CSMA/CD, namely, it is assumed that time is quantized into mini-slots of length τ seconds and that all users are synchronized so that transmissions can begin only at the start of a mini-slot. Thus, when a packet is scheduled for transmission during some mini-slot, the user with that packet waits until the end of that mini-slot, senses the channel, and follows the corresponding version of the CSMA/CD protocol. In addition, we assume that both γ and T (the transmission time of a packet) are integer multiples of τ. Thus $\bar{x}$ takes on only values that are certain integer multiples of τ. The analysis is based on the work by Tobagi and Hunt [ToH80].

Throughput of Slotted Nonpersistent CSMA/CD

With the nonpersistent CSMA/CD time alternates between busy periods (that contain both successful and unsuccessful transmission periods) and idle periods. A cycle is a busy period followed by an idle period (see Figure 4.9). We denote, as before, the length of the busy period by $\bar{B}$, the length of the idle period by $\bar{I}$ and the useful time in a cycle by $\bar{U}$. The distribution of the idle period is identical to that computed for slotted nonpersistent CSMA, i.e.,

$$P(\bar{I} = k\tau) = (e^{-g\tau})^{k-1}(1 - e^{-g\tau}) \qquad k = 1, 2, \cdots \qquad (4.14)$$

so the expected length of the idle period is

$$I = \frac{\tau}{1 - e^{-g\tau}} \cdot \qquad (4.15)$$

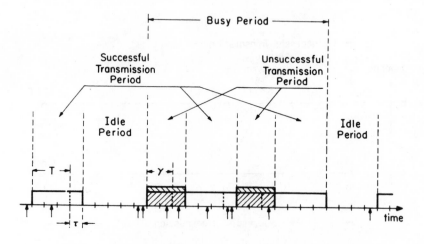

Figure 4.9: Slotted Nonpersistent CSMA/CD Packet Timing

The probability that a certain transmission in a transmission period is successful is the probability that the transmission period contains exactly one packet (given that it contains at least one packet), i.e., the probability of a single arrival in a mini-slot (given that there was at least one arrival):

$$P_{suc} = Prob\,[\ single\ transmission\ |\ at\ least\ one\ transmission\ ]$$

$$= \frac{g\,\tau e^{-g\tau}}{1 - e^{-g\tau}}\,. \tag{4.16}$$

Each transmission period that contains a successful transmission is of length $T+\tau$ seconds while a transmission period with an unsuccessful transmission is of length $\gamma+\tau$ seconds. A busy period will contain l transmission periods if there was at least one arrival in the last mini-slot of each of the first $l-1$ transmission periods, and no arrival in the last mini-slot of the l th transmission period. Therefore, the probability that the busy period contains exactly l ($l\geq1$) transmission periods is $e^{-g\tau}(1-e^{-g\tau})^{l-1}$ and the average number of transmission periods within the busy period is $1/e^{-g\tau}$. In addition, we have that the probability distribution of the length of the busy period is

$$P\!\left[\bar{B} = k\,(T+\tau) + (l-k)(\gamma+\tau)\right]$$

$$= e^{-g\tau}(1-e^{-g\tau})^{l-1}\binom{l}{k}P_{suc}^{k}(1-P_{suc})^{l-k} \quad l = 1,2,\cdots\ ;\ k = 0,1,\cdots,l$$

where l corresponds to the total number of transmission periods in the busy period and k corresponds to the successful transmission periods. Therefore,

$$B = \sum_{l=1}^{\infty}\sum_{k=0}^{l}\left[k\,(T+\tau) + (l-k)(\gamma+\tau)\right]P\!\left[\bar{B}=k\,(T+\tau) + (l-k)(\gamma+\tau)\right]$$

$$= \frac{P_{suc}\,(T + \tau) + (1 - P_{suc})(\gamma + \tau)}{e^{-g\tau}}\,. \tag{4.17}$$

We now turn to compute $U = E\,[\bar{U}]$. Every successful transmission period contributes T to $\bar{U}$ while unsuccessful transmission periods do not contribute anything. Thus,

$$Prob\,[\bar{U} = kT] = Prob\,[\ k\ successful\ transmissions\ periods\ in\ a\ busy\ period]$$

$$= \sum_{l=k}^{\infty}Prob\!\left[\bar{B} = k\,(T + \tau) + (l - k)(\gamma + \tau)\right]$$

from which

$$U = \sum_{k=0}^{\infty}k\cdot T\cdot Prob\,[\bar{U}=kT] = \frac{T}{e^{-g\tau}}P_{suc}\,. \tag{4.18}$$

Combining (4.16), (4.17), and (4.18) we compute the throughput:

$$S = \frac{U}{B+I} = \frac{g\tau T e^{-g\tau}}{g\tau T e^{-g\tau} + [(1 - e^{-g\tau}) - g\tau e^{-g\tau}]\gamma + \tau} \ . \qquad (4.19)$$

In a normalized form:

$$S = \frac{aGe^{-aG}}{aGe^{-aG} + (1 - e^{-aG} - aGe^{-aG})\gamma' + a} \qquad (4.20)$$

where γ' is the ratio between γ and the transmission time of a packet ($\gamma' = \gamma/T$). Notice that when $\gamma' = 1$ the result in (4.20) is identical to slotted nonpersistent CSMA. Figure 4.10 depicts the throughput-load characteristics of the nonpersistent CSMA with collision detection. The improvement in performance is readily apparent.

Throughput of Slotted 1-Persistent CSMA/CD

With the 1-persistent CSMA/CD the time also alternates between busy periods (containing successful and unsuccessful transmission periods) and idle periods, and a cycle is a busy period followed by an idle period (see Figure 4.11). Notice that here a success or failure of a transmission period in the busy period depends (only) on the length of the preceding transmission period, except for the first transmission period that depends on arrivals during the preceding

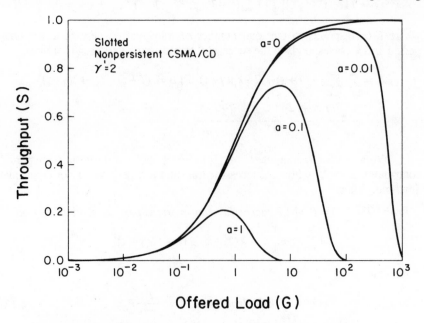

Figure 4.10: Throughput-Load of Slotted Nonpersistent CSMA/CD

mini-slot. Denoting by $\bar{x}_i$ the duration of the i th transmission period in the busy period, then the duration of the $i+1$st transmission period depends only on $\bar{x}_i$. This is so since the type of the i th transmission period (success or collision) is determined by the number of arrivals during the previous transmission period which, in turn, depends only on its duration. Hence, given that a transmission period is of length x, the length of the remainder of the busy period is a function of x, and its average is denoted by $B(x)$. Similarly, given that a transmission period is of length x, the average time the channel is carrying successful transmissions in the remainder of the busy period is denoted by $U(x)$. Let $a_i(x)$ be the probability of i arrivals during a period of length x. Under the Poisson assumption $a_i(x) = (gx)^i e^{-gx} / i!$.

The quantity $B(x)$ is given by:

$$B(x) = \frac{a_1(x)}{1 - a_0(x)} \left[T + \tau + [1 - a_0(T+\tau)]B(T+\tau) \right]$$
$$+ \left[1 - \frac{a_1(x)}{1 - a_0(x)} \right] \left[\gamma + \tau + [1 - a_0(\gamma+\tau)]B(\gamma+\tau) \right] \tag{4.21}$$

The first term in (4.21) corresponds to a successful transmission of the single packet that arrives during x, in which case the remainder of the busy period will be of length $T+\tau$ (the length of a successful transmission period). In addition, if there is at least one arrival within $T+\tau$ (probability $1 - a_0(T+\tau)$), the remainder of the busy period is of length $B(T+\tau)$. The second term in (4.21) corresponds to an unsuccessful transmission due to arrivals during x, in which case the remainder of the busy period will be of length $\gamma+\tau$ (the length of an

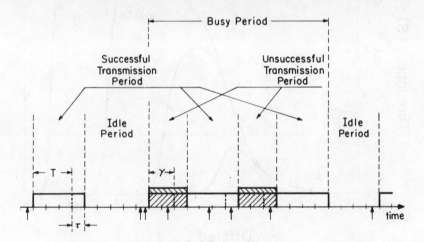

Figure 4.11: Slotted 1-Persistent CSMA/CD Packet Timing

unsuccessful transmission period). In addition, if there is at least one arrival within $\gamma+\tau$, an additional length of $B(\gamma+\tau)$ is the remainder of the busy period. The expected duration of the entire busy period is $B(\tau)$ since x, the argument of $B(\cdot)$ can be interpreted as an arrival period for the next transmission period and clearly the arrival period for the entire busy period is the first mini-slot before it started. Observing (4.21) we notice that substituting τ for x in (4.21) is not quite enough since values of $B(\cdot)$ appear on the right handside as well. This is overcome by setting $x=T+\tau$ and $x=\gamma+\tau$ in (4.21) and obtaining two equations with two unknowns $B(T+\tau)$ and $B(\gamma+\tau)$ which can be solved easily. Having determined these values, $B(x)$ can be determined for any x, in particular $x=\tau$, to yield the expected length of a busy period.

In a similar manner, $U(x)$ is given by

$$U(x) = \frac{a_1(x)}{1-a_0(x)}\left[T + [1-a_0(T+\tau)]U(T+\tau)\right]$$
$$+ \left[1 - \frac{a_1(x)}{1-a_0(x)}\right]\left[[1-a_0(\gamma+\tau)]U(\gamma+\tau)\right] . \tag{4.22}$$

The explanation of (4.22) is similar to that of (4.21). Again, using (4.22) with $x=T+\tau$ and $x=\gamma+\tau$ one obtains two equations with two unknowns $U(T+\tau)$ and $U(\gamma+\tau)$. The average time during a cycle that the channel is carrying

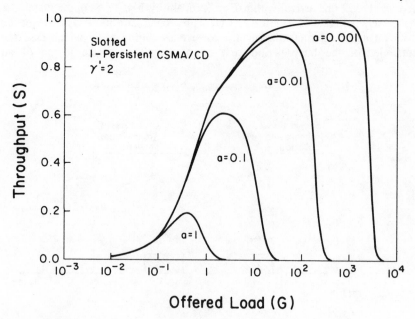

Figure 4.12: Throughput-Load of Slotted 1-Persistent CSMA/CD

successful transmissions, U, is given by $U(\tau)$, expressed in terms of $U(T+\tau)$ and $U(\gamma+\tau)$.

The average length of an idle period is $\tau/(1-e^{-g\tau})$ (see (4.15)), and the throughput is given by

$$S = \frac{U}{B+I} = \frac{U(\tau)}{B(\tau) + \dfrac{\tau}{1-e^{-g\tau}}} \; .$$

While the above evaluation of the throughput does not result in a closed form, computation is straight forward. Figure 4.12 shows the throughput load characteristic of the 1-persistent CSMA with collision detection. As opposed to the nonpersistent case, a rather dramatic change is seen here. For comparison Figure 4.13 shows the characteristics of the slotted nonpersistent and 1-persistent CSMA with and without collision detection, all for $a=0.01$. Superiority of the collision detection mechanism is evident. Moreover, the "gap" in performance between the nonpersistent and the 1-persistent CSMA when collision detection is used has narrowed down. Because of its better performance in

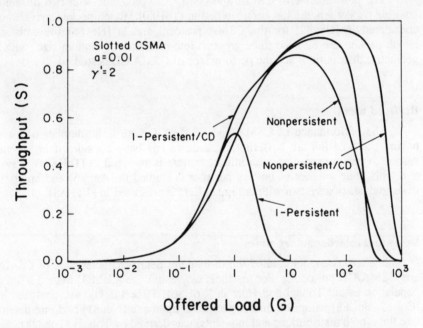

Figure 4.13: Comparison of Throughput-Load of Slotted systems with $a=0.01$
Nonpersistent without collision detection, 1-persistent without collision detection
Nonpersistent with collision detection, 1-persistent with collision detection

low load and because its delay characteristic is favorable the 1-persistent CSMA with collision detection is so popular in local area networks.

4.5. RELATED ANALYSIS

Carrier sensing has become extremely popular in recent years for one major reason--local area networks (LANs). The pioneering technological development was first reported in [MeB76]. This popularity is a result of the ease of implementing collision detection in broadcast LANs. The direct outcome is an enormous amount of research and analysis of these protocols under all types of circumstances. In fact, the amount of published material is so large that it is impossible to cover it all or even classify it properly. In the next few paragraphs we point the reader at some relevant additional work on the subject. For a broader survey the reader is referred to [Tob80].

Variable-length packets

The performance of CSMA and CSMA/CD protocols with two different possible packet lengths has been studied in [ToH80]. Batch packet arrivals are considered in [Hey82] for the CSMA protocol and in [Hey86] the constant length packets are allowed to be grouped into messages of random size (with a geometric distribution) and the performance of CSMA/CD is studied.

Buffered users

The performance of CSMA and CSMA/CD with finite number of users having finite or infinite buffering capabilities has been considered in several works. A two-user system with infinite buffers is analyzed in [TaK85a], a system with finite number of buffers per user is studied in [ApP86] and approximate analysis of a system with infinite buffers is presented in [TTH88].

Delay and interdeparture times

Numerous papers studied the throughput delay characteristics of CSMA and CSMA/CD protocols. For instance, Coyle and Liu [CoL83] treated a finite population as did Tobagi and Hunt in [ToH80]. Packet delay was analyzed in [CoL85, BeC88] using the matrix-geometric approach [Neu81] and interdeparture time (both distributions and moments) was derived by Tobagi [Tob82b].

Ordered users

Most CSMA-type local networks are implemented using a coaxial cable as the transmission means. As such, the attachment of the users to the cable introduces an inherent order, which, if properly used, can improve performance substantially. Such attempts were done by Tobagi and Rom [ToR80, RoT81], by Limb and Flores [LiF82], and by Tobagi and Fine [FiT84]. It was shown by Rom [Rom84] that users can by themselves identify their ordinal number on the network.

Performance improvement

In an attempt to improve the performance of CSMA and CSMA/CD protocols Meditch and Lea [MeL83] derive some optimized versions (keeping stability in mind), Takagi and Yamada [TaY83] proposed to resolve collisions deterministically while Molle and Kleinrock [MoK85] proposed using *virtual time* to resolve collisions. Other versions of virtual time CSMA have been considered in [ZhR87, CuM88]. Several schemes were proposed to incorporate priority structures in carrier sense multiple access environments; typical examples of these are presented in [RoT81, Tob82a, KiK83].

Collision detection in radio systems

Implementing collision detection in local area networks is relatively simple since the transmitted and received signals are of the same order of magnitude. In radio systems the received signal is considerably weaker compared with the transmitted signal and therefore collision detection cannot be implemented via a simple comparison. An idea of how to implement collision detection in radio systems is described in [Rom86] (see Exercises).

EXERCISES

Problem 4.1

Find the throughput of nonpersistent and 1-persistent CSMA for $a \to 0$ and $g \to \infty$. Explain the difference. Find the throughput of a slotted 1-persistent CSMA for $a \to 0$ and compare with the result for an unslotted system.

Problem 4.2

For Nonpersistent CSMA show that

(a)   Increasing a uniformly decreases the throughput.

(b)   There is a single load for which the channel attains its capacity.

Problem 4.3 (CSMA with a heavy user [ScK79])

Consider a network containing one central computer and a large (read: infinite) number of terminals all operating as follows. The terminals each have a single packet buffer and communicate using the slotted ALOHA scheme. The computer has an infinite buffer and uses a modified CSMA protocol (see below). All packets are of equal length T.

To increase the total throughput the slot size is set to $T + 2\tau$ and the terminal packets carry a preamble of length τ (where τ is the propagation delay in the system). That is, a terminal packet transmission consists of τ seconds of carrier followed by T seconds of information (and, of course, τ more seconds to 'clean' the channel). The computer, at the beginning of the slot where transmission is attempted, listens to the channel and will transmit a packet of duration T only if the channel is sensed idle. (Note that the computer has in fact a lower priority since it defers transmission to an ongoing terminal transmission).

Let λ_1 and λ_2 be the Poisson arrival rates (in packets/second) of the computer and the terminals, respectively, and let g be the combined offered load of the terminals. Define, as usual, the partial throughputs $S_1 = \lambda_1 T$, $S_2 = \lambda_2 T$, and the total throughput $S = S_1 + S_2$. (For convenience define $\Lambda_i = \lambda_i(T + 2\tau)$).

(a)   Find the throughputs S_1, S_2, and S.

(b)   When is the throughput maximal? What is the throughput in this case?

(c)   Let $\tilde{x}$ denote the service time of a central computer's packet. The random variable $\tilde{x}$ is the time from the moment the channel is first sensed for that packet until its transmission is complete. Find $E[\tilde{x}]$ and $E[\tilde{x}^2]$.

(d)   From the results of part (c) compute the average delay of a computer packet. What is the average delay under the conditions of part (b)?

Problem 4.4 (Mixed mode CSMA)

Consider the following version of slotted CSMA: Whenever a packet is scheduled for transmission, the corresponding user senses the channel. If the channel is idle the packet is transmitted. If the channel is busy, a coin is flipped; with probability p the packet is scheduled for transmission at some later time (nonpersistent) and with probability $1-p$ the user waits until the channel becomes idle and then transmits the packet (1-persistent).

(a)   Assume $a=0$ and use the standard Poisson assumption to determine the relation between S and G as a function of p. Check your results for $p=0$ and $p=1$.

(b)   Repeat part (a) for $a\neq0$. How should p be chosen to maximize the throughput?

Problem 4.5 (CSMA with a noisy channel)

Consider a slotted nonpersistent CSMA system with a noisy channel. Each slot is noisy with probability p_e which is independent of the system and of the noise in previous slots. When a slot is noisy while a packet is being transmitted, that packet is destroyed. In addition, a user arriving in a noisy slot within an idle period thinks (erroneously) that the channel is busy and behaves accordingly.

To analyze the system we assume an infinite number of users collectively forming a Poisson arrival process with average g packets per second. Let the slot size equal the end-to-end propagation delay τ and let all the packets be of equal length T (assumed to occupy an integer number of slots). For the analysis we define an embedded Markov chain at the beginning and end of each transmission period.

(a)   What is the probability that a given slot in the idle period is not the last slot of that period.

(b)   Compute the throughput of the system. Verify your answer for the case $p_e=0$.

Problem 4.6 (Collision detection in radio systems [Rom86])

This problem deals with a collision detection scheme usable also in radio network. The scheme is essentially a nonpersistent CSMA with the following exception. Each transmitting user pauses during transmission and senses the channel. If the channel is sensed idle transmission proceeds as usual. If the channel is sensed busy the user concludes that his packet collided and will not transmit the entire packet. However, the user will not abort transmission immediately but rather will continue transmitting for some period of time and then abort. The period from the start of transmission to the time of abortion is called the collision detection interval.

The analysis of such a system is based on a slotted nonpersistent CSMA. Let there be infinitely many users collectively generating (on the channel) a Poisson distributed offered load with mean g packets/second. The slot size τ equals the end-to-end propagation delay in the system. All packets are of equal length T and occupy an integer number of slots. The collision detection interval is $R = r\tau$ (where r is an integer) and a transmitting user will pause for one slot randomly and uniformly chosen among the r slots of transmission starting with the second slot.

(a)   Is it necessary for R to be identical for all users?

(b)   Define an embedded Markov chain with which you intend to analyze the system.

(c)   Watching the channel we observe long and short transmission periods. What is the probability of a long transmission period? What is the probability of a short transmission period?

(d)   What is the probability of a successful transmission period?

(e)   Derive an expression for the channel throughput.

(f)   Let r_{opt} be that r that maximizes the throughput. Why does such an r exist? What system parameters does it depend on? What is the value of r_{opt} for low load?

CHAPTER 5

COLLISION RESOLUTION PROTOCOLS

We have seen that the original Aloha protocol is inherently unstable in the absence of some external control. If we look into the philosophy behind the Aloha protocol, we notice that there is no sincere attempt to resolve collisions among packets as soon as they occur. Instead, the attempts to resolve collisions are always deferred to the future, with the hope that things will then work out, somehow, but they never do.

In this chapter we introduce and analyze multiple access protocols with a different philosophy. In these protocols, called *Collision Resolution Protocols* (CRP), the efforts are concentrated on resolving collisions as soon as they occur. Moreover, in most versions of these protocols, new packets that arrive to the system are inhibited from being transmitted while the resolution of collisions is in progress. This ensures that if the rate of arrival of new packets to the system is smaller than the rate at which collisions can be resolved (the maximal rate of departing packets), then the system is stable.

The basic idea behind these protocols is to exploit in a more sophisticated manner the feedback information that is available to the users in order to control the retransmission process so that collisions are resolved more efficiently and without chaotic events.

The underlying model and the assumptions used here are identical to those assumed for the slotted Aloha protocol. The channel is slotted and the users can transmit packets (whose length is one slot) only at beginning of slots. New packets arrive to the system according to a Poisson process with rate λ packets/slot. If two or more packets are transmitted in a slot, a collision occurs and the packets involved in the collision have to be retransmitted. At the end of each slot the users of the system know what happened in the slot, namely, whether the slot was idle (no packet was transmitted), or contained a successful transmission (exactly one packet was transmitted) or there was a collision (at least two packets were transmitted). This is known as the *ternary feedback* model. For some protocols it suffices for the users to know whether the slot contained a collision or not. The latter is referred to as the *binary feedback* model.

5.1. THE BINARY-TREE PROTOCOL

The most basic collision resolution protocol is called the *binary-tree* CRP (or binary-tree protocol) and was proposed almost concurrently by Capetanakis [Cap79], Tsybakov and Mikhailov [TsM78], and Hayes [Hay78]. According to this protocol when a collision occurs, in slot k say, all users that are not involved in the collision wait until the collision is resolved. The users involved in the collision split randomly into two subsets, by (for instance) each flipping a coin. The users in the first subset, those that flipped 0, retransmit in slot $k+1$ while those that flipped 1 wait until all those that flipped 0 transmit successfully their packets. If slot $k+1$ is either idle or contains a successful transmission, the users of the second subset (those that flipped 1) retransmit in slot $k+2$. If slot $k+1$ contains another collision, then the procedure is repeated, i.e., the users whose packets collided in slot $k+1$ (the "colliding users") flip a coin again and operate according to the outcome of the coin flipping, and so on. We refer to a user having a packet that collided (at least once) as a *backlogged user*.

The above explanation shows that the protocol is specified by a recursion: a group of colliding packets is split into two subgroups each of which is subjected to the same procedure as the original group. This recursion will be manifested later when these protocols are analyzed. But even at the description level the recursive operation of the protocol is best described by a binary-tree (see Figure 5.1) in which every vertex corresponds to a time slot. The root of the tree corresponds to the slot of the original collision. Each vertex of the tree also designates a subset (perhaps empty) of backlogged users. Vertices whose subsets contain at least two users (labeled "≥ 2") indicate collisions and have two outgoing branches, corresponding to the splitting of the subset into two new subsets. Vertices corresponding to empty subsets (labeled "0"), or subsets containing one user (labeled "1") are leaves of the tree and indicate an idle and a successful slot, respectively.

To further understand the operation of the protocol we consider in detail the example depicted in Figure 5.1. A collision occurs in slot 1. At this point it is neither known how many users nor who are the users that collided in this slot. Each of the colliding users flip a coin and those that flipped 0 transmit in slot 2. By the rules of the protocol no newly arrived packet is transmitted while the resolution of a collision is in progress, so that only users that collided in slot 1 and flipped 0 transmit in slot 2. Another collision occurs in slot 2 and the users involved in that collision flip a coin again. In this example, all the colliding users of slot 2 flipped 1 and therefore slot 3 is idle. The users that flipped 1 in slot 2 transmit again in slot 4, resulting in another collision and forcing the users involved in it to flip a coin once more. One user flips 0 and transmits (successfully) in slot 5 causing all users that flipped 1 in slot 4 to transmit in slot 6. In this example there is one such user and therefore slot 6 is a successful one. Now that the collision among all users that flipped 0 in slot 1 has been resolved, the users that flipped 1 in that slot transmit (in slot 7). Another collision occurs, and the users involved in it flip a coin. Another collision is observed in slot 8, meaning that at least two users flipped 0 in slot 7. The users that collided in slot 8 flip

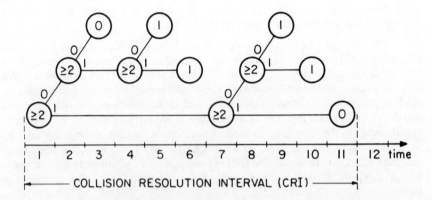

Figure 5.1: Example of the Binary-Tree Protocol Operation

a coin and, as it happens, there is a single user that flipped 0 and it transmits (successfully) in slot 9. Then, in slot 10, transmit the users that flipped 1 in slot 8. There is only one such user, and his transmission is, of course, successful. Finally, the users that flipped 1 in slot 7 must transmit in slot 11. In this example there is no such user, hence slot 11 is idle, completing the resolution of the collision that occurred in slot 7 and, at the same time, the one in the first slot. Observing again Figure 5.1 we see that the order of transmission corresponds exactly to the traversal of the tree.

It is clear from this example that each user can construct the binary-tree shown in Figure 5.1 by following the feedback signals corresponding to each slot. Users that are not involved in the collision, can also follow the binary-tree and thus know exactly when the collision is resolved. In the same manner, each backlogged user can keep track of his own position on that tree (while a collision is being resolved), and thus can determine when to transmit his packet. For the correct operation of the binary-tree protocol, the binary feedback suffices, i.e., users do not have to distinguish idle slots from successful ones.

We say that a collision is *resolved* when the users of the system know that *all* packets involved in the collision have been transmitted successfully. The time interval starting with the original collision (if any) and ending when this collision is resolved is called *collision resolution interval* (CRI). In the above example the length of the CRI is 11 slots.

The binary-tree protocol dictates how to resolve collisions once they occur. To complete the description of the protocol, we need to specify when newly generated packets are transmitted for the first time or, in other words, to specify the first-time transmission rule. One alternative, which we assumed all along (known as the *obvious-access* scheme), is that new packets are inhibited from being transmitted while a resolution of a collision is in progress. That is, packets that arrive to the system while a resolution of a collision is in progress, wait until the collision is resolved, at which time they are transmitted. In the example of Figure 5.1 all new packets arriving to the system during slots 1 through 11 are transmitted for the first time in slot 12.

The operation of the binary-tree protocol can also be described in terms of a stack (see Figure 5.2). This is, in fact, a standard description of tree traversal by a stack representation. In each slot the stack is popped, and all the users that were at the top of the stack transmit their messages. In case of a collision, the stack is pushed with the users that flip 1 and then pushed again with those that flip 0. The users that flip 0 remain therefore at the top of the stack to be popped and transmit in the next slot. In case of a successful transmission or an idle slot no further operations are done on the stack. Clearly then, when the stack empties the collision is resolved, the CRI is over and users with newly arrived packets (if any) are pushed onto the top of the stack and operation proceeds as before.

Performance analysis of binary-tree CRP can be done either with the tree or stack representations reaching, of course, the same results. In this book we confine ourselves to the tree approach. For analysis via the stack representation the interested reader is referred to the work by Fayolle et. al. [FFH85]. In the

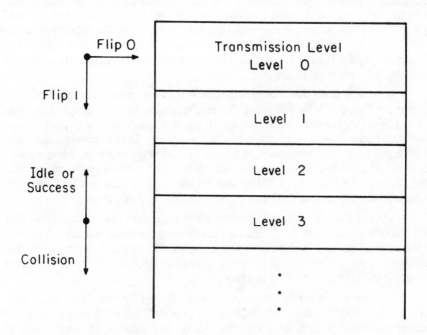

Figure 5.2: Binary-Tree Protocol Stack Representation

following we first compute the moments of the time required to resolve a collision among n packets and obtain tight bounds for these moments. These results are then used to derive the stability condition for this system. Finally, we show that when the system is stable, the expected delay of a packet is bounded. The analysis in this section is based on that of Massey [Mas81].

5.1.1. Moments of the Conditional Length of a CRI

Assume that at some given slot n packets collide. To resolve the collision each participating user flips a coin and proceeds correspondingly. Clearly, the number of slots required to resolve such a collision is a random variable. Denote therefore by $\tilde{B}_n$ the length (in slots) of a CRI given that it starts (in its first slot) with a collision among n packets, and let $B_n = E[\tilde{B}_n]$. The quantity B_n plays a crucial role in the analysis of the binary-tree CRP. Loosely speaking, the ratio n/B_n represents the "effective service rate" of packets in a CRI that starts with the transmission of n packets, since n packets are transmitted successfully during B_n slots. One would expect that if the arrival rate of new packets is smaller than the "effective service rate" even when the system is highly loaded (n is large), then the system is stable. This statement is made rigorous in Section 5.1.2. But first we compute the moments of $\tilde{B}_n$.

When no packet, or a single packet, is transmitted in the first slot of a CRI then the CRI lasts exactly one slot, hence

$$\tilde{B}_0 = \tilde{B}_1 = 1 \ . \tag{5.1}$$

When $n \geq 2$, there is a collision in the first slot of the CRI and the random coin flipping takes place. Let p be the probability that a user flips 0 whenever it flips the binary coin. Then, the probability that exactly i of the n colliding users flip 0 (and hence transmit in the next slot) is

$$Q_i(n) = \binom{n}{i} p^i (1-p)^{n-i} \qquad 0 \leq i \leq n \ . \tag{5.2}$$

Given that i users flipped 0, the length of the CRI is

$$\tilde{B}_{n \mid i} = 1 + \tilde{B}_i + \tilde{B}_{n-i} \qquad n \geq 2 \ . \tag{5.3}$$

The 1 corresponds to the slot of the initial collision among the n users. Then it takes $\tilde{B}_i$ slots to resolve the collision among the i users that flipped 0. Finally, it takes $\tilde{B}_{n-i}$ additional slots to resolve the collision among the $n-i$ users that flipped 1. From the above relation the first moment of $\tilde{B}_n$ can be recursively derived as follows. First, from equation (5.1) we have

$$B_0 = B_1 = 1 \tag{5.4}$$

Then, from equation (5.3)

$$B_{n \mid i} = E[\tilde{B}_{n \mid i}] = 1 + B_i + B_{n-i} \qquad n \geq 2$$

leading to

$$B_n = 1 + \sum_{i=0}^{n} Q_i(n)(B_i + B_{n-i}) \qquad n \geq 2 . \tag{5.5}$$

In this last equation B_n appears on both sides of the equation; solving for B_n we obtain the recursion

$$B_n = \frac{1 + \sum_{i=0}^{n-1} Q_i(n)B_i + \sum_{i=1}^{n} Q_i(n)B_{n-i}}{1 - Q_0(n) - Q_n(n)} \tag{5.6}$$

$$= \frac{1 + \sum_{i=0}^{n-1} [Q_i(n) + Q_{n-i}(n)]B_i}{1 - Q_0(n) - Q_n(n)} \qquad n \geq 2$$

where equation (5.4) provides the initial values.

Computation of a similar nature can be done for any moment desired. However, a more general approach is that of the generating function $G_n(z) \stackrel{\Delta}{=} E[z^{\tilde{B}_n}]$. To compute this generating function notice that the random variables $\tilde{B}_i$ and $\tilde{B}_{n-i}$ are independent and thus

$$G_n(z) = E[z^{\tilde{B}_n}] = \sum_{i=0}^{n} Q_i(n)E[z^{1+\tilde{B}_i+\tilde{B}_{n-i}}] = \sum_{i=0}^{n} Q_i(n)zE[z^{\tilde{B}_i}]E[z^{\tilde{B}_{n-i}}] \qquad n \geq 2$$

or

$$G_n(z) = z\sum_{i=0}^{n} Q_i(n)G_i(z)G_{n-i}(z) \qquad n \geq 2 . \tag{5.7}$$

In equation (5.7) $G_n(z)$ appears on both sides so, as we did before, solving for $G_n(z)$ we obtain:

$$G_n(z) = \frac{z\sum_{i=1}^{n-1} Q_i(n)G_i(z)G_{n-i}(z)}{1 - z^2[Q_0(n) + Q_n(n)]} \qquad n \geq 2$$

and the initial conditions of equation (5.1) translate into

$$G_0(z) = G_1(z) = z \tag{5.8}$$

allowing recursive computation of $G_n(z)$. From this generating function the moments of $\tilde{B}_n$ can be computed recursively by taking derivatives at $z=1$. Taking the first derivative at $z=1$ leads, obviously, to the result of equation (5.6). We now proceed to calculate the second moment.

Let V_n be the second moment of $\tilde{B}_n$ i.e., $V_n = E[\tilde{B}_n^2]$. From (5.1) we immediately have

$$V_0 = V_1 = 1 .$$

To compute the second moment for higher values of n we differentiate equation (5.7) twice with respect to z and obtain

$$\ddot{G}_n(z) = 2\sum_{i=0}^{n}Q_i(n)\dot{G}_i(z)G_{n-i}(z) + 2\sum_{i=0}^{n}Q_i(n)G_i(z)\dot{G}_{n-i}(z)$$

$$+ 2z\sum_{i=0}^{n}Q_i(n)\dot{G}_i(z)\dot{G}_{n-i}(z) + z\sum_{i=0}^{n}Q_i(n)\ddot{G}_i(z)G_{n-i}(z) \qquad (5.9)$$

$$+ z\sum_{i=0}^{n}Q_i(n)G_i(z)\ddot{G}_{n-i}(z) \qquad n\geq 2 .$$

Substituting $z=1$ in (5.9) and using the facts that $\dot{G}_n(1)=B_n$ and $\ddot{G}_n(1)=V_n-B_n$ we obtain

$$V_n - B_n = 2\sum_{i=0}^{n}Q_i(n)(B_i + B_{n-i} + B_iB_{n-i})$$

$$+ \sum_{i=0}^{n}Q_i(n)(V_i - B_i + V_{n-i} - B_{n-i}) \qquad (5.10)$$

$$= B_n - 1 + 2\sum_{i=0}^{n}Q_i(n)B_iB_{n-i} + \sum_{i=0}^{n}Q_i(n)(V_i + V_{n-i}) \qquad n\geq 2$$

where we used (5.5). Solving for V_n we obtain the following recursion:

$$V_n = \frac{2B_n - 1 + 2\sum_{i=0}^{n}Q_i(n)B_iB_{n-i} + \sum_{i=0}^{n-1}[Q_i(n) + Q_{n-i}(n)]V_i}{1 - Q_0(n) - Q_n(n)} \qquad n\geq 2 . \qquad (5.11)$$

The recursive nature of equations (5.6) and (5.11) are sometimes inconvenient to work with and a direct expression might be preferred. Indeed, it is possible to obtain closed-form expressions for the moments of $\tilde{B}_n$. The derivations of these expressions are quite lengthy and for the interested reader are given in Appendix A at the end of this chapter. The resulting expressions are:

$$B_n = 1 + \sum_{k=2}^{n}\begin{bmatrix}n\\k\end{bmatrix}\frac{2(k-1)(-1)^k}{[1-p^k-(1-p)^k]} \qquad n\geq 2 , \qquad (5.12)$$

$$V_n = 1 + \sum_{k=2}^{n}\frac{2n!}{(n-k)![1-p^k-(1-p)^k]}\left[B_k^* + \sum_{i=0}^{k}B_i^*B_{k-i}^*\right]$$

$$+ \sum_{k=2}^{n}\begin{bmatrix}n\\k\end{bmatrix}\frac{4(k-1)(-1)^k}{[1-p^k-(1-p)^k]} \qquad n\geq 2$$

where

$$B_0^* = 1 ; \quad B_1^* = 0 ; \quad B_k^* = \frac{2(k-1)(-1)^k}{k![1-p^k-(1-p)^k]} \qquad k\geq 2 .$$

It is interesting to investigate the behavior of B_n as a function of p. Differentiating (5.12) twice with respect to p we note that independent of n, at $p=\frac{1}{2}$ the first derivative vanishes while the second derivative is positive. In fact, $p = \frac{1}{2}$ is the only real value for which the first derivative vanishes. We conclude therefore, that B_n is minimized for $p = \frac{1}{2}$ for all n. Table 4.1 contains some of the values of B_n and V_n when $p = \frac{1}{2}$ along with values of the "effective service rate" n/B_n. Judging by the values of n/B_n it is interesting to note that the protocol resolves collisions among a small number of packets more efficiently than collisions among a large number of packets. We return to this topic in Section 5.2.2.

Bounds on the Moments

In the previous section the first two moments of the conditional length of a CRI are computed. In this section we derive upper bounds for these moments. We are seeking an upper bound for B_n of the form

$$B_n \leq \alpha_m n - 1 \qquad n \geq m \qquad (5.13)$$

for some arbitrary m and with some $\alpha_m > 0$. The motivation for a bound of this form is that it guarantees a strictly positive "effective service rate" (n/B_n) for large n. If indeed a bound of that form can be found then one would be able to write

$$\frac{n}{B_n} \geq \frac{1}{\alpha_m} + \frac{1}{\alpha_m B_n} \qquad n \geq m$$

and hence the effective service rate is guaranteed to be larger than $1/\alpha_m$. This

n	0	1	2	3	4
B_n	1.0000	1.0000	5.0000	7.6667	10.5238
n/B_n	0.0000	1.0000	0.4000	0.3913	0.3801
V_n	1.0000	1.0000	33.000	68.555	124.28
n	6	7	8	9	10
B_n	16.3131	19.2010	22.0854	24.9691	27.8532
n/B_n	0.3678	0.3646	0.3622	0.3604	0.3590
V_n	286.42	392.36	514.82	653.89	809.63
n	11	12	13	14	15
B_n	30.7382	33.6238	36.5097	39.3955	42.2813
n/B_n	0.3579	0.3569	0.3561	0.3554	0.3548
V_n	982.05	1171.1	1376.9	1599.3	1838.4

Table 4.1: The first and second moments of $\bar{B}_n$ for $p = \frac{1}{2}$.

also motivates looking for the smallest α_m for which the bound holds.

The approach to determine α_m is as follows. We fix m $(m \geq 2)$ and choose some α_m so that $B_n \leq \alpha_m n - 1$ for $n = m$ (any $\alpha_m \geq (B_m + 1)/m$ is feasible). Next, we assume that (5.13) holds up to $j-1$, i.e., $B_n \leq \alpha_m n - 1$ for $n = m, m+1, \cdots, j-1$ and by induction establish the validity of (5.13) for j.

The point of departure is equation (5.6), i.e.,

$$B_j[1 - Q_0(j) - Q_j(j)] = 1 + \sum_{i=0}^{j-1}[Q_i(j) + Q_{j-i}(j)]B_i$$

$$= 1 + \sum_{i=0}^{m-1}[Q_i(j) + Q_{j-i}(j)]B_i + \sum_{i=m}^{j-1}[Q_i(j) + Q_{j-i}(j)]B_i \ .$$

Applying the induction hypothesis we obtain

$$B_j[1 - Q_0(j) - Q_j(j)] \leq 1 + \sum_{i=0}^{m-1}[Q_i(j) + Q_{j-i}(j)]B_i$$

$$+ \sum_{i=m}^{j-1}[Q_i(j) + Q_{j-i}(j)](\alpha_m i - 1)$$

$$= 1 + \sum_{i=0}^{m-1}[Q_i(j) + Q_{j-i}(j)](B_i - \alpha_m i + 1)$$

$$+ \sum_{i=0}^{j}[Q_i(j) + Q_{j-i}(j)](\alpha_m i - 1) - [Q_0(j) + Q_j(j)](\alpha_m j - 1)$$

$$= 1 + \sum_{i=0}^{m-1}[Q_i(j) + Q_{j-i}(j)](B_i - \alpha_m i + 1)$$

$$+ \alpha_m j - 2 - [Q_0(j) + Q_j(j)](\alpha_m j - 1)$$

$$= \sum_{i=0}^{m-1}[Q_i(j) + Q_{j-i}(j)](B_i - \alpha_m i + 1) + [1 - Q_0(j) - Q_j(j)](\alpha_m j - 1)$$

where we used the facts that $\sum_{i=0}^{j} Q_i(j) = 1$, $\sum_{i=0}^{j} i\, Q_i(j) = jp$ and $\sum_{i=0}^{j} i\, Q_{j-i}(j) = j(1-p)$. Therefore,

$$B_j \leq (\alpha_m j - 1) + \frac{\displaystyle\sum_{i=0}^{m-1}[Q_i(j) + Q_{j-i}(j)](B_i - \alpha_m i + 1)}{1 - Q_0(j) - Q_j(j)} \ . \tag{5.14}$$

It thus follows that (5.13) holds if we choose α_m so that the summation in (5.14) is non-positive for all $j > m$, i.e., such that

$$\sum_{i=0}^{m-1}[Q_i(j) + Q_{j-i}(j)](B_i - \alpha_m i + 1) \leq 0 \qquad j > m$$

or,

$$\alpha_m \geq \frac{\sum\limits_{i=0}^{m-1}(B_i+1)[Q_i(j)+Q_{j-i}(j)]}{\sum\limits_{i=0}^{m-1}i[Q_i(j)+Q_{j-i}(j)]} \qquad j > m \ . \qquad (5.15)$$

Having computed previously the values of B_i, the right hand side of equation (5.15) can also be computed for any desired value of m. Table 4.2 contains some of the values of the expression on the right side of (5.15) for $p=\frac{1}{2}$. Recall that we started with α_m that satisfies $B_m \leq \alpha_m m - 1$. Therefore, if we choose α_m as the maximum between $(B_m+1)/m$ and the following supremum:

$$\sup_{j>m}\left\{\frac{\sum\limits_{i=0}^{m-1}(B_i+1)[Q_i(j)+Q_{j-i}(j)]}{\sum\limits_{i=0}^{m-1}i[Q_i(j)+Q_{j-i}(j)]}\right\} \qquad (5.16)$$

the induction step follows and hence (5.13) holds.

To summarize, for a given m, after computing B_i for $i < m$ (using (5.6) or (5.12)), one can compute the supremum in (5.16) and hence determine α_m as the maximum between that supremum and $(B_m+1)/m$.

We recall that B_n is minimized for $p=\frac{1}{2}$. Hence, the best bound of the form (5.13) is obtained when $p=\frac{1}{2}$. For example, choosing say, $m=6$, we see from Table 4.2 that the supremum is 2.886 when $p=\frac{1}{2}$, thus

$$B_n \leq 2.886n - 1 \qquad n \geq 6 \ . \qquad (5.17)$$

Although inequality (5.17) does not hold for $n < 6$, it is very easy to bound B_n for all $n \geq 0$ (by using (5.17) and Table 4.1) by

$m\backslash j$	3	4	5	6	7	8	9	10	11
2	2.667	2.500	2.400	2.333	2.286	2.250	2.222	2.200	2.182
3		2.875	2.880	2.889	2.898	2.907	2.914	2.920	2.926
4			2.885	2.889	2.892	2.894	2.895	2.896	2.896
5				2.886	2.886	2.887	2.887	2.886	2.886
6					2.886	2.886	2.886	2.885	2.885
7						2.886	2.886	2.886	2.885
8							2.886	2.886	2.886
9								2.886	2.886

Table 4.2: Values of right side of (5.15) for $p=\frac{1}{2}$

$$B_n \leq 2.886n + 1 \qquad n \geq 0 \ . \tag{5.18}$$

We conclude that the "effective service rate", n/B_n, for large n is $1/2.886 \cong 0.346$ and thus the system is expected to be stable for arrival rates smaller than 0.346. This effective rate is smaller than e^{-1}--the maximum throughput of the slotted Aloha protocol; we shall shortly present improved versions of the binary-tree protocol that yield much better performance. In subsequent computations of system parameters and performance we shall take the value $\alpha_m = 2.886$.

Using the above methodology, it is possible to develop a bound on the second moment of the conditional length of a CRI, V_n, of the form

$$V_n \leq \alpha_m^2 n^2 + 1 \qquad n \geq m \tag{5.19}$$

where α_m is the same one used to bound B_n and is determined by the procedure described above. This bound will be required in developing an upper bound for the expected delay of a packet.

We first check the validity of (5.19) for $n=m$. For $p=\frac{1}{2}$, $m=6$, and $\alpha_m = 2.886$ we see from Table 4.1 that (5.19) holds. Next, we assume that (5.19) holds for all values of n up to $j-1$ i.e., $V_n \leq \alpha_m^2 n^2 + 1$ for $n=m,m+1,\cdots,j-1$ and by induction establish the validity of (5.19) for j. The point of departure is equation (5.11) that can be rewritten for $j \geq 2$ (using (5.5)) as

$$V_j = \frac{1 + 2\sum_{i=0}^{j} Q_i(j)(B_i + B_{j-i} + B_i B_{j-i}) + \sum_{i=0}^{j-1}[Q_i(j) + Q_{j-i}(j)]V_i}{1 - Q_0(j) - Q_j(j)} \ . \tag{5.20}$$

Using (5.13) we have

$$2\sum_{i=0}^{j} Q_i(j)(B_i + B_{j-i} + B_i B_{j-i}) \leq 2\sum_{i=0}^{m-1} Q_i(j)(B_i + B_{j-i} + B_i B_{j-i})$$

$$+ 2\sum_{i=m}^{j} Q_i(j)[\alpha_m i - 1 + \alpha_m(j-i) - 1 + (\alpha_m i - 1)(\alpha_m(j-i) - 1)]$$

$$= 2\sum_{i=0}^{m-1} Q_i(j)(B_i + B_{j-i} + B_i B_{j-i}) + 2\sum_{i=m}^{j} Q_i(j)[\alpha_m^2 i(j-i) - 1]$$

$$= 2\sum_{i=0}^{m-1} Q_i(j)[B_i + B_{j-i} + B_i B_{j-i} - \alpha_m^2 i(j-i) + 1] \tag{5.21}$$

$$+ 2\sum_{i=0}^{j} Q_i(j)[\alpha_m^2 i(j-i) - 1]$$

$$= 2\sum_{i=0}^{m-1} Q_i(j)[B_i + B_{j-i} + B_i B_{j-i} - \alpha_m^2 i(j-i) + 1]$$

$$+ 2\alpha_m^2[j^2p - jp(1-p) - j^2p^2] - 2 \ .$$

Similarly, assuming that $V_i \le \alpha_m^2 i^2 + 1$ up to $i \le j-1$ we have

$$\sum_{i=0}^{j-1}[Q_i(j) + Q_{j-i}(j)]V_i \le \sum_{i=0}^{m-1}[Q_i(j) + Q_{j-i}(j)]V_i$$

$$+ \sum_{i=m}^{j-1}[Q_i(j) + Q_{j-i}(j)](\alpha_m^2 i^2 + 1)$$

$$= \sum_{i=0}^{m-1}[Q_i(j) + Q_{j-i}(j)](V_i - \alpha_m^2 i^2 - 1)$$

$$\tag{5.22}$$

$$+ \sum_{i=0}^{j}[Q_i(j) + Q_{j-i}(j)](\alpha_m^2 i^2 + 1) - [Q_0(j) + Q_j(j)](\alpha_m^2 j^2 + 1)$$

$$= \sum_{i=0}^{m-1}[Q_i(j) + Q_{j-i}(j)](V_i - \alpha_m^2 i^2 - 1)$$

$$+ \alpha_m^2[2jp(1-p) + j^2p^2 + j^2(1-p)^2] + 2 - [Q_0(j) + Q_j(j)](\alpha_m^2 j^2 + 1) \ .$$

Substituting (5.21) and (5.22) in (5.20) we obtain:

$$V_j \le \alpha_m^2 j^2 + 1 + \frac{2\sum_{i=0}^{m-1} Q_i(j)[B_i + B_{j-i} + B_i B_{j-i} - \alpha_m^2 i(j-i) + 1]}{1 - Q_0(j) - Q_j(j)}$$

$$+ \frac{\sum_{i=0}^{m-1}[Q_i(j) + Q_{j-i}(j)](V_i - \alpha_m^2 i^2 - 1)}{1 - Q_0(j) - Q_j(j)} \ .$$

Therefore, for the induction hypothesis to hold we require that

$$2\sum_{i=0}^{m-1} Q_i(j)[B_i + B_{j-i} + B_i B_{j-i} - \alpha_m^2 i(j-i) + 1]$$

$$\tag{5.23}$$

$$+ \sum_{i=0}^{m-1}[Q_i(j) + Q_{j-i}(j)](V_i - \alpha_m^2 i^2 - 1) \le 0 \qquad j > m \ .$$

The correctness of (5.23) for $p = \frac{1}{2}$, $m = 6$ and $\alpha_m = 2.886$ can be checked directly.

By analogous arguments to those we used to establish upper bounds of the first two moments of $\bar{B}_n$, it is possible to establish lower bounds on these moments. For instance, it can be shown that (see [Mas81])

$$B_n \ge 2.881n - 1 \qquad n \ge 6 \tag{5.24}$$

and therefore one can show that the system is unstable for arrival rate that is larger than $1/2.881 \cong 0.347$.

5.1.2. Stability Analysis

One of the most important properties of the binary-tree CRP is its stable behavior to which we alluded in previous sections. We are now ready to prove this claim. When the binary-tree CRP is executed, then along the time axis we observe a sequence of collision resolution intervals. Let $\tilde{B}(k)$ be an integer-valued random variable that represents the length (in slots) of the kth CRI. When the obvious access scheme is employed, the chain $\{\tilde{B}(k), k=0,1,2,\cdots\}$ forms a Markov chain because the length of the $k+1$st CRI is determined by the number of packets transmitted in its first slot. This number equals the number of packets arriving during the kth CRI and depends only on the length of the kth CRI. The system is said to be stable if the Markov chain $\{\tilde{B}(k), k=0,1,2,\cdots\}$ is ergodic. (We shall see in the next section that when the system is stable, the expected delay of a packet is finite).

To obtain sufficient conditions for which the Markov chain $\{\tilde{B}(k), k=0,1,2,\cdots\}$ is ergodic, we use again Pakes' Lemma (see Section 3.4). We first notice that the chain is irreducible, aperiodic and homogeneous. To be ergodic, it is sufficient that the chain fulfill the following two conditions:

(a) $|E[\tilde{B}(k+1) - \tilde{B}(k)|\tilde{B}(k) = i]| < \infty \quad \forall i$;

(b) $\limsup_{i \to \infty} E[\tilde{B}(k+1) - \tilde{B}(k)|\tilde{B}(k) = i] < 0$.

We start by computing the following conditional expectation:

$$E[\tilde{B}(k+1)|\tilde{B}(k) = i]$$

$$= \sum_{n=0}^{\infty} E[\tilde{B}(k+1)|\tilde{B}(k)=i, \text{ number of arrivals in the } k\text{-th CRI} = n]\frac{(\lambda i)^n e^{-\lambda i}}{n!}$$

$$= \sum_{n=0}^{\infty} E[\tilde{B}(k+1)|\tilde{B}(k)=i, n \text{ packets transmitted at start of } \tilde{B}(k+1)]\frac{(\lambda i)^n e^{-\lambda i}}{n!}$$

$$= \sum_{n=0}^{\infty} E[\tilde{B}(k+1)| n \text{ packets transmitted at start of } \tilde{B}(k+1)]\frac{(\lambda i)^n e^{-\lambda i}}{n!}$$

$$= \sum_{n=0}^{\infty} B_n \frac{(\lambda i)^n e^{-\lambda i}}{n!} \tag{5.25}$$

where B_n is the expected length (in slots) of a CRI given that it started with a collision among n packets and λ is the expected number of packets that arrive to the system in a slot. In (5.25) we used the fact that the distribution of the length of a CRI, given that it starts with the transmission of n packets, does not depend on the length of the previous CRI, and that the arrival process is Poisson.

In the previous section we have shown that B_n is finite for $n \geq 0$ and, moreover, is bounded by

$$B_n \leq \alpha n + 1 \qquad n \geq 0 \tag{5.26}$$

where $\alpha = 2.886$. Substituting this bound in (5.25) we have

$$E[\bar{B}(k+1)\,|\,\bar{B}(k)=i] \le \sum_{n=0}^{\infty} (\alpha n + 1)\frac{(\lambda i)^n e^{-\lambda i}}{n!} = \alpha \lambda i + 1 \ .$$

Therefore

$$E[\bar{B}(k+1) - \bar{B}(k)\,|\,\bar{B}(k)=i]$$
$$= E[\bar{B}(k+1)\,|\,\bar{B}(k)=i] - E[\bar{B}(k)\,|\,\bar{B}(k)=i] \qquad (5.27)$$
$$= E[\bar{B}(k+1)\,|\,\bar{B}(k)=i] - i \le (\alpha\lambda - 1)i + 1 \ .$$

From (5.27) we see that conditions (a) and (b) of Pakes' Lemma hold if

$$\lambda < \frac{1}{\alpha} \ .$$

It follows then, that a sufficient condition for stability of the system is that λ, the arrival rate of new packets, be less than $1/\alpha$. Consequently, the system is stable for arrival rates that are smaller than 0.346 (packets per slot).

5.1.3. Bounds on Expected Packet Delay

Let $\bar{D}$ be the delay of a randomly chosen packet (a "tagged" packet), namely, the difference between its arrival time to the system and the time it is transmitted successfully. The purpose of this section is to show that the expected delay $D = E[\bar{D}]$ of a randomly chosen packet is finite when $\lambda < \alpha^{-1}$ where $\alpha^{-1} = 0.346$.

We already proved that the Markov chain $\{\bar{B}(k), k=0,1,2,\cdots\}$ is ergodic when $\lambda < \alpha^{-1}$. Let $\bar{A}(k)$ be the number of packets transmitted at the beginning of the kth CRI. We now show that the Markov chain $\{\bar{A}(k), k=0,1,2,\cdots\}$ is also ergodic when $\lambda < \alpha^{-1}$. Since the arrival process of new packets is Poisson we have

$$E[\bar{A}(k+1)\,|\,\bar{A}(k)=i] = \lambda B_i \qquad (5.28)$$

and therefore,

$$E[\bar{A}(k+1) - \bar{A}(k)\,|\,\bar{A}(k)=i] = \lambda B_i - i \le (\lambda\alpha - 1)i - \lambda \ .$$

Testing conditions (a) and (b) of Pakes' Lemma for the chain $\{\bar{A}(k), k=0,1,2,\cdots\}$ we conclude that it is ergodic when $\lambda < \alpha^{-1}$.

Being ergodic Markov chains, steady-state distributions of $\bar{B}(k)$ and $\bar{A}(k)$ exist. Let $\bar{B}$ denote the length of a CRI in steady-state and let B and $\overline{B^2}$ be the first and second moments of $\bar{B}$, respectively, namely, $B = E[\bar{B}]$ and $\overline{B^2} = E[(\bar{B})^2]$. Similarly, let $\bar{A}$ denote the number of packets transmitted at the beginning of a CRI in steady-state and let A and $\overline{A^2}$ be the first and second moments of $\bar{A}$, namely, $A = E[\bar{A}]$ and $\overline{A^2} = E[(\bar{A})^2]$. From (5.28) we see that $A = \lambda B$. In addition we have that

$$E[(\bar{A}(k+1))^2\,|\,\bar{B}(k)=l] = \lambda l + (\lambda l)^2$$

which implies

$$\overline{A^2} = \lambda B + \lambda^2 \overline{B^2} = A + \lambda^2 \overline{B^2} . \tag{5.29}$$

Let $\vec{B}^{(a)}$ denote the length of the CRI in progress when the tagged packet arrives at the system and let $\vec{B}^{(d)}$ be the length of the subsequent CRI during which the tagged packet departs from the system. Then

$$D \le E[\vec{B}^{(a)}] + E[\vec{B}^{(d)}] \tag{5.30}$$

since at the earliest the tagged packet arrives at the beginning of the interval whose length is $\vec{B}^{(a)}$ and at the latest it will be transmitted successfully at the end of the next interval whose length is $\vec{B}^{(d)}$.

Let $\vec{A}^{(d)}$ be the number of packets transmitted in steady-state at the beginning of the CRI in which the packet leaves the system. By definition,

$$E[\vec{B}^{(d)} \mid \vec{A}^{(d)} = n] = B_n$$

and therefore with the help of (5.18),

$$E[\vec{B}^{(d)} \mid \vec{A}^{(d)} = n] \le \alpha n + 1$$

where $\alpha = 2.886$. Unconditioning with respect to $\vec{A}^{(d)}$, we obtain

$$E[\vec{B}^{(d)}] \le \alpha E[\vec{A}^{(d)}] + 1 . \tag{5.31}$$

Similarly to (5.28) we have

$$E[\vec{A}^{(d)}] = \lambda E[\vec{B}^{(a)}] . \tag{5.32}$$

Combining (5.30), (5.31) and (5.32) we have

$$D \le (1 + \lambda\alpha)E[\vec{B}^{(a)}] + 1 .$$

Lastly, the residual life theorem states that (see Appendix)

$$E[\vec{B}^{(a)}] = \frac{\overline{B^2}}{B}$$

and since $B \ge 1$ we have

$$D \le (1 + \lambda\alpha)\overline{B^2} + 1 \tag{5.33}$$

and therefore we only have to bound $\overline{B^2}$ in order to bound D.

We have that

$$\overline{B^2} = E[(\vec{B})^2] = \sum_{n=0}^{\infty} E[(\vec{B})^2 | \vec{A} = n] Prob[\vec{A} = n]$$

$$= \sum_{n=0}^{\infty} V_n Prob[\vec{A} = n] \le \sum_{n=0}^{\infty} (\alpha^2 n^2 + 1) Prob[\vec{A} = n] = \alpha^2 \overline{A^2} + 1 . \tag{5.34}$$

The above along with (5.29) implies that

$$\overline{B^2} \le \alpha^2(A + \lambda^2\overline{B^2}) + 1$$

and since $\lambda < \alpha^{-1}$ we have

$$\overline{B^2} \le \frac{\alpha^2 A + 1}{1 - \lambda^2\alpha^2} \, .$$

Substituting the above result in (5.33) we obtain

$$D \le (1 + \lambda\alpha)\frac{\alpha^2 A + 1}{1 - \lambda^2\alpha^2} + 1 = \frac{\alpha^2 A + 1}{1 - \lambda\alpha} + 1 = \frac{\alpha^2\lambda B + 1}{1 - \lambda\alpha} + 1 \qquad (5.35)$$

where we used the fact that $A = \lambda B$.

Similarly to (5.34) and using (5.18) we have

$$B = E[\vec{B}] = \sum_{n=0}^{\infty} E[\vec{B} \mid \vec{A} = n]Prob[\vec{A} = n] = \sum_{n=0}^{\infty} B_n Prob[\vec{A} = n]$$

$$\le \sum_{n=0}^{\infty} (\alpha n + 1)Prob[\vec{A} = n] = \alpha A + 1 = \alpha\lambda B + 1$$

or

$$B \le \frac{1}{1 - \alpha\lambda} \, . \qquad (5.36)$$

Thus, substituting (5.36) in (5.35) we obtain

$$D \le \frac{\alpha^2\lambda + 1 - \alpha\lambda}{(1 - \lambda\alpha)^2} + 1 \, .$$

Therefore, we showed that when the system is stable, the expected delay of a packet is finite and an explicit upper bound for this quantity is given above.

5.2. ENHANCED PROTOCOLS

The performance of the binary-tree protocol can be improved in two ways. The first is to speed up the collision resolution process by avoiding certain, avoidable, collisions. The second is based on the observation (see Table 4.1) that collisions among a small number of packets are resolved more efficiently than collisions among a large number of packets (compare the ratio n/B_n for small n and for large n). Therefore, if most CRIs start with a small number of packets, the performance of the protocol is expected to improve. These ideas are the basis of the protocols presented in this section.

5.2.1. The Modified Binary-Tree Protocol

Consider again the example depicted in Figure 5.1. In slots 2 and 3 a collision is followed by an idle slot. This implies that in slot 2 all users (and there were at least two of them) flipped 1. The binary-tree protocol dictates that these users must transmit in slot 4, although it is obvious that this will generate a collision that can be avoided. The modified binary-tree protocol is due to Massey [Mas81] and it eliminates such avoidable collisions by letting the users that flipped 1 in slot 2 in the example above, flip coins before transmitting is slot 4. Consequently, the slot in which an avoidable collision would occur is skipped and the evolution of the protocol for the same example of Section 5.1 is depicted in Figure 5.3. Except for eliminating these avoidable collisions, the modified binary-tree protocol evolves exactly as the binary-tree protocol. Note that the correct operation of the modified binary-tree protocol requires ternary feedback, i.e., the users have to be able to distinguish between idle and successful slots.

The analysis of the modified binary-tree protocol is essentially the same as that of the binary-tree protocol. We have

$$\tilde{B}_0 = \tilde{B}_1 = 1$$

and given that a CRI starts with a collision of n ($n \geq 2$) packets and that i users flip 0, the conditional length of the CRI is given by

$$\tilde{B}_{n \mid i} = \begin{cases} 1 + \tilde{B}_i + \tilde{B}_{n-i} & 1 \leq i \leq n \\ 1 + \tilde{B}_n & i = 0 \end{cases}$$

which accommodates for the saving of one slot when no users flip 0 ($i = 0$).

The procedure of determining the expected length of a CRI given that it starts with a collision among n users is entirely analogous to the derivation in the previous section. The equation analogous to (5.6) is,

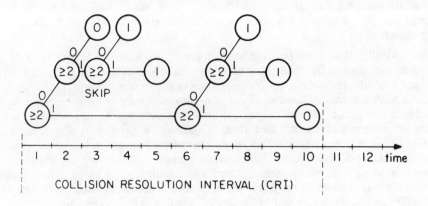

Figure 5.3: Example of the Modified Binary-Tree Protocol Operation

$$B_n = \frac{1 - Q_0(n) + \sum_{i=0}^{n-1}[Q_i(n) + Q_{n-i}(n)]B_i}{1 - Q_0(n) - Q_n(n)} \qquad n \geq 2$$

with the initial values $B_0 = B_1 = 1$.

The equation analogous to (5.12) is,

$$B_n = 1 + \sum_{k=2}^{n} \binom{n}{k} \frac{(-1)^k[k(1+p) - 1 - p^k]}{[1 - p^k - (1-p)^k]} \qquad n \geq 2 . \qquad (5.37)$$

In this case, however, the B_n are not minimized for $p = \frac{1}{2}$. Moreover, there is no single value of p that minimizes all the B_n. If we choose $p = \frac{1}{2}$, we can establish an upper bound on B_n of the form (5.13) with $\alpha_m = 2.664$, while if we use $p = 0.4175$, we can establish an upper bound on B_n with $\alpha_m = 2.623$. This implies that when the modified binary-tree protocol is employed with fair coins, then the system is stable for arrival rates up to $1/2.664 \cong 0.375$ while if biased coins are used, then the system is stable for arrival rates up to $1/2.623 \cong 0.381$ which is higher than e^{-1}--the maximal throughput of the slotted Aloha protocol.

5.2.2. The Epoch Mechanism

From Table 4.1 we see that $1/B_1 = 1$, $2/B_2 = 0.4$, $3/B_3 = 0.3913$ and when n is large (5.17) and (5.24) imply that $n/B_n \cong 0.346$. The conclusion is that the binary-tree protocol resolves collisions among a small number of packets more efficiently than among a large number of packets. When obvious access is employed, it is very likely that a CRI will start with a collision among a large number of packets when the previous CRI was long. When the system operates near its maximal throughput most CRIs are long, hence, collisions among a large number of packets have to be resolved frequently, yielding non efficient operation.

Ideally, if it were possible to start each CRI with the transmission of exactly one packet, the throughput of the system would have been 1. Since this is not possible, one should try to design the system so that in most cases a CRI starts with the transmission of about one packet. There are several ways to achieve this goal by determining a first-time transmission rule, i.e., when packets are transmitted for the first time. One way, suggested by Capetanakis [Cap79], is to have an estimate on the number of packets that arrived in the previous CRI and divide them into smaller groups, each having an expected number of packets on the order of one and handling each group separately. Another way, known as the *epoch mechanism* has been suggested by Gallager [Gal78] and by Tsybakov and Mikhailov [TsM80], and is described next.

Consider the arrivals of packets to the system and divide the time axis into consecutive epochs (called the arrival epochs), each of length Δ slots (Δ is not necessarily an integer). The ith arrival epoch is the time interval $(i\Delta, (i+1)\Delta)$. Packets that arrive during the ith arrival epoch are transmitted for the first time in the first slot after the collision among packets that arrived during the $(i-1)$st arrival epoch is resolved. The parameter Δ is chosen to optimize the performance of the system. The operation of the epoch mechanism is illustrated in Figure 5.4. On the channel we observe a sequence of collision resolution intervals each corresponding to arrivals during some time interval on the arrival axis. If we number these collision resolution intervals sequentially then in the ith CRI all packets (if any) that arrive during the ith epoch are successfully transmitted. All the packets arriving in the 0-th epoch, i.e., in the period $(0,\Delta)$ are transmitted in the first slot of CRI-0; they collide, and a resolution process starts (see Figure 5.4). In the meantime, newly arrived packets wait and when CRI-0 ends all packets belonging to the first epoch, i.e., those arriving in the period $(\Delta,2\Delta)$, are transmitted, and so on. An interesting phenomenon occurs at the end of CRI-2 in our example, since the CRI-2 ended before the third epoch. There are two options at this point (corresponding to two different protocols): one could shorten the third arrival epoch to match the end of CRI-2 or, as is shown in the figure (and analyzed in this section), enter a waiting period lasting from the end of CRI-2 to the end of the third epoch. It turns out that throughput in both cases is the same although the average delay in the latter method is slightly higher (see Huang and Berger [HuB85]).

When the epoch mechanism is employed as the first-time transmission rule, it is possible to describe the binary-tree protocol via interval splitting. Whenever the transmission of packets that arrive during some interval results in a collision, the interval is split in two. The users whose messages arrived in the left part correspond to users that would have flipped 0 in the binary-tree protocol and the users whose messages arrived in the right part correspond to users that would have flipped 1. In this way, it is guaranteed that packets are transmitted in the order they arrive (FCFS). The example of Section 5.1 is depicted again in Figure 5.5 to demonstrate the interval splitting procedure. Slot number 1 is the first slot of a CRI whose corresponding arrival epoch is the period (a,g) in the figure; thus all packets that arrived during (a,g) are transmitted in slot 1. Since a collision occurred one needs to split the group but instead of flipping a coin we split the interval in two halves: all those users whose messages arrived

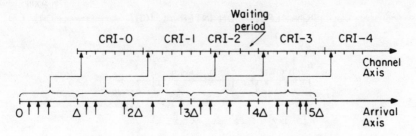

Figure 5.4: Example of the Epoch Mechanism

during (a,d) behave as if they flipped 0 while all those whose message arrived during (d,g) behave as if they flipped 1. This results in another collision in slot 2, requiring further splitting of the interval (a,d) so that in slot 3 transmit those users whose message arrived during (a,b)--none in our example. This causes packets that arrived during (b,d) to be transmitted in slot 4, and so on. Note that the probability p that a user flips 0 corresponds here to the interval splitting ratio. Thus, when $p = \frac{1}{2}$ the interval is halved, and when $p = 0.3$ the left part of the split interval is 0.3 times the length of the original interval.

We now turn to evaluate the performance of this protocol. Since the arrival process is Poisson the arrival points in every given interval are uniformly distributed. Thus, splitting an interval is completely equivalent to flipping a coin. This means that the values B_n and V_n are identical to those of the binary-tree CRP. The main difference lies in the region of stable throughput.

When the epoch mechanism is employed as the first-time transmission rule, there are no statistical dependencies among the corresponding collision resolution intervals. If $\tilde{A}(k)$ denotes the number of new packets that are transmitted at the beginning of the kth CRI, then $\tilde{A}(0), \tilde{A}(1), \tilde{A}(2), \cdots$ is a sequence of independent and identically distributed (i.i.d.) random variables. Since the length of the kth CRI is completely determined by the number of packets transmitted in its first slot, we conclude that the sequence $\tilde{B}(0), \tilde{B}(1),$

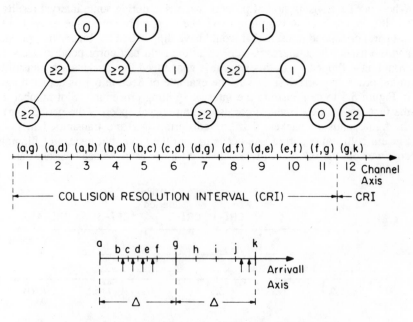

Figure 5.5: Interval-Splitting Procedure for the Epoch Mechanism

$\tilde{B}(2)$, $\cdots$ is also a sequence of independent and identically distributed random variables. Let $\tilde{A}$ and $\tilde{B}$ denote an arbitrary pair $\tilde{A}(k)$ and $\tilde{B}(k)$. Since the arrival process is Poisson, we have

$$Prob\,[\tilde{A} = n] = \frac{(\lambda\Delta)^n e^{-\lambda\Delta}}{n!} \ .$$

Also,

$$Prob\,[\tilde{B} = i] = \sum_{n=0}^{\infty} Prob\,[\tilde{B} = i\,|\,\tilde{A} = n\,]Prob\,[\tilde{A} = n\,]$$

$$= \sum_{n=0}^{\infty} Prob\,[\tilde{B}_n = i]Prob\,[\tilde{A} = n\,] \qquad i \geq 1$$

from which we obtain,

$$B = E[\tilde{B}] = \sum_{n=0}^{\infty} B_n Prob\,[\tilde{A} = n\,] \ ; \qquad \overline{B^2} = E[\tilde{B}^2] = \sum_{n=0}^{\infty} V_n Prob\,[\tilde{A} = n\,]$$

where B_n and V_n are given by (5.6) and (5.11), respectively.

The system can be viewed as a (discrete-time) queueing system in which packets that arrive during the interval $(i\Delta,(i+1)\Delta)$ are served in the ith CRI. The total service time of these arrivals has a first and a second moment B and B^2, respectively. In order for the "server" not to fall behind the arrivals we need that

$$B < \Delta \qquad\qquad\qquad\qquad (5.38)$$

or in other words, the time it takes, on the average, to successfully transmit all packets that arrive in a period of duration Δ must be less than Δ. The quantity $B - \Delta$ is the expected change in the time backlog of the system, namely the expected change in the difference between the current time and the time of the last epoch whose packets were transmitted successfully. When condition (5.38) holds, the system is stable, and if $\overline{B^2}$ is finite, the expected delay of a packet is finite.

Condition (5.38) can be written as:

$$\sum_{n=0}^{\infty} B_n \frac{(\lambda\Delta)^n e^{-\lambda\Delta}}{n!} < \Delta$$

and rewritten as:

$$\lambda < \frac{\lambda\Delta}{\displaystyle\sum_{n=0}^{\infty} B_n \frac{(\lambda\Delta)^n e^{-\lambda\Delta}}{n!}} = \frac{z}{\displaystyle\sum_{n=0}^{\infty} B_n \frac{z^n e^{-z}}{n!}} \triangleq f(z) \qquad (5.39)$$

where $z \triangleq \lambda\Delta$. The function $f(z)$ is depicted in Figure 5.6 for various values of p (recall that p is the probability that a user will flip 0 and it is equivalent to the splitting ratio of the interval when a collision is observed). For $p = \frac{1}{2}$ the function $f(z)$ is maximized for $z^* = 1.15$ and the maximum value is 0.429. Hence, the system is stable for arrival rates $\lambda < 0.429$. The maximal value of $f(z)$ is smaller for other values of p. The fact that $z^* = \lambda \Delta^* = 1.15$ is not surprising. It conforms with the intuition that most of the CRIs should start with the transmission of a single packet. The fact that z^* is slightly higher than 1 is due to the waste incurred by idle slots. The length Δ^* that should be chosen to obtain the maximal throughput is $\Delta^* = 1.15/0.429 = 2.68$. From Figure 5.6 we observe that the function $f(z)$ is not very sensitive to small changes in z, especially for values of z larger than z^*. The conclusion is that slightly longer epochs (slightly larger Δ) will not cause the maximal achievable throughput to deteriorate by a large amount.

The description and the analysis above corresponds to use of the epoch mechanism and resolving collisions as done in the binary-tree protocol. When the epoch mechanism is used with the modified binary-tree collision resolution protocol, the analysis is the same, except that in (5.39) one should use the values of B_n that correspond to this protocol (equation (5.37)). The results are as follows: When $p = \frac{1}{2}$ the system is stable for $\lambda < 0.462$ and when $p = 0.4175$ the system is stable for input rates up to $\lambda < 0.468$.

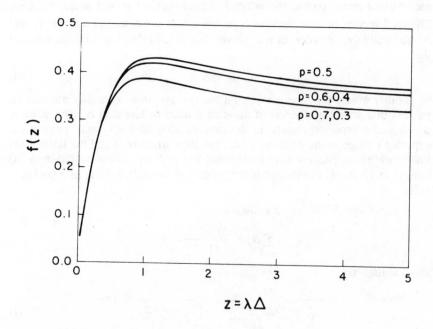

Figure 5.6: Determining Permissible Arrival Rates for the Epoch Mechanism

5.2.3. The Clipped Binary-Tree Protocol

In the previous analysis we made the point that to improve performance a CRI should start with the transmission of about one packet. However, that idea was not fully exploited by the above enhancements. To see why, assume that the epoch mechanism is employed and consider what happens when a collision is followed by another collision (see slots 1 and 2 in Figure 5.5). The collision in the first slot is among the packets that arrived during an interval of length Δ. The users whose packets collided are divided into two groups by splitting the interval into two parts (for explanation purposes we assume $p = \frac{1}{2}$ so the length of either of the two parts equals $\Delta/2$). The packets that arrived in the left part are then transmitted in slot 2 and collide again. By repeated interval splitting all packets in the left part are eventually successfully transmitted (slot 6 in our example). At this point the packets that arrived during the right part of the original interval are transmitted. It is at this point that we have not done as best we can. The underlying observation is that there is no information regarding the number of packets in the part we attempt to resolve, yet the expected number of arrivals during that period is different from the desired quantity, namely, slightly larger than one. Indeed, if the distribution of the number of packets in that part is as that of new packets i.e., Poisson with parameter λ, then the transmission of packets in that part is identical to starting a CRI with half the optimal expected number of packets. To remedy this, it would be better to choose a new interval of length Δ and let packets that arrived in this interval transmit. Protocols based on this observation have been suggested by Gallager [Gal80] and Tsybakov and Mikhailov [TsM80].

To incorporate this strategy into the protocol we adopt the rule that whenever a collision is followed by two successive successful transmissions, a new epoch of length Δ from the arrival axis is enabled, that is, the packets that arrived in that interval are transmitted. The protocol that results from such an operation will be called the *clipped binary-tree protocol*, since part of the binary-tree is clipped and not enabled (see Figure 5.7). One might add that the clipping idea can be used with the original binary-tree protocol (Section 5.1) as well as the modified one (Section 5.2.1), i.e., the one that avoids transmission of packets that are guaranteed to collide (the latter is called the *modified clipped binary tree protocol*). The example of Sec. 5.1 is depicted in Figure 5.7 when the clipped binary-tree protocol is employed. Note that in slot 7 a new CRI is started, corresponding to the arrival epoch (d,i), rather than enabling the interval (d,f) as would be the case in the regular epoch mechanism. In the modified clipped binary-tree protocol the collision in slot 3 will be avoided (skipped) as was the case in the example depicted in Figure 5.3.

The argument that leads to the enhancement described above is based on the assertion that the distribution of the number of packets in the right part of the interval is the same as that of the newly arrived ones i.e., those that arrived in the part of the arrival axis that was never explored. This assertion is not as trivial as it first appears, since after receiving the feedback indicating that a collision took place, it is not clear that the distribution of the right part remains Poisson with the same parameter as before. To show this property, let $\tilde{x}$ be the

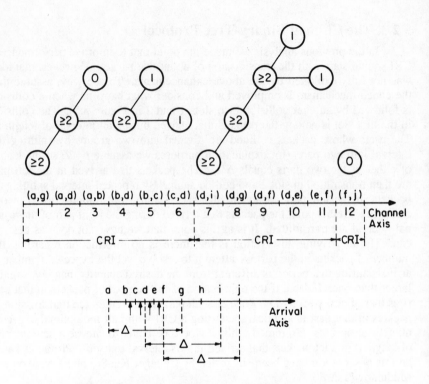

Figure 5.7: Example of the Clipped Binary-Tree Protocol Operation

number of packets involved in the first collision and let $\bar{x}_l$ and $\bar{x}_r$ be the number of packets in the left part and the right part of the interval, respectively. We need to show that if it is known that $\bar{x} = \bar{x}_l + \bar{x}_r \geq 2$ and $\bar{x}_l \geq 2$ then the distribution of $\bar{x}_r$ is Poisson. We compute

$$Prob\,[\bar{x}_r = i \mid \bar{x}_l + \bar{x}_r \geq 2\,,\,\bar{x}_l \geq 2] = Prob\,[\bar{x}_r = i \mid \bar{x}_r \geq 0\,,\,\bar{x}_l \geq 2]$$

$$= Prob\,[\bar{x}_r = i \mid \bar{x}_l \geq 2] = Prob\,[\bar{x}_r = i] = \frac{(\lambda\Delta/2)^i\, e^{-\lambda\Delta/2}}{i!}$$

where we used the fact that $\bar{x}_r$ and $\bar{x}_l$ are independent, a result stemming from the known property of the Poisson process that the number of events in nonoverlapping intervals are independent. Generally, receiving the collision feedback, results in a non-Poisson distribution of the number of colliding packets; but, receiving the additional feedback of a collision in the left part of the interval means that the number of packets that arrived in the right part is greater or equal to zero--information we had to start with--meaning that we have the same Poisson distribution.

The analysis of the clipped binary-tree protocol is similar to that of the binary-tree protocol. We present the analysis for the modified clipped binary-tree (see Section 5.2.1) in which definite collisions, i.e., those that can be predicted beforehand, are avoided. Denote, as before, by $\bar{B}_n$ the length of the collision resolution interval that starts with a collision of n packets and by $\tilde{B}_{n\,|\,i}$ the length of the collision resolution interval that starts with a collision of n packets, i of which arrived in its left part, and by B_n and $B_{n\,|\,i}$ their respective expected values. For $n=0$ and $n=1$ we have

$$\tilde{B}_0 = \tilde{B}_1 = 1 .$$

Consider a CRI that starts with a collision of n $(n \geq 2)$ packets, i of which arrived in the left part and $n-i$ in the right part $(0 \leq i \leq n)$. If $i=0$ then the length of the CRI will include the original collision slot followed by the need to still resolve the collision among all n packets. If $i=1$ then the CRI includes the original collision slot, the successful slot for the left part, and then the number of slots needed to resolve the collision among the remaining $n-1$ packets. Finally, when $2 \leq i \leq n$ the CRI includes the original collision slot and then the number of slots needed to resolve the the collision among the i packets that arrived in the left part. Note that in the latter case (that is unique to the clipped tree protocol) the resolution of the remaining $n-i$ packets is not a part of the current CRI. The conditional length of a CRI for the clipped binary-tree protocol can therefore be summarized by:

$$\tilde{B}_{n\,|\,i} = \begin{cases} 1 + \tilde{B}_i & 2 \leq i \leq n \\ 2 + \tilde{B}_{n-1} & i = 1 \\ 1 + \tilde{B}_n & i = 0 \end{cases}$$

and correspondingly the expected values are

$$B_{n\,|\,i} = \begin{cases} 1 + B_i & 2 \leq i \leq n \\ 2 + B_{n-1} & i = 1 \\ 1 + B_n & i = 0 . \end{cases} \tag{5.40}$$

Denoting, as before, by $Q_i(n)$ the probability that in an interval containing n arrivals i occurred in its left part, we can write, based on equation (5.40), an expression for B_n:

$$B_n = E[B_{n\,|\,i}] = \sum_{i=0}^{n} B_{n\,|\,i} Q_i(n)$$

$$= 1 + Q_0(n)B_n + Q_1(n)(1 + B_{n-1}) + \sum_{i=2}^{n} Q_i(n)B_i \qquad n \geq 2$$

or

$$B_n = \frac{1 + Q_1(n)(1 + B_{n-1}) + \sum_{i=2}^{n-1} Q_i(n)B_i}{1 - Q_0(n) - Q_n(n)} \qquad n \geq 2 . \tag{5.41}$$

The quantity B_n can be computed recursively from (5.41) with the initial values $B_0 = B_1 = 1$.

With the clipped binary-tree protocol not all packets that collide in the first slot of a CRI are successfully transmitted during that CRI (since part of the tree is clipped). For instance, in the example depicted in Figure 5.7, during the CRI that starts with a collision among four packets, only two packets are transmitted successfully (the rest will be part of the next CRI). To evaluate the performance of the protocol, one must compute the rate of successful transmissions during a CRI. To that end, let $\tilde{U}_n$ be a random variable representing the number of packets that are successfully transmitted during a CRI given that it started with the transmission of n packets and $\tilde{U}_{n\,|\,i}$ be the same variable conditioned on having i packets in the left part, and by U_n and $U_{n\,|\,i}$ their respective expected values. For $n=0$ and $n=1$ we have

$$U_0 = 0 \qquad U_1 = 1$$

and for $n \geq 2$, similarly to equation (5.40), we have

$$U_{n\,|\,i} = \begin{cases} U_i & 2 \leq i \leq n \\ 1 + U_{n-1} & i = 1 \\ U_n & i = 0 \ . \end{cases} \qquad (5.42)$$

Leading to

$$U_n = Q_0(n)U_n + Q_1(n)(1 + U_{n-1}) + \sum_{i=2}^{n} Q_i(n)U_i \qquad n \geq 2$$

or

$$U_n = \frac{Q_1(n)(1 + U_{n-1}) + \sum_{i=2}^{n-1} Q_i(n)U_i}{1 - Q_0(n) - Q_n(n)} \qquad n \geq 2 \qquad (5.43)$$

and U_n can be computed recursively from (5.43) with the initial values $U_0 = 0$ and $U_1 = 1$.

Values of B_n and U_n are given in Table 4.3 for $p = \frac{1}{2}$. It is interesting to note the slow growth of B_n with n compared to the almost linear growth of B_n with n when the binary-tree protocol is employed (see Table 4.1). In addition, observe that the expected number of packets transmitted successfully during a CRI is almost a constant for $n \geq 3$.

The expected length of a CRI, B, and the expected number of packets that are successfully transmitted during a CRI, U, are given by

$$B = E[B_n] = \sum_{n=0}^{\infty} B_n \frac{(\lambda\Delta)^n e^{-\lambda\Delta}}{n!} \ , \qquad (5.44)$$

$$U = E[U_n] = \sum_{n=0}^{\infty} U_n \frac{(\lambda\Delta)^n e^{-\lambda\Delta}}{n!} \ .$$

The expected number of packets transmitted in the first slot of a CRI is $\lambda\Delta$ and

n	0	1	2	3	4
B_n	1.0000	1.0000	4.0000	5.8333	6.4762
U_n	0.0000	1.0000	2.0000	2.5000	2.5714
n	6	7	8	9	10
B_n	6.8363	7.0286	7.2180	7.3894	7.5406
U_n	2.4977	2.4958	2.5008	2.5052	2.5075
n	11	12	13	14	15
B_n	7.6741	7.7937	7.9027	8.0035	8.0980
U_n	2.5079	2.5073	2.5064	2.5055	2.5049

Table 4.3: The first moment of $\bar{B}_n$ and $\bar{U}_n$ for $p = \frac{1}{2}$.

therefore the fraction of packets successfully transmitted during a CRI is $U/\lambda\Delta$. The Poisson process has an interesting property that given a number of arrivals in an interval, the arrival points are uniformly distributed in the interval. Consequently, if a fraction $U/\lambda\Delta$ of the packets are successfully transmitted it means that $U/\lambda\Delta$ is also the fraction of the interval resolved. Hence, $(U/\lambda\Delta)\Delta = U/\lambda$ is, on the average, the portion of the resolved interval measured in slots. On the other hand, on the average, it takes B slots to resolve a collision. Thus, for the system to remain stable, it must be able to resolve collisions at least at the rate in which time progresses, or

$$B < U/\lambda$$

which, upon substitution of equation (5.44) leads to

$$\lambda < \frac{\displaystyle\sum_{n=0}^{\infty} U_n \frac{(\lambda\Delta)^n e^{-\lambda\Delta}}{n!}}{\displaystyle\sum_{n=0}^{\infty} B_n \frac{(\lambda\Delta)^n e^{-\lambda\Delta}}{n!}} = \frac{\displaystyle\sum_{n=0}^{\infty} U_n \frac{z^n e^{-z}}{n!}}{\displaystyle\sum_{n=0}^{\infty} B_n \frac{z^n e^{-z}}{n!}} \tag{5.45}$$

where we have substituted $z \triangleq \lambda\Delta$. The right handside is a function of z (with parameter p). For a given p this function can be plotted (the curves obtained are similar to those in Figure 5.6) and its maximal value found. For $p = \frac{1}{2}$ the right side of (5.45) is maximized for $z = 1.26$ and the maximum value is 0.487 packets/slot. Thus, the system is stable for arrival rates $\lambda < 0.487$ and the length Δ that should be chosen is $\Delta = 1.26/0.487 = 2.60$ slots. When the splitting probability p is optimized it is possible to slightly increase the throughput to 0.4877 as was demonstrated by Mosley and Humblet [MoH85].

The analysis presented above was carried out for the modified clipped binary-tree protocol, i.e., avoidable collisions are eliminated. When the modification is not used, the only change in the analysis is the addition of $Q_0(n)$

to the numerator of equation (5.41), and the resulting maximal throughput is 0.449.

5.3. LIMITED SENSING PROTOCOLS

The protocols described so far require every user to monitor the channel feedback at all times, even if that user has no packet to transmit. This is necessary because a newly generated packet can be transmitted for the first time only at the end of the current CRI, requiring every user to positively determine the end of the CRI. This kind of feedback monitoring is known as *full-sensing*. This mode of operation is quite impractical because a user that crashed can never again join the system and, furthermore, a user that due to some fault did not receive properly all signals may actually disturb the others and decrease the efficiency of the protocol. Thus, it is desirable that users monitor the feedback signals only during limited periods, preferably after having generated a packet for transmission and until the packet is transmitted successfully. This kind of monitoring is known as *limited-sensing*, and protocols with such monitoring are referred to as protocols operating in a limited sensing environment.

Several collision resolution protocols have been devised for the limited-sensing environment. The simplest, albeit not the most efficient one, is the *free-access* protocol analyzed by Mathys and Flajolet [MaF83] and by Fayolle et. al. [FFH85]. In this protocol, new packets are transmitted as soon as possible, i.e., at the beginning of the slot subsequent to their arrival time; thereafter, a user that transmitted a new packet monitors the feedback signals and continues operating as if he were an "old" user. This protocol works in conjunction with both the basic binary-tree protocol (see Section 5.1) or the modified binary-tree protocol (see Section 5.2.1). The maximal throughput of this limited sensing protocol when the modified binary-tree protocol is employed is 0.360.

To date, the most efficient protocol for a limited-sensing environment is the one introduced by Humblet [Humb86] and Georgiadis and Papantoni-Kazakos [GeK87] which is essentially an adaptation of the (full-sensing) modified clipped binary-tree protocol described in Section 5.2.3. As mentioned earlier, a crucial feature required for the correct operation of the full sensing protocols is the ability of all users to determine the end of a CRI. This is necessary so that users with new packets know exactly when they may transmit for the first time in a manner that would not interfere with an ongoing resolution of a collision. The major change involved in the adaptation of the clipped binary-tree protocol to the limited sensing environment is therefore controlling the extent of CRIs so that their end remains uniquely and easily detectable. As before, newly generated packets are not considered for transmission until the ongoing collision resolution is done (and all waiting users receive sufficient feedback to detect the end of a CRI). A collision feedback obviously indicates that a CRI is in progress; the difficulty is to realize whether or not a collision resolution is in progress when a series of idle and successful slots is observed, and then to detect the end of a CRI.

Going back to the clipped binary-tree protocol described in Section 5.2.3, we recall that the end of a CRI that started with a collision is characterized by two consecutive successful slots. In addition, there are CRIs that consist of a single slot, either an idle one or a successful one. Thus, if we have a successful slot followed by either an idle slot or another successful slot, we are assured that a CRI just ended. We take this event to be the end-of-CRI marker, that is, a successful slot followed immediately by an idle slot or another successful slot denotes the end of the CRI. Such marking is, however, not enough. Observing the channel once the system becomes idle with no user having a new packet to transmit, reveals a sequence of idle slots. A user generating a new packet at this state will wait forever for the end-of-CRI marker. To overcome this potential deadlock, the end-of-CRI marker is augmented to include an event consisting of $R+1$ idle slots, where R is a globally known protocol parameter. Thus, a user that observes $R+1$ consecutive idle slots concludes that a CRI ended. This indication of the end of a CRI is correct only if $R+1$ consecutive idle slots never occur during an actual resolution of a collision. Yet, in the modified clipped binary-tree protocol, such an event is possible since the protocol dictates to avoid definite collisions, i.e., those that are guaranteed to occur. Consequently, in the limited sensing environment, we avoid definite collisions at most $R-1$ times in succession. Users that participate in a collision resolution and observe R consecutive idle slots, retransmit in the next slot to cause a collision, and continue regularly thereafter. In summary, a user that generates a new packet at some slot will be able to decide whether or not a CRI is in progress within at most $R+1$ slots and if he finds out that a CRI is in progress, he will be able to determine its end.

There is a clear performance tradeoff in the choice of R. A large value for R may cause a packet arriving to an idle system to wait quite long before it can determine that the system is idle, but it will eliminate more definite collisions. A small value for R requires fairly often to retransmit a packet unnecessarily, only to announce an ongoing CRI, but the delay incurred by a new packet upon arrival to an idle system will be small. Observe that the case $R=1$ corresponds to elimination of the modification introduced in Section 5.2.1, while when R is very large, the protocol is similar to the clipped binary-tree protocol.

To complete the specification of the protocol, we must define the behavior of the users involved in the resolution process. One of the rules has already been defined, and requires a participating user to retransmit his packet after having sensed R consecutive idle slots. The other rules define the exact transmission schedules and are similar to the rules of the clipped binary-tree protocol, namely, upon detection of the end of a CRI, a new epoch is chosen and packets that arrived during this epoch are transmitted; upon a collision the epoch is split in two, and so forth. To describe how new epochs are chosen and how epochs are split we note that at each point in time all users having packets awaiting transmission, both the newly arrived and the old, nontransmitted, ones can be divided into three classes. Class A contains those users that cannot decide thus far whether or not some CRI is in progress. Class B contains those users that definitely know a CRI is in progress (they heard a collision feedback) but do not know when it started. Class C contains those users that know a CRI is in progress as well as the time it started. While all users in class C can simultaneously decide which epoch will be chosen for transmission, those in classes A and B cannot. The beginning of the CRI is not known to the users since they start monitoring the channel only upon a packet arrival meaning that the only common time reference is the end of the CRI (which is known to all class C users). Since it is desirable to select an initial epoch whose length is optimal we select it so that its *end* coincides with the latest class C slot. In other words, the protocol in the limited sensing environment evolves in such a way that the epochs for transmission are chosen so that the most recent arrivals belonging to class C attempt transmission first. In this sense the protocol is a last-come first-served protocol.

Figure 5.8 presents seven snapshots, taken at seven consecutive slots, of a system with $R = 2$. Each snapshot is taken at the time marked CT (Current Time) and depicts the time axis starting at some time t_0, a moment for which all previously arrived packets have already left. The up-arrows indicate arrival instants of packets, the numbers are packet numbers used for explanation, and the feedback for the slot starting at CT is shown above the axis ('0' = idle, '1' = success, '≥2' = collision). Such a diagram is often called the arrival time-axis diagram.

Figure 5.8(a) depicts the initial situation and shows the arrival times of the various classes. All but those users that generated packets in the last slot before CT belong to class C while those that arrived in the last slot belong to class A since they have not sensed a collision and cannot decide, based on a single slot, whether some activity is going on. At this time, a portion of the rightmost part of the class C time is enabled namely, packets that arrive during this transmission interval (marked TI in the figure) are transmitted, and a collision between packets 2 and 3 occurs. Users that previously belonged to class A have now sensed a collision and therefore belong to class B. The same applies to packet 4 that arrived during the most recent slot. This is depicted in snapshot (b).

At this point in time the rightmost half of the previous TI is enabled, and since it contains no packets an idle slot occurs and therefore it is concluded that the left part contains at least two packets and its rightmost half is enabled, as illustrated in Figure 5.8(c). Another idle slot occurs and it is concluded that the corresponding left part contains at least two packets. However, having sensed two idle slots in a system with $R = 2$ the entire left part of the previous TI is enabled, causing a (definite) collision as is illustrated in Figure 5.8(d). Note that the two idle slots, depicted in snapshots (b) and (c) do not increase the extent of class B users since two idle slots leave all users arriving during these slots in uncertainty--they have not sensed a collision and cannot determine whether or not the system is idle. Having sensed a collision (snapshot (d)) all class A users become class B users.

After the collision of snapshot (d), operation continues as before. The previously enabled interval is halved and packet 3 is transmitted successfully (snapshot (e)) after which packet 2 is transmitted successfully (snapshot (f)). At

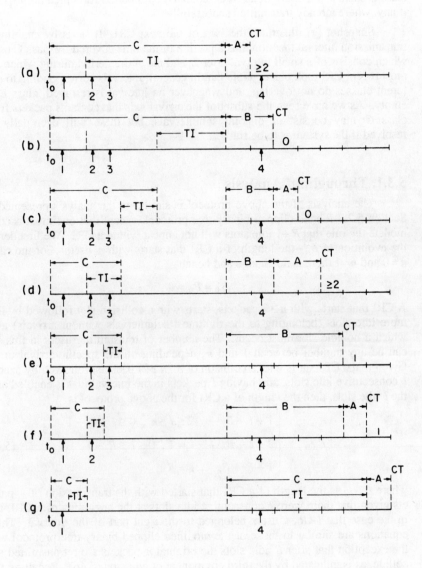

Figure 5.8: Enabled Intervals in Limited Sensing

this point two consecutive successful slots took place and an end-of-CRI marker is detected. All users but those arriving in the most recent slot join class C while those arriving in the most recent slot join class A (having sensed a single success they know the system is not idle). Note that the extent of time covered by class C users is not contiguous--it is separated by a period for which all arrivals, if any, where already transmitted successfully.

Snapshot (g) illustrates the start of the next CRI. It starts by enabling a transmission interval that contains a portion of the time covered by class C users which consists of a small interval after t_0 and the entire period during which the most recent CRI took place. Note that in general, intervals corresponding to different classes do not overlap, and whenever an interval is resolved, class B is empty. As we have seen the subset of the arrival axis that contains packets from class C may consist of disjoint subintervals, but these will eventually be resolved if the system is to be stable.

5.3.1. Throughput Analysis

The analysis of the above protocol is similar to the analysis presented in Section 5.2.3 for the clipped binary-tree protocol, except that one must accommodate the rule that $R+1$ idle slots will not appear within a CRI. We first derive the evolution of $\bar{B}_n$--the length of a CRI that starts with n users. For the cases $n=0$ and $n=1$ there is no change and hence

$$\bar{B}_0 = \bar{B}_1 = 1 .$$

A CRI that starts with $n \geq 2$ packets, starts with a collision slot followed by 0 or more idle slots (belonging to the rightmost subintervals without arrivals) after which a nonidle slot must occur. The number of transmitting users in this slot can be any number between 1 and n, depending on the specific arrival times. Given that a CRI starts with a collision of n $(n \geq 2)$ packets, followed by exactly l consecutive idle slots, and having i packets in the interval that is enabled after the l idle slots, then the length of a CRI for the above protocol is

$$\bar{B}_{n \mid i,l} = \begin{cases} 1 + l + \bar{B}_i & 2 \leq i \leq n , \ 0 \leq l \leq R - 1 \\ 2 + l + \bar{B}_{n-1} & i = 1 , \ 0 \leq l \leq R - 1 \\ 1 + R + \bar{B}_n & l = R \end{cases} \qquad (5.46)$$

where $\bar{B}_{n \mid i,l}$ is the length of a CRI that started with the transmission of n packets given that there were l consecutive idle slots at the beginning of a CRI, and in the case that $l < R$, i users belonged to the right part of the interval. These equations are similar to those of the modified clipped binary-tree protocol with the exception that after R idle slots the original n packets are retransmitted and collide, as is indicated by the third component of equation (5.46). Recalling that $Q_i(n)$ is the probability of i arrivals occurring during the right portion of the an interval containing n arrivals (see equation (5.2)) we obtain from (5.46) in the same manner as before

$$B_n = 1 + [Q_0(n)]^R (R + B_n)$$
$$+ \sum_{l=0}^{R-1} [Q_0(n)]^l \left[Q_1(n)(1 + l + B_{n-1}) + \sum_{i=2}^{n} Q_i(n)(l + B_i) \right] \qquad n \geq 2$$

or after some algebra we have for $n \geq 2$ that

$$B_n = \frac{1 - Q_0(n) + \left[1 - [Q_0(n)]^R \right] \left[Q_0(n) + Q_1(n)(1 + B_{n-1}) + \sum_{i=2}^{n-1} Q_i(n) B_i \right]}{\left[1 - [Q_0(n)]^R \right] \left[1 - Q_0(n) - Q_n(n) \right]}$$

and B_n is computed recursively from the above equation with the initial values $B_0 = B_1 = 1$.

The derivation of the expected number of packets transmitted successfully during a CRI is identical to that presented for the clipped binary-tree (see Section 5.2.3 equations (5.42) and (5.41)). The maximal throughput of the protocol is given by equation (5.44). When $R = 1$ the maximal throughput is 0.449--the same throughput obtained for the clipped binary-tree protocol (without the modification). When R is large (for that matter $R = 5$ is already large enough), the maximal throughput is 0.487, the same as the throughput for the full-sensing environment.

5.4. RELATED ANALYSIS

Numerous variations of the environment under which collision resolution protocols operate have been addressed in the literature and excellent surveys on the subject have been written by Gallager [Gal85] and Tsybakov [Tsy85]. Chapter 4 in Bertsekas and Gallager's book [BeG87] is also an excellent source on collision resolution protocols. We considered but a very small number of these variations: slotted time, infinite population, Poisson arrivals and reliable ternary feedback. In the following we list a few of the other variations.

Bounds on throughput

Considerable effort has been spent on finding upper bounds to the maximum throughput that can be achieved in an infinite population model with Poisson arrivals and ternary feedback [Pip81, Mol82, MiT81, CrH82, TML83, BeZ88]. The best upper bound known to-date is 0.568 and is due to Tsybakov and Likhanov [TsL88].

Feedback types

In the text we considered mainly the ternary feedback distinguishing among idle, successful and collision slots, and the binary feedback that informs the users only whether or not there was a conflict in the slot. There are two other binary feedback types that can be considered: (i) Something/Nothing feedback that informs the users whether or not a slot was idle; (ii) Success/Failure feedback that informs the users whether or not a slot contained exactly one packet. Collision resolution protocols for these binary feedback channels have been studied in [MeB84].

In some cases it might be possible to increase the amount of feedback detail by using an extra control channel for reservation [HuB85, ToV87], or by indicating the exact number of users involved in a collision. The latter information can be obtained by using energy or power detectors and this kind of feedback is termed *known multiplicity feedback* [Tsy80] and [GeP82].

When a packet is transmitted successfully it is possible to use the contents of the packet in the feedback in order to improve the performance of the CRP. A protocol that uses an extra bit that can be read only when a packet is transmitted successfully is presented in [KeS88].

Multiple access protocols without feedback have been considered in [TsL83, MaM85].

Noise errors, erasures and captures

Practical multiple access communication systems are prone to various types of errors. The most common are the *noise errors* that are intrinsic in any physical radio channel. Such errors cause the feedback to indicate a collision although no user or a single user transmitted. Another type of errors are *erasures*. These errors correspond to situations in which one or several nodes are transmitting, but the feedback detected by the users indicates that the slot was idle. Reasons for erasures in practical systems are mobile users that may occasionally be hidden (for example, because of physical obstacles) or because of fading problems. The *capture* phenomenon can also be considered as erroneous operation of the system, corresponding to the ability to receive a packet successfully although more than one packet is transmitted at the same time. Collision resolution protocols that operate in presence of noise errors, erasures and captures have been studied in [VvT83, SiC85, CiS85, CiS87, CKS88].

Group testing

Group testing, a branch of applied statistics, addresses the problem of classifying items of some population as either defective or non-defective. It has been discovered that group testing ideas and algorithms can be applied in the design of protocols, similar to the collision resolution protocols, for random access communication. The basic idea is that a defective item in the group testing problem corresponds to an active user in the communication problem and a non-defective item corresponds to an idle user. Collision resolution protocols based on group testing ideas have been developed in [BMT84] for a homogeneous population of users and in [KuS88] for a nonhomogeneous population of users.

General arrival processes

In the analysis of the collision resolution protocols it has been assumed that the arrival process of new packets to the system is a stationary Poisson process. Furthermore, some of the parameters of the protocols were carefully tuned, based on the Poisson assumption, to yield the best performance (the epoch length Δ, for instance). It is not difficult to realize, though, that the performance of some of the algorithms is not sensitive to the specific arrival process. For instance, the maximal throughput of the basic binary-tree protocol with the obvious access scheme is 0.346, independently of the arrival process. Collision resolution protocols yielding high throughputs for general arrival processes (even if their statistics are unknown) were developed in [GFL87] and [CiS88].

Delay analysis

Several delay analyses of collision resolution protocols appear in the literature. The expected packet delay of the binary-tree protocol has been derived in [TsM78, MaF85, FFH85]. Bounds on the expected packet delay of the clipped binary-tree with the epoch mechanism have been obtained in [TsM80, GMP87]. Other variations of delay analysis appear in [HuB85, PMV87].

EXERCISES

Problem 5.1

For the binary-tree protocol we found that (see eq. (5.12))

$$B_n = 1 + \sum_{k=2}^{n} \binom{n}{k} \frac{2(k-1)(-1)^k}{[1-p^k-(1-p)^k]} \qquad n \geq 2 .$$

For $p = \frac{1}{2}$ prove:

(a)

$$B_n = 3 + \sum_{k=2}^{n} \binom{n}{k} \frac{2(k-1)(-1)^k}{2^{k-1}-1} \qquad n \geq 2 .$$

(b)

$$B_n = B_{n-1} + 2(n-1)\sum_{k=1}^{\infty} 2^{-k}(1-2^{-k})^{n-2} \qquad n \geq 3 .$$

Problem 5.2

Prove equation (5.37) and determine the corresponding equation for V_n in this case.

Problem 5.3 (Noise errors)

Assume that the binary-tree protocol with the epoch mechanism is employed. Assume that the channel is noisy, so that an idle slot is interpreted as a collision with probability $\pi_{0,c}$ and a slot that contains a single transmission is interpreted as a collision with probability $\pi_{1,c}$ (in the latter event the user that transmitted has to retransmit his packet again according to the protocol). All error events are independent of each other and of the system state.

(a) Compute B_0, B_1 and write recursive relations for computing B_n, $n \geq 2$ for this system. What are the conditions on the error probabilities to insure that these quantities are finite?

(b) Write an expression for computing the throughput.

(c)   Let

$$B(z) \stackrel{\Delta}{=} \sum_{n=0}^{\infty} B_n \frac{z^n e^{-z}}{n!} .$$

Prove that

(i) $B(0) = B_0$; $\dfrac{dB(z)}{dz} \big|_{z=0} = B_1 - B_0$.

(ii) $B(z) - 2B(z/2) = 1 - (1+z)(1+B_0)e^{-z}$.

(iii) The optimal z that maximizes the throughput (z^*) does not depend on $\pi_{1,C}$. How would you explain this phenomenon?

(d)   For $\pi_{0,C} = \pi_{1,C} = 1/4$ determine z^* and the maximal throughput.

Problem 5.4 (Power capture [CKS88])

This problem deals with the capture phenomenon employing a model similar to that of Problem 3.4. As explained there a capture means receiving correctly a packet even when other packets are transmitted during the same time. The model used is typical to *power capture,* namely, that some nodes transmit with higher power than others.

When $n \geq 2$ users are transmitting in a slot, a capture occurs with probability $\pi_{n,1}$, namely, one of the n transmitted packets is successfully received and the other $n-1$ packets have to be retransmitted.

Assume that the users are executing the binary-tree protocol with the epoch mechanism. Also assume that when a transmission succeeds, the users are informed which packet was received correctly. The latter implies that the users transmitting during a slot that contained a capture, know of that event (but other users are not aware that a capture occurred). We therefore assume that in case of success all users (including those that transmitted and failed in that slot) behave as if the slot was successful. The question then is when will the users whose packets failed due to a capture retransmit their packets. Consider the following alternatives: (i) They transmit immediately in the subsequent slot after the capture occurs *(persist scheme).* (ii) They wait until the current CRI ends and retransmit in the first slot of the subsequent CRI *(wait scheme).*

Let $\bar{A}_k$ be the number of new packets transmitted at the beginning of the kth CRI and let $\bar{Y}_k$ be the number of packets that due to captures are not transmitted successfully during the kth CRI and hence are transmitted at the beginning of the $(k+1)$st CRI. Let $\bar{X}_k = \bar{A}_k + \bar{Y}_{k-1}$ and for $n \geq 0$, $0 \leq l \leq n$ let $P_n(l) = Prob[\bar{Y}_k = l \mid \bar{X}_k = n]$.

(a)   Write recursive equations for $P_n(l)$ for the wait and the persist schemes. Indicate the order in which $P_n(l)$ should be computed.

(b)   Let $p(n_2 \mid n_1) = Prob[\bar{Y}_k = n_2 \mid \bar{Y}_{k-1} = n_1]$. How would you compute $p(n_2 \mid n_1)$ from $P_n(l)$?

(c)   Let B_n be the expected length of a CRI that starts with the transmission of n packets. Write recursive equations for computing B_n, $n \geq 0$ for the wait and the persist schemes.

(d)   Write an expression for the throughput of the protocol as a function of B_n, $n \geq 0$ and $P_Y(l)$-- the probability that $\tilde{Y}_k = l$ in steady-state. How would you compute $P_Y(l)$?

Problem 5.5 (Known Multiplicity [Tsy80, GeP82])

Consider a system in which at the end of each slot the users are informed of the exact number of users that transmitted during the slot. Assume that the epoch mechanism is used and devise a collision resolution protocol for this system. Compute the maximal throughput of your protocol.

Problem 5.6 (Erasures, lost packets)

Consider a system that uses the binary-tree CRP with the epoch mechanism. Assume that whenever n ($n \geq 1$) packets are transmitted, there is a possibility that all these packets will be *erased*, i.e., they will be lost and the feedback signal will indicate all users that the slot was empty. Denote by π_n the probability of this event. Assume that lost packets are never retransmitted.

(a)   Write expressions for the expected length of a CRI that starts with the transmission of n packets.

(b)   Write expressions for the expected number of packets that are transmitted successfully during a CRI that starts with the transmission of n packets.

(c)   Write expressions for the expected number of packets that are lost during a CRI that starts with the transmission of n packets.

(d)   Derive the throughput of this system when the arrival rate is λ and the epoch length is Δ. What is the rate (packets/slot) in which packets are lost in this case.

(e)   Let $\pi_1 = 0.5$; $\pi_i = 0$ $i \geq 2$. How should $\lambda\Delta$ be chosen in order to maximize the throughput. How would you compute the optimal epoch length in this case.

(f)   Repeat (a)-(e) when the modified binary-tree CRP is used.

APPENDIX A

Moments of Collision Resolution Interval Length

In this appendix we derive a closed form expression for the moments of $\bar{B}_n$. The reader must bear with the lengthy (yet straight forward) algebraic manipulation involved in this derivation.

We first demonstrate the method to obtain a closed form expression for B_n. Define the exponential generating function of B_n by

$$B(z) \triangleq \sum_{n=0}^{\infty} B_n \frac{z^n}{n!} \ . \tag{5A.1}$$

Multiplying equation (5.5) by $z^n/n!$ and summing both sides for $n \geq 2$ we obtain

$$\sum_{n=2}^{\infty} B_n \frac{z^n}{n!} = \sum_{n=2}^{\infty} \frac{z^n}{n!} + \sum_{n=2}^{\infty} \frac{z^n}{n!} \sum_{i=0}^{n} Q_i(n)(B_i + B_{n-i}) \ .$$

Using (5A.1) we have

$$B(z) - z - 1 = e^z - z - 1 + \sum_{n=0}^{\infty} \frac{z^n}{n!} \sum_{i=0}^{n} Q_i(n)(B_i + B_{n-i})$$

$$- \left[\sum_{n=0}^{1} \frac{z^n}{n!} \sum_{i=0}^{n} Q_i(n)(B_i + B_{n-i}) \right]$$

or (using (5.1))

$$B(z) = e^z + \sum_{n=0}^{\infty} \frac{z^n}{n!} \sum_{i=0}^{n} Q_i(n)(B_i + B_{n-i}) - \left[2 + 2z[1 - p + p] \right]$$

$$= e^z - 2(1 + z) + \sum_{n=0}^{\infty} \sum_{i=0}^{n} \frac{z^n}{i!(n-i)!} p^i (1-p)^{n-i}(B_i + B_{n-i})$$

$$= e^z - 2(1 + z) + \sum_{i=0}^{\infty} \sum_{n=i}^{\infty} \frac{z^n}{i!(n-i)!} p^i (1-p)^{n-i}(B_i + B_{n-i})$$

$$= e^z - 2(1 + z) + \sum_{i=0}^{\infty} \sum_{n=i}^{\infty} \frac{[z(1-p)]^{n-i}}{(n-i)!} \cdot \frac{[zp]^i}{i!}(B_i + B_{n-i})$$

$$= e^z - 2(1 + z) + \sum_{i=0}^{\infty} \frac{[zp]^i}{i!} B_i \sum_{n=i}^{\infty} \frac{[z(1-p)]^{n-i}}{(n-i)!}$$

$$+ \sum_{i=0}^{\infty} \frac{[zp]^i}{i!} \sum_{n=i}^{\infty} \frac{[z(1-p)]^{n-i}}{(n-i)!} B_{n-i}$$

$$= e^z - 2(1 + z) + B(zp)e^{z(1-p)} + B(z(1-p))e^{zp} .$$

Therefore,

$$e^{-z}B(z) = 1 - 2e^{-z}(1 + z) + B(zp)e^{-zp} + B(z(1-p))e^{-z(1-p)} . \quad (5A.2)$$

It is convenient to define

$$B^*(z) \triangleq e^{-z}B(z) \tag{5A.3}$$

which transforms (5A.2) to

$$B^*(z) - B^*(zp) - B^*(z(1-p)) = 1 - 2e^{-z}(1 + z) . \tag{5A.4}$$

Expanding both sides of (5A.4) to a Taylor series around $z=0$, letting $B^*(z) = \sum_{k=0}^{\infty} B_k^* z^k$ and equating the coefficients of z^k on both sides of (5A.4) we get for $k \geq 2$

$$B_k^* - p^k B_k^* - (1-p)^k B_k^* = -2\frac{(-1)^k}{k!} - 2\frac{(-1)^{k-1}}{(k-1)!} = \frac{2(k-1)(-1)^k}{k!}$$

or

$$B_k^* = \frac{2(k-1)(-1)^k}{k![1 - p^k - (1-p)^k]} \qquad k \geq 2 . \tag{5A.5}$$

From the definitions (5A.1) and (5A.3) we obtain

$$\sum_{n=0}^{\infty} B_n \frac{z^n}{n!} = B(z) = e^z B^*(z) = \sum_{j=0}^{\infty} \frac{z^j}{j!} \sum_{k=0}^{\infty} B_k^* z^k = \sum_{k=0}^{\infty} \sum_{j=0}^{\infty} \frac{B_k^*}{j!} z^{k+j}$$

from which, by equating corresponding coefficients of z^n, we obtain:

$$\frac{B_n}{n!} = \sum_{k=0}^{n} \frac{B_k^*}{(n-k)!} .$$

Finally, since $B_0^* = 1$ and $B_1^* = 0$, and using (5A.5) we obtain

$$B_n = 1 + \sum_{k=2}^{n} \binom{n}{k} \frac{2(k-1)(-1)^k}{[1 - p^k - (1-p)^k]} \qquad n \geq 2 \tag{5A.6}$$

which is the closed form expression for B_n we were seeking.

In almost the same manner, a closed form expression for V_n can be obtained. Let

$$V(z) \triangleq \sum_{n=0}^{\infty} V_n \frac{z^n}{n!} .$$

Then from (5.10) we obtain

$$V(z) = 2B(z) - e^z - 4(1 + z) + 2B(zp)B(z(1-p))$$
$$+ V(zp)e^{z(1-p)} + V(z(1-p))e^{zp}$$

and with a definition $V^*(z) = e^{-z} V(z)$ we get

$$V^*(z) - V^*(zp) - V^*(z(1-p))$$
$$= 2B^*(z) - 1 - 4e^{-z}(1+z) + 2B^*(zp)B^*(z(1-p))$$

from which

$$V_n = 1 + \sum_{k=2}^{n} \frac{2n!}{(n-k)![1 - p^k - (1-p)^k]} \left[B_k^* + \sum_{i=0}^{k} B_i^* B_{k-i}^* \right]$$
$$+ \sum_{k=2}^{n} \binom{n}{k} \frac{4(k-1)(-1)^k}{[1 - p^k - (1-p)^k]} \qquad n \geq 2 .$$

CHAPTER 6

ADDITIONAL TOPICS

The field of multiple access systems is much too broad to be contained in a single book. Although we treated in depth many fundamental protocols and systems, we were able to uncover just the tip of the iceberg. Many important and interesting subjects in this field were not discussed in the book, either because they are beyond the scope we planned for the book or because they are still in a formative and fragmentary stage of research. This section is devoted to short descriptions of several of these subjects.

Multihop Networks

The basic topology assumed throughout this book is the single-hop topology in which all users hear one another, or there is a common receiver that can hear all transmissions in the network. An important topology, known as a *multihop* network, is characterized by the feature that each user is in reception range of only a subset of the users and similarly the transmission of a user is heard by a subset of all users. A transmission is successful only if it is the only transmission currently being heard by the *receiving* node. The term "multihop" alludes to the need of packets to hop over several intermediate users in order to arrive at their destinations, since not all pairs of users communicate directly. This gives rise to routing issues i.e., which of the receiving users should forward a received packet towards its destination. The multihop topology allows for concurrent successful transmissions, provided each receiver receives only a single transmission at a time; this property is utilized to increase the capacity of the total network by an approach called *spatial reuse*

Multihop networks appear naturally in radio networks with low powered transmitters or in interconnected local area networks. The fact that each receiver hears a subset of transmitters rather than all of them renders the analysis of multihop systems far more complex than that of single-hop systems. Yet, some of the basic protocols such as the pure and the slotted Aloha are still applicable in multihop systems. Carrier sensing can also be used, although it will not be as effective as in single-hop systems since a transmission cannot be sensed by all users. To improve the effectiveness of carrier sensing, the idea of *busy-tone* can be used (see ToK75, SiS81, BrT85, CiR86]). The application of collision resolution or controlled Aloha protocols require substantial revisions of the protocols since it is difficult to obtain the correct feedback information at the end of each slot in a multihop environment.

A detailed description of multihop packet radio technology appears in [KGB78]. An approach to solving for the throughput of multihop networks for several access protocols was first presented in [BoK80] and refined in [BKM87] and [KBC87]. An extensive survey of recent developments in the analysis of multihop systems appears in [Tob87]. Other relevant papers are [SiK83, TaK85b, KlS87, ShK87, PYS87].

Multistation Networks

The multihop topology assumes that every user in the network can and should serve as a repeater for packets it receives from its neighbors and that needs to be forwarded to their destinations. In many applications of packet-radio networks, the population of users is not homogeneous: some users are more powerful than others, some are not mobile, etc. In addition, some inherent hierarchy may exist among the users of the network. In such systems it is natural to build a backbone network of *stations* that is responsible for the routing and other network functions.

In the multistation model the users of the network are originators of the data that are transmitted through a shared channel to the stations. The stations may be either the final destinations for some packets sent by the users or can act as relays for other packets, by forwarding them to their respective destinations (other stations or users). The network operates as follows: a packet that is generated at some user, is forwarded to a station via the shared channel by employing some multiple access protocol. The station then forwards it to some other station through the backbone network of stations to be finally transmitted on the station-to-user channel to its destination (cellular phone systems use this approach).

The advantages of the multistation configuration over the single-hop one are that the former allows for lower power transmitters at the users, results in better utilization of the common radio channel due to spatial reuse and allows distribution of control among several stations. It is also advantageous over the multihop configuration because it simplifies both the design and the analysis of the network, it simplifies nodal protocols, and is also adequate for a large number of naturally structured hierarchical networks.

Multistation networks in which a TDMA scheme is used are considered in [RoS89]. Aloha-type protocols in this environment are studied in [SiC88, CiR86], and collision resolution protocols in [BaS88].

Multichannel Systems

The networks considered in this book contain a single shared channel used by the users for communication. Many studies consider *multichannel* networks. These networks are characterized by the ability of the users to communicate via several different, noninterfering, communication channels at different bands. To keep the same level of connectivity as in the single channel environment, the users should be equipped with several receivers. The main advantage of using multiple channels is the reduced interference level among the users. There are two ways in which interference is reduced compared to the single channel environment. The first is obvious--less users use each frequency band. The second is characteristic to carrier sensing systems; since the total available bandwidth is fixed, each frequency band in the multichannel system is narrower and the transmission time of a packet is longer. The propagation delay is constant and hence the ratio between the propagation delay and the packet transmission time becomes smaller, yielding better performance.

Multichannel systems for various Aloha and CSMA protocols are discussed in [MaR83, Tod85, Kim85, MaB87, Kim87, ShK87, ChG88].

REFERENCES

Abr70.   N. Abramson, "The ALOHA System - Another Alternative for Computer Communications," pp. 281-285 in *Proc. of the Fall Joint Computer Conference*, (1970).

Abr77.   N. Abramson, "The Throughput of Packet Broadcasting Channels," *IEEE Trans. on Communications*, **COM-25**(1) pp. 117-128 (January 1977).

ApP86.   T.K. Apostolopoulos and E.N. Protonotarios, "Queueing Analysis of Buffered CSMA/CD Protocols," *IEEE Trans. on Communications*, **COM-34**(9) pp. 898-905 (September 1986).

BaS88.   A. Bar-David and M. Sidi, "Collision Resolution Algorithms in Multi-Station Packet-Radio Networks," pp. 385-400 in *PERFORMANCE' 87*, Brussels (December 1987).

BeB80.   S. Bellini and P. Borgonovo, "On the throughput of an ALOHA channel with variable length packets," *IEEE Trans. Communications*, **COM-28**(11) pp. 1932-1935 (November 1980).

BeC88.   S.L. Beuerman and E.J. Coyle, "The Delay Characteristics of CSMA/CD Networks," *IEEE Trans. on Communications*, **COM-36**(5) pp. 553-563 (May 1988).

BeG87.   D. Bertsekas and R. Gallager, *Data Networks*, Prentice Hall, Inc., New-Jersey (1987).

BeT88.   T. Berger and T.S. Tszan, "An Improved Upper Bound for the Capacity of a Channel with Multiple Random Access," *Problemy Peredachi Informatsii*, **21**(4) pp. 83-87 (January 1985).

BeZ88.   T. Berger and R.Z. Zhu, "Upper Bound for the Capacity of a Random Multiple Access System," *Problemy Peredachi Informatsii*, **17** pp. 90-95 (January 1988).

Bin75.   R. Binder, "A Dynamic Packet Switching System for Satellite Broadcast Channels," pp. 41.1-41.5 in *Proc. of ICC'75*, San Francisco, California (1975).

BKM87.   R.R. Boorstyn, A. Kershenbaum, B. Maglaris, and V. Sahin, "Throughput Analysis in Multihop CSMA Packet Radio Networks," *IEEE Trans. on Communications*, **COM-35**(3) pp. 267-274 (March 1987).

BMT84.   T. Berger, N. Mehravari, D. Towsley, and J. Wolf, "Random Multiple-Access Communication and Group Testing," *IEEE Trans. on Communications*, **COM-32**(7) pp. 769-779 (July 1984).

BoF78. F. Borgonovo and L. Fratta, *SRUC: A Technique for Packet Transmission on Multiple Access Channels Reservation and TDMA schemes*. 1978.

BoK80. R.R. Boorstyn and A. Kershenbaum, "Throughput Analysis of Multihop Packet Radio," pp. 13.6.1-13.6.6 in *Proc. of ICC'80*, Seattle, Washington (1980).

BrT85. J.M. Brazio and F.A. Tobagi, "Throughput Analysis of Spread Spectrum Multihop Packet Radio Networks," pp. 256-265 in *Proceeding of IEEE INFOCOM'85*, Washington, D.C. (March 1985).

CaH75. A.B. Carleial and M.E. Hellman, "Bistable Behavior of ALOHA-type Systems," *IEEE Trans. on Communications*, **COM-23**(4) pp. 401-410 (April 1975).

Cap77. J.I. Capetanakis, "The Multiple Access Broadcast Channel: Protocol and Capacity Considerations," in *Ph.D. Dissertation*, Department of Electrical Engineering, MIT (August 1977).

Cap79. J.I. Capetanakis, "Tree Algorithm for Packet Broadcast Channels," *IEEE Trans. on Information Theory*, **IT-25**(5) pp. 505-515 (September 1979).

CFL79. I. Chlamtac, W.R. Franta, and K.D. Levin, "BRAM: The Broadcast Recognizing Access Mode," *IEEE Trans. on Communications*, **COM-27**(8) pp. 1183-1189 (August 1979).

ChG88. I. Chlamtac and A. Ganz, "Channel Allocation Protocols in Frequency-Time Controlled High Speed Networks," *IEEE Trans. on Communications*, **COM-36**(4) pp. 430-440 (April 1988).

CiR86. I. Cidon and R. Rom, "Carrier Sense Access in a Two Interfering Channels Environment," *Computer Networks and ISDN Systems*, **12**(1) pp. 1-10 (August 1986).

CiS85. I. Cidon and M. Sidi, "The Effect of Capture on Collision-Resolution Algorithms," *IEEE Trans. Communications*, **COM-33**(4) pp. 317-324 (April 1985).

CiS87. I. Cidon and M. Sidi, "Erasures and Noise in Multiple Access Algorithms," *IEEE Trans. on Information Theory*, **IT-33**(1) pp. 132-143 (January 1987).

CiS88. I. Cidon and M. Sidi, "Conflict Multiplicity Estimation and Batch Resolution Algorithms,," *IEEE Trans. on Information Theory*, **IT-34**(1) pp. 101-110 (January 1988).

CKS88. I. Cidon, H. Kodesh, and M. Sidi, "Erasure, Capture and Random Power Level Selection in Multiple-Access Systems," *IEEE Trans. Communications*, **COM-36**(3) pp. 263-271 (March 1988).

CoB80. S.D. Conte and C. de Boor, *Elementary Numerical Analysis: An Algorithmic Approach (3rd ed.)*, McGraw Hill (1980).

CoL83.   E.J. Coyle and B. Liu, "Finite Population CSMA-CD Networks,"
          IEEE Trans. on Communications, **COM-31**(11) pp. 1247-1251
          (November 1983).

CoL85.   E.J. Coyle and B. Liu, "A Matrix Representation of CSMA/CD Net-
          works," *IEEE Trans. on Communications,* **COM-33**(1) pp. 53-64
          (January 1985).

CPR78.   D.D. Clark, K.T. Pogran, and D.P. Reed, "Introduction to Local Area
          Networks," *Proc. of the IEEE,* **66**(11) pp. 1497-1517 (November
          1978).

CrH82.   R. Cruz and B. Hajek, "A New Upper Bound to the Throughput of a
          Multi-Access Broadcast Channel," *IEEE Trans. on Information
          Theory,* **IT-28** pp. 402-405 (May 1982).

CRW73.   W. Crowther, R. Rettberg, D. Walden, S. Ornstein, and F. Heart, "A
          System for Broadcast Communication: Reservation-ALOHA," pp.
          371-374 in *Proc. of the 6th Hawaii International Conference on Sys-
          tems Sciences,* Honolulu, Hawaii (1973).

CuM88.   G.A. Cunningham and J.S. Meditch, "Distributed Retransmission
          Controls for Slotted, Nonpersistent, and Virtual Time CSMA," *IEEE
          Trans. on Communications,* **COM-36**(6) pp. 685-691 (June 1988).

DaG80.   D.H. Davis and S.A. Gronemeyer, "Performance of Slotted ALOHA
          Random Access with Delay Capture and Randomized Time of
          Arrival," *IEEE Trans. on Communications,* **COM-28**(5) pp. 703-710
          (May 1980).

EpZ87.   A. Ephremides and R.Z. Zhu, "Delay Analysis of Interacting Queues
          with an Approximate Model," *IEEE Trans. on Communications,*
          COM-35(2) pp. 194-201 (February 1987).

Fer75.   M.J. Ferguson, "On the Control, Stability, and Waiting Time in a
          Slotted ALOHA Random-Access System," *IEEE Trans. on Com-
          munications,* **COM-23**(11) pp. 1306-1311 (November 1975).

Fer77a.   M.J. Ferguson, "A Bound and Approximation of Delay Distribution
          for Fixed-Length Packets in an Unslotted ALOHA Channel and a
          Comparison with Time Division Multiplexing (TDM)," *IEEE Trans.
          on Communications,* **COM-25**(1) pp. 136-139 (January 1977).

Fer77b.   M.J. Ferguson, "An Approximate Analysis of Delay for Fixed and
          Variable Length Packets in an Unslotted ALOHA Channel," *IEEE
          Trans. on Communications,* **COM-25**(7) pp. 644-654 (July 1977).

FFH85.   G. Fayolle, P. Flajolet, M. Hofri, and P. Jacquet, "Analysis of a Stack
          Algorithm for Random Multiple-Access Communication," *IEEE
          Trans. Information Theory,* **IT-31**(2) pp. 244-254 (March 1985).

FiT84.   M. Fine and F.A. Tobagi, "Demand Assignment Multiple Access
          Schemes in Broadcast Bus Local Area Networks," *IEEE Trans.
          Computers,* **C-33**(12) pp. 1130-59 (December 1984).

FLB74.   G. Fayolle, J. Labetoulle, D. Bastin, and E. Gelenbe, "The Stability Problem of Broadcast Packet Switching Computer networks," *Acta Informatica,* **4**(1) pp. 49-53 (1974).

Gal78.   R.G. Gallager, "Conflict Resolution in Random Access Broadcast Networks," pp. 74-76 in *Proc. AFOSR Workshop Communication Theory and Applications,* Provincetown (September 1978).

Gal85.   R.G. Gallager, "A Perspective on Multiaccess Channels," *IEEE Trans. on Information Theory,* **IT-31**(2) pp. 124-142 (March 1985).

GeK87.   L. Georgiadis and P. Papantoni-Kazakos, "A 0.487 Throughput Limited sensing Algorithm," *IEEE Trans. on Information Theory,* **IT-33**(2) pp. 233-237 (March 1987).

GeP82.   L. Georgiadis and P. Papantoni-Kazakos, "A Collision Resolution Protocol for Random Access Channels with Energy Detectors," *IEEE Trans. on Communications,* **COM-30**(11) pp. 2413-2420 (November 1982).

GFL87.   A.G. Greenberg, P. Flajolet, and R.E. Ladner, "Estimating the Multiplicities of Conflicts to Speed Their Resolution in Multiple Access Channels," *Journal of the ACM,* **34**(2) pp. 289-325 (April 1987).

GMP87.   L. Georgiadis, L.F. Merakos, and P. Papantoni-Kazakos, "A Method for the Delay Analysis of Random Multiple-Access Algorithms whose Delay Process is Regenerative," *IEEE Journal on Selected Areas in Communications,* **SAC-5**(6) pp. 1051-1062 (July 1987).

HaL82.   B. Hajek and T. Van Loon, "Decentralized Dynamic Control of a Multiaccess Broadcast Channel," *IEEE Trans. on Automatic Control,* **AC-27** pp. 559-569 (June 1982).

HaO86.   J.L. Hammond and P.J.P. O'Reilly, *Performance Analysis of Local Computer Networks,* Addison-Wesley Publishing Company (1986).

HaS79.   L.W. Hansen and M. Schwartz, "An Assigned-Slot Listen-Before-Transmission Protocol for a Multiaccess Data Channel," *IEEE Trans. on Communications,* **COM-27**(6) pp. 846-856 (June 1979).

Hay78.   J.F. Hayes, "An Adaptive Technique for Local Distribution," *IEEE Trans. on Communications,* **COM-26**(8) pp. 1178-1186 (August 1978).

Hay84.   J.F. Hayes, *Modeling and Analysis of Computer Communications Networks,* Plenum Press, New York (1984).

Hey82.   D.P. Heyman, "An Analysis of the Carrier-Sense Multiple-Access Protocol," *Bell System Technical Journal,* **61** pp. 2023-2051 (October 1982).

Hey86.   D.P. Heyman, "The Effects of Random Message Sizes on the Performance of the CSMA/CD Protocol," *IEEE Trans. on Communications,* **COM-34**(6) pp. 547-553 (June 1986).

HoR87.   M. Hofri and Z. Rosberg, "Packet Delay Under the Golden Ration Weighted TDM Policy in a Multiple Access Channel," *IEEE Trans. on Information Theory*, **IT-33**(3) pp. 341-349 (1987).

HuB85.   J.C. Huang and T. Berger, "Delay Analysis of Interval-Searching Contention Resolution Algorithms," *IEEE Trans. on Information Theory*, **IT-31**(2) pp. 264-273 (March 1985).

HuB86.   J.C. Huang and T. Berger, "Delay Analysis of 0.487 Contention Resolution Algorithms," *IEEE Trans. on Communications*, **COM-34**(9) pp. 916-926 (September 1986).

Hum86.   P.A. Humblet, "On the Throughput of Channel Access Algorithms with Limited Sensing," *IEEE Trans. Communications*, **COM-34**(4) pp. 345-347 (April 1986).

ItR84.   A. Itai and Z. Rosberg, "A Golden Ratio Control Policy for a Multiple-Access Channel," *IEEE Trans. Automatic Control*, **AC-29**(8) pp. 712-718 (August 1984).

Jen80.   Y.C. Jenq, "On the Stability of Slotted ALOHA Systems," *IEEE Trans. Communications*, **COM-28**(11) pp. 1936-1939 (November 1980).

KBC87.   A. Kershenbaum, R. Boorstyn, and M.S. Chen, "An Algorithm for Evaluation of Throughput in Multihop Packet Radio Networks with Complex Topologies," *IEEE Journal on Selected Areas in Communications* **SAC-5**(6) pp. 1003-1012 (July 1987).

Kel85.   F.P Kelly, "Stochastic Models of Computer Communication Systems," *Journal of the Royal Statistical Society*, **47**(1)(1985).

KeS88.   I. Kessler and M. Sidi, "Mixing Collision Resolution Algorithms Exploiting Information of Successful Messages," *IEEE Trans. on Information Theory*, **IT-34**(3) pp. 531-536 (May 1988).

KGB78.   R.E. Kahn, A.A. Gronemeyer, J. Burchfiel, and R.C. Kunzelman, "Advances in packet radio technology," *Proceedings of the IEEE*, **66**(11) pp. 1468-1496 (November 1978).

KiK83.   W.M. Kiesel and P.J. Kuehn, "A new CSMA-CD protocol for local area networks with dynamic priorities and low collision probability," *IEEE Journal on Selected Areas in Communications* **SAC-1**(5) pp. 869-876 (November 1983).

Kim85.   G. Kimura, "An Analysis of the Multi-channel CSMA/CD Protocol by Nonslotted Model," *Trans. of the Japanese Inst. Electronics and Communication Engineering*, **J68B** (Part B)(12) pp. 1341-1348 (December 1985).

Kim87.   G. Kimura, "An Analysis of the Multi-Channel CSMA/CD Protocol by Nonslotted Model," *Trans. of the Japanese Inst. Electronics and Communication Engineering*, **70**(5) pp. 78-85 (May 1987).

Kle76.   L. Kleinrock, *Queueing Systems (Vols. I, II)*, J. Wiley (1975, 1976).

KlL75.   L. Kleinrock and S.S. Lam, "Packet Switching in a Multiaccess Broadcast Channel: Performance Evaluation," *IEEE Trans. on Communications*, **COM-23**(4) pp. 410-423 (April 1975).

KlS80.   L. Kleinrock and M. Scholl, "Packet Switching in Radio Channels: New Conflict-Free Multiple Access Schemes," *IEEE Trans. on Communications*, **COM-28**(7) pp. 1015-1029 (July 1980).

KlS87.   L. Kleinrock and J. Silvester, "Spatial Reuse in Multihop Packet Radio Networks," *Proceedings of the IEEE*, **75**(1) pp. 156-167 (January 1987).

KlT75.   L. Kleinrock and F.A. Tobagi, "Packet Switching in Radio Channels: Part I - Carrier Sense Multiple-Access Modes and Their Throughput Delay Characteristics," *IEEE Trans. on Communications*, **COM-23**(12) pp. 1400-1416 (December 1975).

KlY78.   L. Kleinrock and Y. Yemini, "An optimal adaptive scheme for multiple access broadcast communication," in *Proc. of ICC'78*, Toronto, Canada (1978).

KSY84.   J.F. Kurose, M. Schwartz, and Y. Yemini, "Multiple-access protocols and time-constrained communication," *Computer Survey* **16**(1) pp. 43-70 (March 1984).

KSY88.   J.F. Kurose, M. Schwartz, and Y. Yemini, "Controlling window protocols for time-constrained communication in multiple access networks," *IEEE Trans. on Communications*, **COM-36**(1) pp. 41-49 (January 1988).

Kuo81.   F.F. Kuo, *Protocols and Techniques for Data Communication Networks*, Prentice Hall, New Jersey (1981).

KuS88.   D. Kurtz and M. Sidi, "Multiple Access Algorithms via Group Testing for Heterogeneous Population of Users," *IEEE Trans. Communications*, **COM-36**(12) pp. 1316-1323 (December 1988).

LaK75.   S.S. Lam and L. Kleinrock, "Packet Switching in a Multiaccess Broadcast Channel: Dynamic Control Procedures," *IEEE Trans. on Communications*, **COM-23**(9) pp. 891-904 (September 1975).

Lam77.   S.S. Lam, "Delay Analysis of a Time Division Multiple Access (TDMA) Channel," *IEEE Trans. on Communications*, **COM-25**(12) pp. 1489-1494 (December 1977).

Lam80.   S.S. Lam, "Packet Broadcast Networks-a Performance Analysis of The R-ALOHA Protocol," *IEEE Trans. on Computers*, **C-29**(7) pp. 596-603 (July 1980).

Lee87.   C.C. Lee, "Random Signal Levels for Channel Access in Packet Broadcast networks," *IEEE Journal on Selected Areas in Communications* **SAC-5**(6) pp. 1026-1034 (July 1987).

LeP87.   J.S. Lehnert and M.B. Pursley, "Error Probabilities for Binary Direct-Sequence Spread-Spectrum Communications with Random Signature Sequence," *IEEE Trans. on Communications,* **COM-35**(1) pp. 87-98 (January 1987).

LiF82.   J.O. Limb and C. Flores, "Description of Fasnet, a Unidirectional Local Area Communication Network," *Bell System Technical Journal,* **61 (Part** 1)(7)(September 1982).

MaB87.   M.A. Marsan and M. Bruscagin, "Multichannel ALOHA Networks with Reduced Connections," pp. 268-275 in *IEEE INFOCOM'87,* San Francisco, CA (April 1987).

MaF83.   P. Mathys and P. Flajolet, "Q-ary Collision Resolution Algorithms in Random-access Systems with Free or Blocked Channel-Access," *IEEE Trans. Information Theory,* **IT-31**(2) pp. 217-243 (March 1985).

MaM85.   J.L. Massey and P. Mathys, "The Collision Channel Without Feedback," *IEEE Trans. on Information Theory,* **IT-31**(2) pp. 192-204 (March 1985).

Mar78.   J. Martin, *Communication Satellite Systems,* Prentice-Hall, New Jersey (1978).

MaR83.   M.A. Marsan and D. Roffinella, "Multichannel Local Area Network Protocols," *IEEE Journal on Selected Areas in Communications,* **SAC-1**(5) pp. 885-897 (November 1983).

Mas81.   J.L. Massey, "Collision Resolution Algorithms and Random-Access Communications," pp. 73-137 in *Multi-User Communications Systems (CISM Courses and Lectures Series),* ed. G. Longo, Springer-Verlag, New York (1981).   (Also in UCLA Technical Report UCLA-ENG-8016, April 1980)

MeB76.   R.M. Metcalfe and D.R. Boggs, "ETHERNET: Distributed Packet Switching for Local Computer Networks," *Communications of the ACM* **19**(7) pp. 395-403 (1976).

MeB84.   N. Mehravari and T. Berger, "Poisson Multiple-Access Contention with Binary Feedback," *IEEE Trans. Information Theory,* **IT-30**(5) pp. 745-751 (September 1984).

MeK85.   L. Merakos and D. Kazakos, "On Retransmission Control Policies in Multiple-Access Communication Networks," *IEEE Trans. Automatic Control,* **AC-30**(2) pp. 109-117 (February 1985).

MeL83.   J.S. Meditch and C.T.A. Lea, "Stability and Optimization of the CSMA and CSMA/CD Channels," *IEEE Trans. on Communications,* **COM-31**(6) pp. 763-774 (June 1983).

Met73.   R.M. Metcalfe, "Steady-State Analysis of a Slotted and Controlled Aloha System with Blocking," in *Proc. 6-th Hawaii International Conference on System Sciences,* (January 1973).

Met76.   J.J. Metzner, "On Improving Utilization in ALOHA Networks," *IEEE Trans. on Communications*, **COM-24**(4) pp. 447-448 (April 1976).

MiT81.   V.A. Mikhailov and B.S. Tsybakov, "Upper Bound for the Capacity of a Random Multiple Access System," *Problemy Peredachi Informatsii*, **17**(1) pp. 90-95 (January 1981).

MoH85.   J. Mosley and P.A. Humblet, "A Class of Efficient contention Resolution Algorithms for Multiple Access Channels," *IEEE Trans. on Communications*, **COM-33**(2) pp. 145-151 (February 1985).

MoK85.   M.L. Molle and L. Kleinrock, "Virtual Time CSMA: Why Two Clocks are Better Than One," *IEEE Trans. on Communications*, **COM-33**(6) pp. 919-933 (June 1985).

Mol82.   M.L. Molle, "On the Capacity of Infinite Population Multiple Access Protocols," *IEEE Trans. Information Theory*, **IT-28**(3) pp. 396-401 (May 1982).

MoR84.   L.F.M. De Moraes and I. Rubin, "Message Delays for a TDMA Scheme under a Nonpreemptive Priority Discipline," *IEEE Trans. on Communications*, **COM-32**(5) pp. 583-8 (May 1984).

Mue56.   D.E. Mueller, "A Method of Solving Algebraic Equations Using an Automatic computer," *Mathematical Tables and Other Aids to Computation (MTAC)*, **10** pp. 208-215 (1956).

Neu81.   M.F. Neuts, *Matrix-Geometric Solutions in Stochastic Models: An Algorithmic Approach*, The John Hopkins Press (1981).

OnN85.   Y. Onozato and S. Noguchi, "On the Thrashing Cusp in Slotted ALOHA Systems," *IEEE Trans. on Communications*, **COM-33**(11) pp. 1171-1182 (November 1985).

Pak69.   A.G. Pakes, "Some Conditions of Ergodicity and Recurrence of Markov Chains," *Operations Research*, **17** pp. 1058-1061 (1969).

Pip81.   N. Pippenger, "Bounds on the Performance Of Protocols for a Multiple-Access Broadcast Channel," *IEEE Trans. Information Theory*, **IT-27**(2) pp. 145-151 (March 1981).

PMV87.   G.C. Polyzos, M.L. Molle, and A.N. Venetsanopoulos, "Performance Analysis of Finite Nonhomogeneous Population Tree Conflict Resolution Algorithms using Constant Size Window Access," *IEEE Trans. on Communications*, **COM-35**(11) pp. 1124-1138 (November 1987).

Pur77.   M.B. Pursley, "Performance Evaluation for Phase-Coded Spread-Spectrum Multiple-Access Communication (part I: System analysis)," *IEEE Trans. on Communications*, **COM-25**(8) pp. 795-799 (August 1977).

Pur87.   M.B. Pursley, "The Role of Spread Spectrum in Packet Radio Networks," *Proceedings of IEEE,*, (1) pp. 116-34 (January 1987).

PYS87.   E. Pinsky, Y. Yemini, and M. Sidi, "The canonical approximation in the performance analysis of packet radio networks," pp. 140-162 in *Current advances in distributed computing and communications, Ed. Y. Yemini*, Computer Science Press, (1987).

Riv87.   R.L. Rivest, "Network Control by Bayesian Broadcast," *IEEE Trans. on Information Theory*, IT-33(3) pp. 323-328 (May 1987).

Rob72.   L.G. Roberts, "ALOHA Packet System With and Without Slots and Capture," *Computer Communications Review* 5(2) pp. 28-42 (April 1975). (Originally published as ARPANET Satellite System Note 8 (NIC 11290), 1972)

Rob75.   L.G. Roberts, "Dynamic Allocation of Satellite Capacity Through Packet Reservation," in *Computer communication networks*, ed. R.L. Grimsdale and F.F. Kuo, Noordhoff Internat Publishing, Groningen, Netherlands (1975).

Rom84.   R. Rom, "Ordering Subscribers on Cable Networks," *ACM Transaction on Computer Systems*, 2(4) pp. 322-334 (November 1984).

Rom86.   R. Rom, "Collision Detection in Radio Channels," pp. 235-249 in *Local Area and Multiple Access Networks*, Computer Science Press, (1986).

Ros72.   S.M. Ross, *Introduction to Probability Models*, Academic Press, New York (1972).

RoS89.   Z. Rosberg and M. Sidi, "TDM Policies in Multistation Packet-Radio Networks," *IEEE Trans. on Communications*, COM-37(1) pp. 31-38 (January 1989).

RoT81.   R. Rom and F.A. Tobagi, "Message-Based Priority Functions in Local Multiaccess Communication Systems," *Computer Networks*, 5(4) pp. 273-286 (July 1981).

Rub77.   I. Rubin, "Message Delays in FDMA and TDMA Communication Channels," *IEEE Trans. on Communications*, COM-27(5) pp. 769-777 (May 1979).

Rub78.   I. Rubin, "Group Random-Access Disciplines for Multi-Access Broadcast Channels," *IEEE Trans. on Information Theory* IT-24(5) pp. 578-592 (September 1978).

Rub79.   I. Rubin, "Access Control Disciplines for Multi-Access Communications Channels: Reservation and TDMA schemes," *IEEE Trans. on Information Theory* IT-25(5) pp. 516-536 (September 1979).

Sac88.   S.R. Sachs, "Alternative Local Area Network Access Protocols," *IEEE Communications Magazine* 26(3) pp. 25-45 (March 1988).

SaE81.   T.N. Saadawi and A. Ephremides, "Analysis, Stability and Optimization of Slotted ALOHA with a Finite Number of Buffered Users," *IEEE Trans. on Automatic Control*, AC-26(3) pp. 680-689 (June 1981).

San80.   D. Sant, "Throughput of unslotted ALOHA channels with arbitrary packet interarrival time distributions," *IEEE Trans. Communications*, **COM-28**(8 (part 2)) pp. 1422-1425 (August 1980).

ScK79.   M. Scholl and L. Kleinrock, "On a Mixed Mode Multiple Access Scheme for Packet-Switched Radio Channels," *IEEE Trans. on Communications*, **COM-27**(6) pp. 906-911 (June 1979).

Sha84.   N. Shacham, "Throughput-Delay Performance of Packet-Switching Multiple-Access Channel with Power Capture," *Performance Evaluation*, **4**(3) pp. 153-170 (August 1984).

ShH82.   N. Shacham and V.B. Hunt, "Performance Evaluation of the CSMA-CD 1-Persistent Channel Access Protocol in Common Channel Local Networks," pp. 401-414 in *Proc. of the International Symposium on Local Computer Networks*, IFIP TC-6, Florence, Italy (April 1982).

ShK87.   N. Shacham and P.J.B. King, "Architectures and Performance of Multichannel Multihop Packet Radio Networks," *IEEE Journal Selected Areas Communications*, **SAC-5**(6) pp. 1013-1025 (20 July 1987).

SiC85.   M. Sidi and I. Cidon, "Splitting Protocols in Presence of Capture," *IEEE Trans. Information Theory*, **IT-31** pp. 295-301 (March 1985).

SiC88.   M. Sidi and I. Cidon, "A Multi-Station Packet-Radio Network," *Performance Evaluation*, **8**(1) pp. 65-72 (February 1988).

SiK83.   J.A. Silvester and L. Kleinrock, "On the Capacity of Multihop Slotted ALOHA Networks with Regular Structure," *IEEE Trans. on Communications*, **COM-31**(8) pp. 974-982 (August 1983).

SiS81.   M. Sidi and A. Segall, "A Busy-Tone Multiple-Access Type Scheme for Packet-Radio Networks," pp. 1-10 in *The International Conference on Performance of Data Communication Systems and their Applications*, Paris, France (14-16 September 1981).

SiS83.   M. Sidi and A. Segall, "Two Interfering Queues in Packet-Radio Networks," *IEEE Trans. on Communications*, **COM-31**(1) pp. 123-129 (January 1983).

SMV87.   K. Sohraby, M.L. Molle, and A.N. Venetsanopoulos, "Comments on `Throughput Analysis for Persistent CSMA Systems´," *IEEE Trans. on Communications*, **COM-35**(2) pp. 240-243 (February 1987).

Sta85.   W. Stallings, *Data and Computer Communications*, Macmillan Inc., New York (1985).

Szp86.   W. Szpankowski, "Bounds for queue lengths in a contention packet broadcast system," *IEEE Trans. Communications*, **COM-34**(11) pp. 1132-1140 (November 1986).

TaI84.   S. Tasaka and Y. Ishibashi, "A Reservation Protocol for Satellite Packet communication-a Performance Analysis and Stability

Considerations," *IEEE Trans. on Communications*, **COM-32**(8) pp. 920-7 (August 1984).

TaK85. H. Takagi and L. Kleinrock, "Mean Packet Queueing Delay in a Buffered Two-User CSMA/CD system," *IEEE Trans. on Communications*, **COM-33**(10) pp. 1136-1139 (October 1985).

TaK85a. H. Takagi and L. Kleinrock, "Throughput Analysis for Persistent CSMA Systems," *IEEE Trans. on Communications*, **COM-33**(7) pp. 627-638 (July 1985). (Corrected February 1987)

TaK85b. H. Takagi and L. Kleinrock, "Output Processes in Contention Packet Broadcasting Systems," *IEEE Trans. on Communications*, **COM-33**(11) pp. 1191-1199 (November 1985).

TaK87. H. Takagi and L. Kleinrock, "Correction to 'Throughput Analysis for Persistent CSMA Systems'," *IEEE Trans. on Communications*, **COM-35**(2) pp. 243-245 (February 1987).

Tan81. A.S. Tannenbaum, *Computer Networks*, Prentice Hall, Inc., New Jersey (1981).

Tas86. S. Tasaka, *Performance Analysis of Multiple Access Protocols*, MIT Press, Cambridge, Mass. (1986).

TaY83. A. Takagi and S. Yamada, "CSMA/CD with Deterministic Contention Resolution," *IEEE Journal on Selected Areas in Communications*, **SAC-1**(5) pp. 877-884 (November 1983).

TML83. B.S. Tsybakov, V.A. Mikhailov, and N.B. Likhanov, "Bounds for Packet Transmission Rate in a Random-Multiple-Access System," *Probl. Information Transmission*, **19**(1) pp. 50-68 (January-March 1983).

Tob80. F.A. Tobagi, "Multiaccess Protocols in Packet Communication Systems," *IEEE Trans. on Communications*, **COM-28**(4) pp. 468-488, (April 1980).

Tob82a. F.A. Tobagi, "Carrier Sense Multiple Access With Message-Based Priority Functions," *IEEE Trans. on Communications*, **30**(1, part 2) pp. 185-200 (January 1982).

Tob82b. F.A. Tobagi, "Distributions of Packet Delay and Interdeparture Time in Slotted ALOHA and Carrier Sense Multiple Access," *Journal of the ACM*, **29**(4) pp. 907-927 (October 1982).

Tob87. F.A. Tobagi, "Modeling and Performance Analysis of Multihop Packet Radio Networks," *Proc. of the IEEE*, **75**(1) pp. 135-155 (January 1987).

Tod85. T.D. Todd, "Throughput in Slotted Multichannel CSMA/CD Systems," pp. 276-280 in *GLOBECOM'85*, New Orleans, LA (December 1985).

ToH80. F.A. Tobagi and V.B. Hunt, "Performance Analysis of Carrier Sense Multiple Access with Collision Detection," *Computer Networks*,

4(5) pp. 245-259 (October/November 1980).

ToK75.   F.A. Tobagi and L. Kleinrock, "Packet Switching in Radio Channels: Part II - The Hidden Terminal Problem in Carrier Sense Multiple-Access and the Busy Tone Solution," *IEEE Trans. on Communications,* COM-23(12) pp. 1417-1433 (December 1975).

ToK76.   F.A. Tobagi and L. Kleinrock, "Packet Switching in Radio Channels: Part III - Polling and (Dynamic) Split-Channel Reservation Multiple-Access," *IEEE Trans. on Communications,* COM-24(8) pp. 832-845 (August 1976).

ToK77.   F.A. Tobagi and L. Kleinrock, "Packet Switching in Radio Channels: Part IV - Stability Considerations and Dynamic Control in Carrier Sense Multiple-Access," *IEEE Trans. on Communications,* COM-25(10) pp. 1103-1119 (October 1977).

ToR80.   F.A. Tobagi and R. Rom, "Efficient Round Robin and Priority Schemes in Unidirectional Broadcast Systems," in *Proc. of the IFIP-WG 6.4 Local Area Networks Workshop,* Zurich (August 1980).

ToV82.   D. Towsley and G. Venkatesh, "Window Random Access Protocols for Local Computer Networks," *IEEE Trans. on Computers* C-31(8) pp. 715-722 (August 1982).

ToV87.   D. Towsley and P.O. Vales, "Announced arrival random access protocols," *IEEE Trans. on Communications,* COM-35(5) pp. 513-521 (May 1987).

TsB88.   B.S. Tsybakov and V.L. Bakirov, "Stability Analysis of a Packet Switching Network and Its Application to Asynchronous Aloha Radio Networks," *Problemy Peredachi Informatsii,* 24(2) pp. 139-151 (October 1988).

TsC86.   D. Tsai and J.F. Chang, "Performance Study of an Adaptive Reservation Multiple Access Technique for Data Transmissions," *IEEE Trans. on Communications,* COM-34(7) pp. 725-727 (July 1986).

Tsi87.   J.N. Tsitsiklis, "Analysis of a Multiaccess Control Scheme," *IEEE Trans. on Automatic Control,* AC-32(11) pp. 1017-1020 (November 1987).

TsL83.   B.S. Tsybakov and N.B. Likhanov, "Packet Switching in a Channel Without Feedback," *Probl. Information Transmission,* 19 pp. 69-84 (April-June 1983).

TsL88.   B.S. Tsybakov and N.B. Likhanov, "Upper Bound on the Capacity of a Random Multiple Access System," *Problemy Peredachi Informatsii,* 23(3) pp. 224-236 (January 1988).

TsM78.   B.S. Tsybakov and V.A. Mikhailov, "Free Synchronous Packet Access in a Broadcast Channel with Feedback," *Probl. Information Transmission,* 14(4) pp. 259-280 (October-December 1978).

TsM79. B.S. Tsybakov and V.A. Mikhailov, "Ergodicity of a slotted ALOHA system," *Probl. Information Transmission*, **15**(4) pp. 301-312 (October-December 1979).

TsM80. B.S. Tsybakov and V.A. Mikhailov, "Random Multiple Packet Access: Part-and-Try Algorithm," *Probl. Information Transmission*, **16**(4) pp. 305-317 (October-December 1980).

Tsy80. B.S. Tsybakov, "Resolution of a Conflict of Known Multiplicity," *Prob. Information Transmission*, **16**(2) pp. 134-144 (April-June 1980).

Tsy85. B.S. Tsybakov, "Survey of USSR Contributions to Multiple-Access Communications," *IEEE Trans. on Information Theory*, **IT-31**(2) pp. 143-165 (March 1985).

TTH88. T. Takin, Y. Takahashi, and T. Hasegawa, "An Approximate Analysis of a Buffered CSMA/CD," *IEEE Trans. on Communications*, **COM-36**(8) pp. 932-941 (August 1985).

VvT83. N.D. Vvedenskaya and B.S. Tsybakov, "Random Multiple Access of Packets to a Channel With Errors," *Prob. Information Transmission*, **19**(2) pp. 131-147 (April-June 1983).

ZhR87. W. Zhao and K. Ramamritham, "Virtual Time CSMA Protocols for Hard Real-Time Communication," *IEEE Trans. Software Engineering*, **SE-13**(8) pp. 938-952 (August 1987).

APPENDIX A

MATHEMATICAL FORMULAE AND BACKGROUND

This appendix summarizes some of the important properties and results regarding queueing and Markov processes that are used in the text. This is only a list; the reader is expected to be acquainted with the items on the list (and with stochastic processes in general) to the extent that he/she understands them and knows how to make use of them. This appendix is included here so that basic results in the text can be referenced rather than derived, and is by no means sufficient for studying the subject. The material here is based on textbooks by Ross [Ros72] and Kleinrock [Kle76].

In this appendix as well as throughout the text we adopt a consistent notation as follows. A random variable is denoted by a letter with a tilde, e.g., $\tilde{x}$. For this random variable we denote by $F_{\tilde{x}}(x)$ its probability distribution function, by $f_{\tilde{x}}(x)$ its probability density function, by $F_{\tilde{x}}^{*}(s)$ the Laplace transform of $f_{\tilde{x}}(x)$, and by $\overline{x^k}$ its kth moment. If $\tilde{x}$ is a discrete random variable then $X(z)$ denotes its generating function. The expectation is denoted by $\bar{x}$ or just x. In general, a discrete stochastic process is denoted by $\{\tilde{x}_n, n \geq 0\}$.

Markov Chains

Consider a finite or countable set $E = \{E_0, E_1, \cdots\}$ and a stochastic process $\{\tilde{x}_n, n \geq 0\}$ in which $\tilde{x}_n \in E$ designates the state of the process. We say that the process is in state j at time n if $\tilde{x}_n = E_j$. For conciseness we consider the states as being the set of integers, i.e., $E_j = j$. Such a stochastic process is a Markov chain if

$$Prob[\tilde{x}_n = j \mid \tilde{x}_{n-1} = i, \tilde{x}_{n-2} = i_2, \cdots, \tilde{x}_0 = i_0] = Prob[\tilde{x}_n = j \mid \tilde{x}_{n-1} = i] \triangleq p_{ij}^n$$

that is, the probability that at time n the process is in state j depends only on its state at time $n-1$ and not on prior history. The quantities p_{ij}^n are called the one-step transition probabilities of the process at time n. When the transition probabilities are time independent, i.e., $p_{ij}^n = p_{ij}$ for all n, the chain is called *homogeneous*. The m-step transition probability of a homogeneous Markov chain is defined as

$$p_{ij}^{(m)} = Prob\,[\bar{x}_{m+n}=j \mid \bar{x}_n=i]$$

and is the probability of transitioning from state i to state j in exactly m steps. The one-step probabilities can be arranged in a matrix P called the transition matrix.

Two states of a Markov chain are said to communicate if and only if there is a positive probability that the process ever be in state j after having been in state i, and vice versa. In fact all communicating states form a class of states. A Markov chain having but one class of states is called irreducible. There is a variety of other ways to characterize states in Markov chains, notably periodicity and ergodicity (whose definition we leave out); in this textbook we are interested only in irreducible, aperiodic and homogeneous chains. Since ergodicity plays an important role in the analyses the proof of ergodicity is included in the text in the appropriate places.

The result most frequently used in the text stems from the following theorem:

For an irreducible ergodic Markov chain the limit

$$\pi_j \triangleq \lim_{m \to \infty} p_{ij}^{(m)}$$

exists and the values π_j are the unique nonnegative solutions of the set of equations

$$\pi_j = \sum_i \pi_i\, p_{ij} \;,$$

$$1 = \sum_i \pi_i \;.$$

Several remarks and corollaries result from the above theorem. First, the set of equations can be written in matrix form as

$$\pi = \pi P$$

where π is the row vector of the values π_i. This notation is especially useful when the number of states is finite as the tools of linear algebra can be put to work. It can also be shown that if the set of equations has a solution such that $\sum \pi_i < \infty$ then the chain is ergodic. The probabilities π_i are (interchangeably) referred to in the literature as limiting probabilities, steady-state probabilities, stationary probabilities, or invariant probabilities. In general the term "steady-state" refers to the operation of the process after a long time, i.e., for large values of n. The limiting probability π_i is the steady state probability that the process is in state i; it is also the proportion of time that the process stays in state i (the latter remains true for periodic chains).

Recurrent Markov chains are members of another family of stochastic processes known as regenerative processes. This special family of processes possesses the property that there exist times $t_0, t_1, \cdots$ such that the behavior of the process after time t_{i+1} is a repetition, in a probabilistic sense, of the behavior of the process after time t_i. Referring to the time between two regeneration points as a cycle, we have that

$$Proportion\ of\ time\ in\ state\ j = \frac{Expected\ time\ in\ state\ j\ in\ a\ cycle}{Expected\ cycle\ length} .$$

This relation is used extensively in the textbook when a (regenerative) system is modeled as having two states--useful and useless--the ratio of which is a good measure of efficiency.

Residual Life

Consider a stochastic (renewal) process that marks time instants on the time axis in a way that the length of the marked intervals, denoted $\bar{x}_n$, $n \geq 0$, are independent and identically distributed (i.i.d.) according to a common distribution $F_{\bar{x}}(x)$ (or density $f_{\bar{x}}(x)$) and expected value $E[\bar{x}] = \bar{x}$. At some random time t, while the process is ongoing, it is sampled and we are interested in the distribution and moments of the residual time i.e., the time until the next marked point.

If $\bar{y}$ denotes the residual time then

$$f_{\bar{y}}(y) = \frac{1 - F_{\bar{x}}(y)}{\bar{x}} ,$$

$$F_{\bar{y}}^*(s) = \frac{1 - F_{\bar{x}}^*(s)}{s\bar{x}} ,$$

$$E[\bar{y}] = \frac{\overline{x^2}}{2\bar{x}} , \quad E[\bar{y}^2] = \frac{\overline{x^3}}{3\bar{x}}$$

where $F^*(\cdot)$ is the Laplace transform of the corresponding probability density function. The age of the process, i.e., the time from the beginning of the interval to the sampled point has the same distribution as $\bar{y}$.

The M/G/1 Queue

Consider a queueing system in which arrivals occur according to a Poisson process with parameter λ and in which $\bar{x}$--the service rendered to the customers--is distributed according to a distribution $B(t)$. In such a queueing system the number of customers in the system as seen by an outside observer equals that seen by an arriving customer which equals that left behind a departing customer. With this in mind we make the following notation:

$b(t)$ -- Probability density function of the service time.

$B^*(t)$ -- Laplace transform of $b(t)$.

$\rho = \lambda\bar{x}$ -- Load factor

$\bar{q}$ -- Steady state number of customers in queue

$Q(z)$ -- Generating function of $\bar{q}$

$\tilde{D}$ -- Time spent in the system (delay time)
D -- Average delay time
$\tilde{W}$ -- Queueing time (time spent in queue)
W -- Average queueing time

The following holds for an M/G/1 queueing system:

$$Q(z) = B^*(\lambda - \lambda z) \frac{(1-\rho)(1-z)}{B^*(\lambda - \lambda z) - z} \quad,$$

$$E[\tilde{q}] = \rho + \frac{\lambda^2 \overline{x^2}}{2(1-\rho)} \quad,$$

$$W^*(s) = \frac{(1-\rho)s}{s - \lambda + \lambda B^*(s)} \quad,$$

$$W = \frac{\lambda \overline{x^2}}{2(1-\rho)} \quad,$$

$$D^*(s) = B^*(s) \frac{(1-\rho)s}{s - \lambda + \lambda B^*(s)} \quad,$$

$$D = x + W = x + \frac{\lambda \overline{x^2}}{2(1-\rho)} \quad.$$

GLOSSARY OF NOTATION

Symbol	Meaning (Forms of usage)
a	Arrival per slot (a_i, $\bar{a}$)
	Normalized end-to-end delay
A	Number of arrivals ($\bar{A}$, $A(z)$, $A_k(z)$)
B	Busy period, length of CRI ($\bar{B}$, B, B_n, $B_{n\mid i}$)
b	Backlog departure rate (b, $b_i(n)$)
C	Cycle length ($\tilde{C}$)
c	Constant (c, c_n)
D	Delay ($\bar{D}$, D, $\tilde{D}$, $D^*(s)$, $D(k)$)
d	Distance between assignments (Generalized TDMA) ($d(k)$)
E	Expectation ($E[\cdot]$)
F	General function (usually distribution) ($F(\cdot)$)
f	General function ($f(\cdot)$)
G	Normalized channel (offered) load
	Generating function ($G(z)$, $G_n(z)$)
g	Channel (offered) load
I	Idle period ($\bar{I}$, I)
L	Number of packets in a message ($\bar{L}$, L, $\overline{L^2}$, $L(z)$, $L^*(s)$)
M	Number of users in the system
N	Population size ($\bar{N}$, N, $\bar{N}_k$)
P	Packet size (P, $\bar{P}$)
	Probabilities (P_{suc}, P_n)
p	probability (p, p_i, p_{ij})
P	Transition matrix
Q	Generating function of q ($Q(z)$, $Q_k(z)$)
	Probabilities ($Q_i(n)$)
q	Number of packets in queue ($\bar{q}$, $\bar{q}_j$, $q(k)$)
R	Channel transmission rate
S	Throughput (S, S_n, $S_n(k)$)
s	Laplace variable
T	Slot size
	Packet length (time)
	Transmission period ($\tilde{T}$, $\tilde{T}_i$, T, T_i, T_c)
t	General time ($\bar{t}$, t)
U	Useful (successful) time in a cycle ($\bar{U}$, U $\bar{U}_n$, U_n)
V	Second moment of CRI length (V_n, $V(z)$)
W	Waiting time

Symbol	Meaning (Forms of usage)
x	General variable (x, x_i, x_l, x_r)
	General service time $(\hat{x}, \bar{x})$
z	Generating function variable
α	CRI length bound (α_m)
β	Root of unity (β_m)
δ	Impulse function $(\delta(\cdot))$
	General (bounding) number
Δ	Step function $(\Delta(\cdot))$
	CRI epoch length
γ	Collision detection time (CSMA/CD)
λ	Arrival rate
ν	General probability
π	Invariant probabilities (π_i), Probability vector $(\boldsymbol{\pi})$
ρ	Load factor
σ	General probability
τ	Minislot duration, end-to-end propagation delay

INDEX